PRAISE FC

The Purpose of Power

"Alicia Garza offers a smart, thoughtful, introspective and unflinchingly self-reflective narrative of how she became a movement organizer and what she has learned along the way. . . . Garza is a gifted storyteller. . . . *The Purpose of Power* is an admirable, endearing and genuinely illuminating book. It reflects the lessons that a brilliant Black woman distilled over twenty years in her quest to make the world around her a better place. Garza projects idealism, pragmatism and realism."

—*The Washington Post*

"Garza traces where the movement came from and where it could go, taking readers back through her first lessons in politics taught by her mom, to watching the 1992 L.A. riots on television as a child, to the birth of the Black Lives Matter movement and the Ferguson uprising. In a year when a long overdue reckoning with racism is once again in the spotlight, Garza's call to action to create a sustainable movement bigger than hashtags and social media followings is urgent and critically necessary. 'Our movements must reflect the best of who we are and who we can be,' she writes. In *The Purpose of Power*, Garza shows us what that vision of the future looks like."

—*TIME*

"[Garza's] goals extend beyond the struggle against police brutality or even the criminal justice system. She is primarily interested in the larger question of how to move from engaging in protests and mobilization to acquiring the political power necessary to transform the conditions in poor and working-class Black communities. . . . Garza and other organizers are grappling with how to raise a level of accountability while also opening doors to new people who are not schooled in this kind of political culture. They are asking different kinds of questions. . . . A large part of what is appealing about Garza's book is how honestly and directly she delves into political debates within the B.L.M. movement. . . . Nothing short of mass movements to uproot, overturn, and radically reconstruct can produce the new America envisioned here. Garza's excellent and provocative new book is a gateway to these urgent debates."

—KEEANGA-YAMAHTTA TAYLOR, *The New Yorker*

"*The Purpose of Power* is a must-read for those who want a better understanding of the current state of Black America. This book highlights the work necessary not only to transform the conscience of our nation but also to disrupt the policies that contribute to systemic racism so we can successfully build a country where Black lives matter. Alicia Garza has created a guidebook for building coalitions to bring about transformational change. By combining activism with electoral politics, she is reflecting the influence of the strength and brilliance of her late mother, who I know is smiling down from on high with pride and love. As we face challenging times in our nation, anyone interested in turning the page of our contemptible past toward a brighter future should put this book on their reading list."

—CONGRESSWOMAN BARBARA LEE

"Alicia Garza has articulated the aspiration of generations of Black people to be valued, protected, respected, and free. This beautiful, important, and timely memoir is insightful, compelling, and necessary in this critical moment of reckoning with our history."

—BRYAN STEVENSON, author of *Just Mercy*

" 'Black lives matter' was Alicia Garza's love letter read around the world. *The Purpose of Power* is another love letter that should be read around the world. It speaks to all that molded Garza, all that molds organizers, all that molds movements. It is story. It is lesson. It is power."

—IBRAM X. KENDI, author of *How to Be an Antiracist*

"Damn. *The Purpose of Power* changes everything. I suppose I shouldn't be shocked at this book's audacity, because it's written by a young Black woman who literally changed everything. But the art of building a movement and the art of building a textured book to chronicle and guide future movements are wholly different endeavors. Somehow—and I think the how is in the way the sentences and chapters put pressure on yesterday and tomorrow—Alicia Garza has written a book that is more dynamic, daring, and rigorous than the most expansive movement of my lifetime, a movement she helped create and sustain. Very few books become national monuments. Even fewer help shape social movements. *The Purpose of Power* is that rare book that is a monumental movement. It is a liberatory offering. Damn."

—KIESE LAYMON, author of *Heavy*

"In this magnificent and engaging text, Alicia Garza deftly combines revealing personal memoir, thorough social history, astute political theory, and pragmatic strategic advice. Through this exquisite narrative, Garza shows why she is a singular figure of her generation—a generation about which everyone was convinced, she writes, 'that there was something inherently wrong with us.' Combining personal and national history, Garza reveals all that is right about a generation forged in the fire of the Clinton-era carceral state and coming of age in the era of Obama-enforced respectability. Refusing to romanticize any moment or movement, Garza explains both the why and the how of meaningful, impactful organizing for and with black communities. Never cruel but unflinchingly honest, Garza analyzes the external and internal opponents that have marked Black people's long struggle for justice in this country. She teaches clearly, corrects lovingly, demands boldly, and proceeds fearlessly to fight for the lives of all Black people. This is a text everyone needs to read, to discuss, to debate, to challenge, and to absorb. Alicia Garza is our Ella Baker."

—MELISSA HARRIS-PERRY, Maya Angelou Presidential Chair and professor of politics and international affairs at Wake Forest University

"In the difficult work of building movements, one of our most important resources is leadership, the people who hold the lanterns, light the path, and serve as our guides through the darkness. I can think of no greater guide than Alicia Garza and no greater tome of wisdom for this age than *The Purpose of Power*, a precious offering to a nation navigating unprecedented crises, for whom movements remain our only saving grace."

—AI-JEN POO, executive director of the National Domestic Workers Alliance and author of *The Age of Dignity*

"Like the movement she launched into the world, Alicia Garza's book will pull you in, break your heart, and make it bigger all at once. *The Purpose of Power* cements Garza as a generational leader whose unflinching yet generous wisdom will shape our approach to activism for years to come."

—HEATHER MCGHEE, author of *The Sum of Us*

"With *The Purpose of Power*, Alicia Garza has provided us simultaneously with a necessary political history, an expansive theory of liberation, and a personal testament to the power of movement building. If we are serious about the work of dismantling all the systems of oppression that have caused pain and suffering for generations, we would do well to listen as Garza helps guide us to greater understanding and faith in our prospects for revolutionary change."

—MYCHAL DENZEL SMITH, author of *Stakes Is High*

"Moving a jaded populace from 'spectators to strategists' is not for the faint of heart, but Alicia Garza knows how to do it. With eloquence, intimacy, and electric clarity, Black Lives Matter cofounder Garza has delivered a dynamic story of how a multiracial, Black-led movement for rights and dignity came of age. Accessible and hands on, *The Purpose of Power* is part generous autobiography, part manual for building multiracial coalitions and political majorities strong enough to overcome anti-Black racism in the modern era. The book reveals Garza as not only a superb strategist but a master storyteller, breaking down complex narratives of displacement, police violence, and worker disenfranchisement to serve up the incredible blend of movement building know-how and community organizing how-to that today's generation of activists desperately needs.

"Make no mistake, Garza's words are no ride-along. Every page resuscitates the reader, dashes our myths about how change happens, and invites us into the simple but powerful truth that at the end of the day, the future will be built by people. From the streets to the battlefields of popular culture, news, and the Internet, *The Purpose of Power* delivers wisdom for the seasoned organizer and an incredible story for the impassioned newbie. This layered book is for anyone who understands that surviving with dignity is a practice, but fighting for both dignity and survival is a skill. From end to end, Garza honors the political moment, the new and diverse leadership, all the while reminding us of this simple truth: Hashtags don't build movements, people do."

—MALKIA DEVICH CYRIL, senior fellow and
founding director of Media Justice

"Alicia Garza is a leader for our times, a deeply erudite strategist and thinker who leads heart first. In this book, she puts us back together again, reminding us that when things fall apart, as they inevitably do, it is we who hold the puzzle pieces, and coming together, we can begin again."

—BRITTNEY COOPER, professor at Rutgers University
and author of *Eloquent Rage*

THE PURPOSE OF POWER

THE
PURPOSE
OF POWER

HOW WE COME TOGETHER
WHEN WE FALL APART

ALICIA GARZA

FOREWORD BY RASHAD ROBINSON

ONE WORLD
NEW YORK

2021 One World Trade Paperback Edition

Published in the United States by One World, an imprint of Random House, a division of Penguin Random House LLC, New York.

ONE WORLD and colophon are registered trademarks of Penguin Random House LLC.

Originally published in hardcover in the United States by One World, an imprint of Random House, a division of Penguin Random House LLC, in 2020.

Library of Congress Cataloging-In-Publication Data
Names: Garza, Alicia, author.
Title: The purpose of power: how we come together when we fall apart / Alicia Garza.
Description: New York: One World, 2020.
Identifiers: LCCN 2020023583 (print) | LCCN 2020023584 (ebook) | ISBN 9780525509707 (paperback) | ISBN 9780525509691 (ebook)
Subjects: LCSH: Social movements. | Political participation.
Classification: LCC HM881 .G37 2020 (print) | LCC HM881 (ebook)
DDC 303.48/4—dc23
LC record available at https://lccn.loc.gov/2020023583
LC ebook record available at https://lccn.loc.gov/2020023584

PRINTED IN THE UNITED STATES OF AMERICA ON ACID-FREE PAPER

oneworldlit.com

246897531

Illustration by iStock / OlgaLebedeva

For Mumsie

CONTENTS

THE PURPOSE OF POWER

FOREWORD FOR THE PAPERBACK EDITION

RASHAD ROBINSON

IN EIGHT YEARS, THE THREE WORDS "BLACK LIVES MATTER" have never changed. But they have completely transformed. They transformed from a defiant cry into an echo bouncing off protest signs and a rallying force all across the internet and then into one of the greatest social movement banners in American history, into a network of innovative Black leaders and a new brand of Black leadership. And perhaps most significantly, those words transformed into a new and powerful consensus about what our society should be.

In 2013, Black Lives Matter began as an expression of love, hope, and renewal for Black people everywhere. It was also a profound expression of outrage, rising up from Black communities who were determined to make the killing of Trayvon Martin a turning point in this country—to draw a line in the sand on police violence and anti-Black violence in all its many forms. Millions of people drew that line, danced on that line, cried on that line, and refused to give up on that line. And they held that line for years, believing they would find a way to push society to understand it and catch up to it.

The rallying call of Black Lives Matter recognized that a new kind of leadership was needed—then, as now—to actually win change and not just demand it. It challenged those in power to reckon with the deep racism that continues to be dismissed and ignored. But it was also a challenge to all of us: to harness and organize our own power in different and more effective ways, as Black people and all people who want justice.

Today, policies that encourage anti-Black harassment and violence by police are getting tossed out over the line that was drawn with the words Black Lives Matter. Policies like money bail are getting measured by that line, turning the consensus against a practice that keeps hundreds of thousands of people locked up in jail and in harm's way for no other reason than not having the money to pay bail fees that judges and prosecutors deliberately set out of reach. We have forced telecom corporations profiting off mass incarceration to answer to that line, no longer allowing them to exploit their monopoly and charge families outrageous and exploitative rates to talk to their incarcerated loved ones. City councils across the country are drawing lines through police budgets and drawing emphatic circles around the kind of local leadership that can truly bring about security, safety, and freedom for their communities.

That's not only power, it's power with purpose. It is the power we need to keep building and using to transform society: the power to win big change, the power to protect and help our people, and the power to counter and expose the harm of the forces working against us. Those are the types of power we need today, and we need leaders and leadership who are focused firmly on creating them.

In 2021, Black Lives Matter has become a tangible standard

of accountability for eliminating anti-Black racism in every domain of life. This standard is certainly not enforced, or even accepted, everywhere. But it has become an instrumental tool for activists undertaking the massive challenge of changing how society works—changing the equation of decision-making in institutions that have evaded responsibility for their role in perpetuating racial injustice across the centuries. We now have a powerful shared tool for challenging the everyday racism in our lives as well as the systemic racism in society, while having the full force of history on our side. The principle of Black Lives Matter is a line—and more and more, crossing it comes with consequences. Not enough consequences and not in nearly enough areas of society or in nearly enough parts of our lives. But more than ever before.

All of this comes in the face of two types of violence working against us: the widespread violence committed *against* racial justice protesters, which mayors and police departments have enabled, and the widespread violence committed *by* white nationalist insurgents, who were practically welcomed in to raid the U.S. Capitol building in Washington, D.C., who use threats and violence to slow down progress and attack Black leaders in every realm, and who are promoted by social media companies that profit from them.

Black Lives Matter showed us what winning looks like in a time of deep and profound loss, and it defined winning in the most expansive way possible. It's the ability not only to turn out people to vote, but to change the very agenda that people are voting for. It's the power not only to make racial justice a truly majoritarian idea—one that most Americans believe in—but to rally people around specific solutions to ensure that racial equity is a filter by which policies and budgets are evaluated.

Many people in politics relegate Black leaders to the realm of mobilization: turning out protesters and voters in service of someone else's master plan. But, in fact, the racial justice movement that Black Lives Matter stands for has been one of the strongest forces of persuasion we have ever seen in politics. This movement hasn't just changed the way people think about candidates during an election, it's changed the way people think about the world, including their own role in changing it. It has powered participation by people emboldened to live out their values, to reinvent their political lives, work lives, and social lives. This is what Black leadership can do.

Movements run on people power. The essence of people power is the ability to change the rules society lives by, the rules decisions are made by, the rules success is measured by and consequences are dealt by. If we want to change society, we have to change those rules. Alicia Garza's book is for the rule-changer in all of us. And we need more rule-changers than ever right now.

Alicia, one of my closest sisters in justice and liberation, has changed the rules. She has not only made it easier to advance racial justice, she has made it harder for those who benefit from racism to undermine and undo what we have won. She knows that if we don't keep changing the rules, someone else will, and those rules will continue to take away freedom and opportunity from people who have already been denied for far too long.

Black Lives Matter has shown us what Black power can do for all of us: unite millions of people from all walks of life in a movement with clear demands that cannot be ignored and will never run out of fuel.

It should be no surprise that Alicia has a lifetime of experience, insight, inspiration, and learning behind her. I have always benefited from Alicia's insight: how MTV shaped her understanding of the power of culture to win when politics alone can't do it; how Black power starts with Black community; how the difference between feeling powerful and being powerful is the difference between seeing our potential and realizing it—the difference between dreaming of freedom and winning freedom.

This book is a practical guide, written from the heart, for one of the most impractical fights of our time: making racial justice a reality by making all of us, together, more powerful than we thought we could be.

INTRODUCTION

SEVEN YEARS AGO, I STARTED THE BLACK LIVES MATTER Global Network with my sisters Patrisse Cullors and Opal Tometi. BLM went from a hashtag to a series of pages on social media platforms like Facebook and Twitter to a global network. The movement has generated the highest number of protests since the last major period of civil rights. When I started writing this book, that's what I thought it would be about—the story of Black Lives Matter, its origin and most profound lessons.

The funny thing is, when I sat down to write, that's not what came out. The first paragraphs were about my mother and how she trained my eyes to see the world. The opening words turned into a story about my own personal journey—words about lessons I've learned from more than twenty years of organizing and building movements, words that I know I wanted and needed to read when I started doing this work so many years ago, words that, honestly, I need right now.

It's my deepest wish that the words that follow are the ones you need to hear right now too.

Even though I'd been an organizer for more than ten years when Black Lives Matter began, it was the first time I'd been part of something that garnered so much attention. Being catapulted from a local organizer who worked in national coalitions to the international spotlight was unexpected. The OGs in my life would probably say that Black Lives Matter grew me up, but that's not quite true. My experience with BLM toughened my skin and softened my heart. It confirmed things I knew but couldn't express, clarified and sharpened my values, and taught me how to recommit to work that broke my heart every day. BLM accelerated my education in movement building, but it was the decade of organizing prior to Black Lives Matter that grew me up.

My parents used to run an antiques business, so I grew up learning about history through people and the objects they made. For instance: My favorite type of porcelain is a type of Satsuma ware, which has a unique glaze that makes the surface appear to be broken into millions of small pieces. The intention behind the glaze is to make the colors appear deeper and more vibrant, but it also makes the porcelain look old, a trait that implies elegance and aristocracy. As a kid, I found satsuma porcelain beautiful because it looked like broken pieces that had fused together to make something new. I liked to imagine what other lives those shards of pottery might have had if they had been put back together as something else. Or what future lives awaited them: A jewelry box, a teakettle, a dish—what might they become next?

This book is the story of an organizer who comes apart and is put back together many, many times. The words contained within it, the stories that they form, are intended to add richness and depth to that larger story. It is not the story of Black Lives Matter, but it is a story that includes it, that attempts to help make sense of not only where it came from but also the possibilities that it and movements like it hold for our collective future. More than that, this book is meant to offer readers the lessons I've learned along the way, the things I'm still learning, and what my learning may contribute in a time of profound catastrophe and limitless possibility. A time when we desperately need waves of vibrant, effective, and disruptive movements to flow all across America.

I've been asked many times over the years what an ordinary person can do to build a movement from a hashtag. Though I know the question generally comes from an earnest place, I still cringe every time I am asked it. You cannot start a movement from a hashtag. Hashtags do not start movements—people do. Movements do not have official moments when they start and end, and there is never just one person who initiates them. Movements are much more like waves than they are like light switches. Waves ebb and flow, but they are perpetual, their starting point unknown, their ending point undetermined, their direction dependent upon the conditions that surround them and the barriers that obstruct them. We inherit movements. We recommit to them over and over again even when they break our hearts, because they are essential to our survival.

When I say this, the person who asks usually seems . . . confused. Am I keeping the secret of building movements to myself? Being too humble about my contributions? Do I just not know how it happens? No. I promise I am not keeping anything from you when I say this. I am merely attempting to be honest with you while swimming upstream against a tide of bullshit answers that snake oil salespeople have been selling us for generations. You cannot start a movement from a hashtag. Only organizing sustains movements, and anyone who cannot tell you a story of the organizing that led to a movement is not an organizer and likely didn't have much to do with the project in the first place.

Movements are the story of how we come together when we've come apart.

The beginning of this book is about how I came to be, the forces and people that have shaped me and shaped my environment. For me, movements are situated within what the elders would call time, place, and conditions. The political, physical, social, and economic environment, norms and customs, practices and habits of the time shape the content and character of the movement that pushes against them. To understand where each of us fits in a movement and what our best role is and can be, we must first situate ourselves inside a context that makes it make sense. For that reason, the story of how I came to be a part of social movements occupies the first part of this book.

Telling this story also helps to make sense of how we got to where we are now. I then take some time to discuss the emergence of the conservative consensus in America, to help readers understand how we arrived at our present political dilemma. All stories have protagonists and antagonists, heroes and villains. The problem with using this structure to talk about how we got here is that it flattens the narrative to be about good people and bad people rather than providing illuminating stories about how movements succeed and how they fail, stories of strategies and systems. Police do not abuse Black communities because there are good people and bad people on police forces throughout the nation—police abuse Black communities because the system of policing was designed in a way that makes that abuse inevitable. Whether Donald Trump is a good person or a bad person has nothing to do with why he is in power. There are plenty of good people who do terrible things as part of their roles within systems. But the story of how those people whose actions we may deplore came to have power over our lives is a story of how a very powerful movement came together to reshape society as we know it.

I also spend some time in the book talking about the emergence of Black Lives Matter and the uprising that took place in Ferguson, Missouri, in the summer of 2014, a year after Black Lives Matter was created. This part of the book is a bit of connective tissue—a pathway from how I grew up and how I started organizing to the lessons I've learned that shape how I think we can come together again when we've fallen apart. It feels important to say that the story here is not meant to be the definitive story, or even the final one.

Recently I was in a staff retreat with my team at the Black Futures Lab, an organization I started in 2018 to make Black communities powerful in politics. We were discussing a breakdown in communication, trying to get to the root of how it happened, ostensibly so we could avoid it happening again. At a certain point in the conversation, the facilitator interrupted and said, "When I was growing up, and I would get into an argument with my mother, she would say to me, 'What happens between us is half yours and half mine.' I want to encourage you all to take that approach here—how would the story of what happened change if you all acknowledged that what happened between you is half yours and half theirs?"

I found that to be a helpful intervention, and it's one that I offer to contextualize the content of these chapters. I've done my best to tell the story from my perspective—where I enter, what I see as mine and what as yours. I cannot tell the story of Ferguson, nor do I intend to. I've told the story here of my experiences, and mine alone, the experiences that shaped me and continue to shape me.

I can only speak of what I know. There are lots of stories out in the world about what happened in Ferguson and who started

Black Lives Matter; what I can say unequivocally is that Patrisse, Opal, and I set things in motion but there are many leaders in this movement, some of whom have risen to prominence. The stories told here are intended to be honest about the ways that making celebrities out of people in our movement, myself included (half mine, half yours, remember?), have reinforced old paradigms that are ultimately destructive to successful movements. I have been very candid in this book about the phenomenon of celebrity activists and the impact of them/us, with DeRay Mckesson as one, but hardly the only, example of the distorting quality of fame. Our culture values style over substance, as evidenced in the election of Donald J. Trump. Our movements don't have to.

The emergence of the activist-as-celebrity trend matters. It matters for how we understand how change happens (protest and add water), it matters for how we understand what we're fighting for (do people become activists to create personal "influencer" platforms or because they are committed to change?), and it matters for how we build the world we want. If movements can be started from hashtags, we need to understand what's underneath those hashtags and the platforms they appear on: corporate power that is quickly coming together to reshape government and civil society, democracy and the economy.

In some ways, these are also old questions and conflicts. They echo the friction within the Student Nonviolent Coordinating Committee (SNCC) in the 1960s, the type of conflicts that Ella Baker and others had with the Reverend Dr. Martin Luther King, Jr., and so on. But that doesn't mean we can never get past such conflicts. How do we make new mistakes and learn new lessons, rather than continue to repeat the same mistakes and be disillusioned to learn that they merely produce the same results?

The final part of the book looks at some of the components that I believe are necessary to doing just that—making new mistakes. In this section I try to imagine movements that shake the very core of the earth, movements that are so powerful that nothing gets in our way. I imagine movements into which many movements fit, movements that carry us fearlessly further than we've gone before.

My hope is that this book leaves us thinking differently about the moment we're in, how we got here, and where we can go, together—and what gets in the way. I hope this book reinforces your belief in our ability to come together again, after we've fallen very, very far apart.

PART I

A SHORT HISTORY OF HOW WE GOT HERE

CHAPTER ONE

WHERE I'M FROM

FRANTZ FANON SAID THAT "EACH GENERATION MUST, OUT OF relative obscurity, discover its mission, fulfill it, or betray it." This is the story of movements: Each generation has a mission that has been handed to it by those who came before. It is up to us to determine whether we will accept that mission and work to accomplish it, or turn away and fail to achieve it.

There are few better ways to describe our current reality. Generations of conflict at home and abroad have shaped the environment we live in now. It is up to us to decide what we will do about how our environment has been shaped and how we have been shaped along with it. How do we know what our mission is, what our role is, and what achieving the mission looks like, feels like? Where do we find the courage to take up that which has been handed to us by those who themselves determined that the status quo is not sufficient? How do we transform ourselves and one another into the fighters we need to be to win and keep winning?

Before we can know where we're going—which is the first question for anything that calls itself a movement—we need to know where we are, who we are, where we came from, and what we care most about in the here and now. That's where the potential for every movement begins.

We are all shaped by the political, social, and economic contexts of our time. For example, my parents: My mom and dad were both born in the 1950s and came of age during the 1960s and 1970s. My dad was raised in San Francisco, California, by a wealthy Jewish family who became rich through generational transfers of wealth and by owning and operating a successful business. My mother, on the other hand, was born and raised in Toledo, Ohio, the daughter of a long-distance truck driver and a domestic worker. Compared to my father's family, they were working class, but compared to other Black families, they were solidly middle class. Toledo was the home of the Libbey Glass Company and other manufacturers that employed the lion's share of the population. My maternal grandparents' community consisted of Polish immigrant families and other middle-class Black families, until the Polish immigrant families began to move out to the suburbs.

My mother wanted more freedom than her family and her community would allow, so she kept moving: first to New York as a young woman, then joining the army, where she was stationed at Fort McClellan in Alabama for basic training, then Fort Dix in New Jersey for more training, before heading west for a final stint at Fort Ord.

My mom was raised in a context where Black women could aspire to become secretaries, domestic workers, or sales and retail clerks. My father was raised in a context where his family experienced some discrimination based on their Jewish heritage and identity but mostly passed as white people of an elevated economic class, which meant they could reasonably expect every opportunity to be open to them.

And I came of age in a very different context, at a time and in a place that were unique to me. I came to understand the world from a different set of perspectives than those of my parents and most of my peers. And yet here we all are, alive right now, making a world together, our perspectives and experiences sometimes harmonious, sometimes clashing, sometimes unrecognizable to one another. We all came into this world-making project at different times—my parents showed up in a 1966 Chevy Camaro, I arrived in a hybrid, and those who came of age in the 1990s and 2000s came through on rechargeable scooters powered by Citibank—but we're all here now.

Our wildly varying perspectives are not just a matter of aesthetic or philosophical or technological concern. They also influence our understanding of how change happens, for whom change is needed, acceptable methods of making change, and what kind of change is possible. My time, place, and conditions powerfully shaped how I see the world and how I've come to think about change. So, let me tell you who I am, and to tell you who I am, I have to tell you about my mother, who gave me my most enduring lesson in politics: The first step is understanding what really matters.

My mother was twenty-five years old when she found out she was pregnant with me. When she told my biological father, he wasn't thrilled, she says dryly, but he wanted her to keep the baby. I ask her if she wanted to keep the baby. "Were you scared, Mami? I mean, wasn't there any part of you that didn't know if you wanted to have a baby?" I'm trying to coax out of her a genuine answer, trying to make her comfortable enough to say yes if that was her truth. "No. I knew I wanted to have you," she tells me. "I didn't plan it, but when it happened, I was ready to put my big-girl pants on and figure it out." Quintessential Mami. Decisive and strong as an ox at five feet four inches.

There was a time when she was in love with my biological father, but when it went bad, it was over—by then, there wasn't much to do but figure out how to fight for herself and her child. For her, all of this was a long time ago, and she did her best to block it out and move on.

My mother doesn't identify as a feminist; in fact, I don't believe I've ever heard her use the word. She is equally suspicious of men and women: In her experience, men have underestimated and tried to take advantage of her, while some women have tried to undercut her or compete with her—mostly for the attention of men. My childhood was littered with stories of how to protect myself from predatory men and women. "Know when to go home," she would say, warning me to keep my wits about me and predict when a situation was reaching a turning point that might leave me unsafe. "Always know your exits," she would say, in case I needed to escape a predator or some other emergency. "Keep your blessings to yourself," she would say, as if there were someone around the corner ready to snatch a blessing from me.

For her, and for me, the central question wasn't about whether she was a feminist but whether she was able to care for her family and be cared for in return. She grew up during a time when the role of a woman was to raise a family, keep the house together, and make men's lives easier. Mami spent her life rebelling against that, actively and implicitly. She moved to New York at eighteen to be a secretary for a cinematographer and lived alone for two years. When she joined the military, she was the only woman in an all-male platoon, where she refused to take roles reserved for women. She fought off the sexual advances of her married boss when she worked in a California prison. And when the man she thought she would marry began seeing other women while she was pregnant with me, she had to figure out how to take care of herself and her daughter. Her feminism—her politics—was her fight to survive by any means necessary.

One of my earliest memories is asking my mother about a poster that she had hanging up in the apartment we shared with my uncle. The poster featured a beautiful Black woman who looked just like my mother—so much so that I would regularly ask Mami if she was sure she wasn't the woman in the image. Casually wrapped in a goldenrod headscarf, the woman gazes out into the distance next to the words "For Colored Girls Who Have Considered Suicide When the Rainbow Is Enuf."

I didn't know anything about the famous choreopoem, but I had a sense then, as I do now, that there was something unique about the experiences of Black women in a society that in so many ways seems to both fetishize and despise Black people. I recognized the sadness in the eyes of the woman in the poster. It mirrored the sadness in the eyes of my own mother.

Among her many colloquialisms, one of my mother's favorites was "Sex makes babies." For her, the practice of talking about sex was important to the well-being of her Black daughter. She never used phrases like "the birds and the bees" or "down there." There was no stork who brought a baby in a bundle to a house that wanted one. In my house, I would sit at the kitchen table late into the night while my mother would buzz around like a hummingbird. "I can't stand how white people sugarcoat everything," she would say. Buzz. "It's not the birds and the bees, it's sex. Ain't no damn stork. Sex makes babies. And babies are expensive." Buzz.

Our time together, me at the kitchen table, Mami buzzing around prepping everything for the following day, was when we would talk about such intimate topics. At the kitchen table, we would talk about consent. Mami would tell me that I never had to hug or kiss anyone I didn't want to, even family members. She would urge me to tell her or another adult if someone touched me in a way I didn't want to be touched. We would run drills in the kitchen where she would show me how to fight back against someone who was attacking me.

Mami would say, "Okay, baby girl, let's go over it again. What do you do if someone tries to grab you from behind and chokes you around the neck?"

Dutifully, I would reply, "I'm gonna drag my heel down their shin as hard as I can, stomp on their feet, and run as fast as I can."

"That's right, baby girl. Don't try and kick them in the balls. They'll be expecting that."

These were my first lessons in politics: Survival and dignity were priorities, but to fight for them meant taking on overlapping challenges of economics, sex and gender politics, and race. These were also my first lessons in intersectional feminism: Consent, choice, agency, pleasure, access to information, and access to contraception, up to and including abortion, were essential elements of true sexual equality. But before I had read feminist theory or taken an ethnic studies class, I knew that Black women in particular were often denied access to these things. These were not matters of academic or theoretical concern—these were problems I could see just by opening my eyes every morning. But I was also learning what it takes to fight back. My mother's determination to raise a little Black girl child and tell her that she could be as free as she wanted to be, as independent as she wanted to be—and to fight for that little Black girl to be seen as smart enough and capable enough to change the world—was a revolutionary act of liberation. These were the actions of a decidedly feminist Black woman trying to raise a child, support a family, pursue her own dreams, and demand the dignity that she deserved in Marin County, California.

My mother's insistence on living life on her own terms and

never allowing herself to be treated as inferior to anyone has had a significant impact on the way I move through the world, as well as on my vision of the world that I fight for every day—one where we can all live our lives on our own terms. For most of us, whatever we call our politics—leftist, feminist, anti-racist— dignity and survival are our core concerns.

CHAPTER TWO

MY GENERATION

GROWING UP IN THE 1980S AND 1990S, I WOULD READ ABOUT Black revolutionary movements that changed the course of history. They ranged from neighborhood programs set up to serve poor and working-class Black people to lunch counter sit-ins. From massive voter registration programs to rural Black farmers hiding shotguns under their beds to defend themselves from the Klan. From Charles M. Payne to Barbara Ransby to Max Elbaum, many have described that period as one that was expectant with possibility, where, as Elbaum says, "revolution was in the air."

Reading about these movements made me feel like I'd been born too late.

By the time I came into the world, the revolution that many had believed was right around the corner had disintegrated. Communism was essentially defeated in the Soviet Union. The United States, and Black people within it, began a period of economic decline and stagnation—briefly interrupted by catastrophic bubbles—that Black communities have never recovered from. The gulf between the wealthy and poor and working-class communities began to widen. And a massive backlash against the accomplishments won during the 1960s and 1970s saw newly gained rights undermined and unenforced.

But just like in any period of lull, even in the quiet, the seeds of the next revolution were being sown.

Many believe that movements come out of thin air. We're told so many stories about movements that obscure how they come to be, what they're fighting for, and how they achieve success. As a result, some of us may think that movements fall from the sky—Rosa Parks was tired and her feet hurt and she didn't feel like moving to the back of the bus; Black Lives Matter designed a hashtag and suddenly became a global movement.

Those stories are not only untrue, they're also dangerous. Movements don't come out of thin air. Rosa Parks might have been tired, but she also worked with the NAACP, which had been planning a boycott for months prior to kicking it off with Parks's action. Black Lives Matter was introduced to the world as a hashtag, but it didn't become prominent until more than a year after it was created—not to mention the work that went into using that hashtag for the purposes of organizing.

Movements are also not reserved for those of us who want peace, freedom, dignity, and a new way to survive. All movements are organized around a vision, but not all visions are created equal. The following is a story about how a movement shaped my life—and why I became determined to build a different one.

A powerful right-wing conservative movement started to gather steam in the 1970s, and by the early 1980s it had begun to take power. The victories won by progressive and radical social movements over the previous two decades galvanized a wave of backlash. In the 1980s, the social movements of the previous decades receded, and a new movement began to emerge.

What does it mean to be "right wing"? In the United States, "right wing" usually refers to people who are economically, socially, or politically conservative. What does it mean to be "conservative"? I'm using "conservative" to describe people who believe that hierarchy or inequality is a result of a natural social order in which competition is not only inevitable but desirable, and the resulting inequality is just and reflects the natural order. Typically, but not always, the natural order is held to have been determined and defined by God or some form of social Darwinism. The terms "right" and "left" when used to describe political leanings or political values have their origins in the French Revolution, where they were used to describe who sat where in the National Assembly. If you sat to the right as seen from the president's perspective, you were seen as in agreement with the monarchy, which tended toward hierarchy, tradition, and clericalism. We didn't start to use these terms to apply to our political system or political activities until the twentieth century.

Of course, despite how often we hear them, most Americans don't use these words to describe themselves. "Left" and "right" are mostly used by people active in changing or protecting the status quo, people for whom our political system—meaning our government and related institutions, like schools, places of worship, and the media—is the battleground for achieving those goals. Activists, advocates, and organizers use these words to describe ourselves, but most people in America do not. More on this later.

To make matters more complicated, words like "Democrat" and "Republican," referring to members of the two major political parties in the United States, don't neatly fit onto this spectrum of left and right. Of course, Democrats are seen to favor a more socially and economically progressive agenda (for example, advocating for a woman's right to abortion and other family planning services), while Republicans are seen as advocating for a more socially and economically conservative agenda (for example, reducing or eliminating government regulations on commerce). Yet history tells us that not only are these categories not cut and dry but over time, and several times, the parties have entirely switched positions on the political spectrum. Republicans, particularly during the era of the Civil War and Black Reconstruction in the 1860s, were the socially progressive party, and Democrats were the socially conservative one. These dramatic shifts in party ideology were typically caused by major political events and usually related to race.

The conservative movement of today has its roots in the social, political, and economic upheaval of the 1960s and 1970s. The interplay among conservative philosophers, influencers, philanthropists, and politicians helped to grow one of the most successful and influential movements in American history.

Conservatism was unpopular in the post–World War II era. There was a strong national consensus that the New Deal and the nation's success in the war had produced unprecedented prosperity after the catastrophic Great Depression of the 1930s. Conservatives who declared that the expansion of the welfare state threatened individual freedom were seen as irrational and paranoid, angry at the changes taking place in America, unable to embrace the change that seemed inevitable.

This dismissal allowed many to miss how conservatives were going about the business of building an empire. But sure enough, their movement grew. Modern conservative thought was developed in publications like *National Review,* launched in 1955 because its founder, William F. Buckley, Jr., felt that conservative viewpoints were not getting their due in the national media. In 1960, Senator Barry Goldwater published the watershed book *The Conscience of a Conservative,* which sold over 3.5 million copies (the book was actually ghostwritten by Brent Bozell, Buckley's brother-in-law). Goldwater ran for president in 1964 against Lyndon B. Johnson, losing in a landslide, but the conservative movement was learning to contend for power.

And contend they did. In 1966, Ronald Reagan, a Goldwater acolyte who had never run for public office before, ran for governor of California and beat the Democratic incumbent by one million votes. By the early 1970s, two new trends were unfolding within the conservative movement: the new right (which included the Christian or religious right) and the neoconservatives.

What's important to understand about the right as it evolved in this period is that it's a coalition of factions with distinct concerns, viewpoints, long-term and short-term visions, and ideologies. They come together on things they can agree on in the interest of building and maintaining power. This has been key to the right's success and key to its survival.

The new right was a reaction to the attempted takeover of the Republican Party by liberals, and the neoconservative trend was a reaction to the perceived liberal takeover of the Democratic Party. They were not a natural alliance. The new right was suspicious of government and loved the mechanics of politics, while the neoconservatives embraced government and preferred public policy to politics. What brought them together was their shared disdain for communism and liberals. Neoconservatives led the charge here, particularly through their resistance to the counterculture movement characterized by the anti-racist and anti-war struggles of the 1970s.

The new right wanted to cast a wider net, beyond its base of southern segregationists and economic elites, in order to expand its reach and influence into more sectors of society. The Christian right, otherwise known as the religious right, was a fundamental part of that strategy. The Heritage Foundation, created in 1973 to promote the ideas of the new right, was part of this recasting. Paul Weyrich, the strategist who created the Heritage Foundation, was also responsible for the creation of the American Legislative Exchange Council (ALEC) the same year. Originally intended to coordinate the work of religious-right legislators, with a focus on drawing up new legislation on issues such as abortion and the Equal Rights Amendment, it eventually became attractive to corporations. In 1979, Weyrich coined the term "Moral Majority" and turned it into an organization. The Moral Majority would activate and mobilize members of Pentecostal, fundamentalist, and charismatic churches to achieve conservative political goals. This is a constituency that had previously been relatively apolitical.

These new political forces reshaped the Republican Party. Many now believed that their faith called them to weave politics into their everyday lives and, as a cohort, to dominate the political process. The year 1980 was pivotal for the religious right, which registered more than two million voters as Republicans, succeeded in unseating five of the most liberal Democratic incumbents in the U.S. Senate, and gave Ronald Reagan the margin needed to win the election over the incumbent Democrat, President Jimmy Carter. Reagan's ascent to the Oval Office in 1981 marked a movement on the rise, united with a vision of limited government, state authority to determine civil and human rights, and a front to defeat communism once and for all. Ronald Reagan owed much of his success to the new right and its religious foot soldiers.

One component of the successful religious-right strategy included building out an infrastructure of activist organizations that could reach even more people and influence the full range of American politics. These organizations included Concerned Women for America, founded in 1979, which had a reported membership of 500,000 and played an important role in defeating the Equal Rights Amendment through campaigns that included prayer and action meetings; James Dobson's 1977 Focus on the Family radio show and Family Research Council, developed in 1983 to be the political lobbying arm of the radio show; and the Council for National Policy, an umbrella organization of right-wing leaders developed in 1981 to design strategy, share ideas, and fund causes and candidates for their agenda. Another component of their strategy was to take over local and state Republican organizations in order to gain influence and eventually control the national Republican Party.

The religious right developed the wide, more geographically distributed base of voters that the neoconservatives and the new right needed to complete their takeover of the Republican Party. These factions had many differences in approach, long-term objectives, overall vision, values, and ideology. The corporate Republicans wanted deregulation, union busting, and a robust military-industrial complex. The neoconservatives wanted to fight communism and establish global American military hegemony and American control over the world's resources. The social conservatives wanted to roll back the gains of civil rights movements and establish a religious basis and logic for American government. And yet, even amid their differences, where they are powerful is where their interests align; they are able to work through those differences in order to achieve a common goal. A powerful combination of strong and relatable ideas, the transformation of existing social networks into political machines, and a wide net to cast their agenda into every sector of society allowed them to become and to sustain a movement that has changed the landscape of American politics.

And the secret engine of their movement has always been race.

I was born in January 1981. Two weeks later, Ronald Reagan was sworn in as the 40th president of the United States.

Under Reagan's tenure, the rich got richer and the poor got demonized. His infamous slogan, "Government is not the solution to our problem; government is the problem," was the core belief of the now-dominant conservative movement. Idolized by Democratic and Republican voters alike, Reagan was deemed the Great Communicator, but maybe his greatest oratorical gift was his talent for euphemism. Though he wasn't the first, he was probably the most adept politician to deploy a phenomenon that Ian Haney López has named "dog-whistle racism." He could talk about race without ever explicitly mentioning it and in doing so entice millions to vote against their own economic interests. Years of acting made him a charismatic leader, and during his administration, Reagan gave his best performance, in the form of a targeted and effective backlash against Black communities, poor people, and the government itself.

In Reagan, working-class white men were able to find an answer to why their wages were declining after a period of prosperity and economic mobility—wasteful government spending on programs that supported women and people of color. Under Reagan's leadership, a country that had once seemed on the verge of revolution—through movements for civil rights and Black power, against war, and in support of social movements around the world—retreated into silos along race, gender, and class lines. There was now a newly defined and deepening antagonism toward Black communities and civil rights, a backlash against the expansion of social programs and the intervention of the federal government in enforcing civil rights laws.

It was Reagan who helped to usher neoliberalism into the center of American politics. Neoliberalism is a series of economic policies and a school of economic thought that resulted in privatization, corporate subsidies, and tax breaks for the wealthy at the expense of working people, the dismantling of the social safety net, and deregulation. Neoliberalism led to the rolling back of the gains won during the last period of civil rights. And it caused devastating destruction to the economy— particularly for workers. Reagan is infamous for his attacks on air traffic controllers, whom he'd convinced had a friend in him as president when he campaigned. When more than 11,000 air traffic controllers went on strike for better working conditions, he fired them and hired new workers to replace them, sending a clear message that companies could also evade labor regulations and rights with impunity.

He dramatically increased the military budget while slashing funding for programs that supported poor and working-class people or protected consumers and the environment. Internationally, Reagan encouraged the International Monetary Fund and World Bank to impose conditions, such as fiscal austerity and privatization, on their loans to poor countries; these conditions ultimately weaken their economies and increase their dependence on wealthy nations. Those who suffer most are often women, children, and other disadvantaged groups.

Under Reagan's administration, our country saw wealth taken away from working- and middle-class Americans and given instead to the wealthiest tier. As a result, economic inequality increased, including among racial groups, particularly between white and Black communities. Reagan's slashing and burning of safety net programs increased the homeless population exponentially, to 600,000 on any given night and 1.2 million over the course of a year by the late 1980s. Many of those found living on the streets were Vietnam veterans, children, and displaced workers. During his two terms in the White House, the minimum wage was frozen at $3.35 an hour while high inflation raised the cost of living for everyone. On Reagan's watch, on average, more than 33 million people lived beneath the federal poverty line each year. He slashed Medicaid by over $1 billion and eliminated more than 500,000 recipients of Aid to Families with Dependent Children (AFDC). These programs were considered by the conservative movement to be wasteful, giving money to people who did not deserve it. Reagan was successful in racializing these programs, framing them as handouts that Black communities and other poor communities used irresponsibly. It didn't matter that white communities used these programs too.

Reagan's championing of deregulation meant that the government no longer monitored racial discrimination by banks, real estate agents, and landlords. Urban areas were hit particularly hard as he and his administration slashed federal assistance to local governments by 60 percent. Without federal aid, cities with high levels of poverty and a limited base for property taxes suffered. Job training programs, the development of low-income housing, and government assistance were effectively dismantled. When Reagan was elected, federal assistance accounted for approximately 20 percent of the municipal budgets of large cities. By the end of his term, federal assistance would account for only 6 percent of those budgets. The devastating impacts on hospitals, clinics, sanitation services, police and fire departments, and urban schools and libraries continue to this day.

Black people were disproportionately impacted by the "Reagan Revolution," as the most severe cutbacks and backlash were reserved for us. Black unemployment grew to over 21 percent in

1983. For Black families like mine, the Reagan Revolution was a death sentence. Black communities had become the avatar for everything that was wrong with America, victims of a thinly disguised backlash to the powerful Black-led movements of the previous two decades. The Reagan Revolution expertly chipped away at the moral credibility that Black movements had established—whether they wielded guns and served the people or risked their lives to register Black communities to vote. Under Reaganism, personal responsibility became the watchword. If you didn't succeed, it was because you didn't want to succeed. If you were poor, it was because of your own choices. And if you were Black, you were exaggerating just how bad things had become.

Reagan declared a War on Drugs in America the year after I was born. His landmark legislation, the Anti-Drug Abuse Act of 1986, enacted mandatory minimum sentences for drugs. This single piece of legislation was responsible for quadrupling the prison population after 1980 and changing the demographics in prisons and jails, where my mother worked as a guard, from proportionally white to disproportionately Black and Latino. Reagan's plan ushered in new mandatory minimum sentences for crack and powder cocaine, a move that itself was racialized, as crack cocaine was cheaper and tended to be more accessible to Black communities, while powder cocaine was more expensive and more frequently used among white communities. The 100:1 provision of the law meant that possession of one gram of crack cocaine carried the same harsh penalty as one hundred grams of powder cocaine. Reagan stoked public fears about "crack babies" and "crack whores." The Reagan administration was so successful at this manipulation that, in 1986, crack was named the Issue of the Year by *Time* magazine.

Arguably one of Reagan's best-known performances involved selling the American public the image of the Black woman as a "welfare queen" who abused the system. During a campaign rally in January 1976, Reagan said,

> In Chicago, they found a woman who holds the record. She used eighty names, thirty addresses, fifteen telephone numbers to collect food stamps, Social Security, veterans' benefits for four nonexistent deceased veteran husbands, as well as welfare. Her tax-free cash income alone has been running $150,000 a year.

This gross distortion played into lingering fears and racial resentments brought on by economic decline and the earlier tumultuous period of civil rights and Black power. Reagan attacked taxes, welfare, and welfare recipients, and often did it by linking these public goods to Black people and Black communities. He was on record as having opposed the Civil Rights Act of 1964, the Voting Rights Act of 1965, and the Fair Housing Act of 1968. He gutted the Equal Employment Opportunity Commission, fought the extension of the Voting Rights Act, vetoed the Civil Rights Restoration Act, and opposed the creation of Martin Luther King Jr. Day.

Reagan led the popular resistance to the movements fighting against racism and poverty in the Global South that characterized the 1960s and 1970s. Significantly, he alluded to protest movements in the United States being used as tools of violence by the USSR, playing on widespread fears about a communist takeover of the United States and abroad. He also used fears of communism to authorize an invasion of Grenada, a then-socialist Caribbean country, to increase United States morale after a devastating defeat in Vietnam a few years prior, and to increase support for pro-U.S. interventions in El Salvador, Nicaragua, and Guatemala. Reagan also supported the apartheid regime in South Africa.

He carried the tune of "reverse racism" to eliminate any initiative or program aimed at bringing Black people into parity with whites and convinced white Americans that they were unfairly being denied benefits and privileges that they deserved.

Ronald Reagan didn't stop at demonizing Black people—he also provided platforms for well-to-do Black conservatives who could help carry his message, further assuaging any concerns that racism was involved. While Reagan called for "economic emancipation" from welfare and other social programs that he claimed had "enslaved Black America," he appointed a number of Black conservatives, including Clarence Pendleton, Jr., to head the U.S. Commission on Civil Rights. These men worked with Reagan to dismantle civil rights by weakening voting rights, destroying affirmative action programs, halting busing, preventing desegregation, and undermining the commission itself.

Pendleton was particularly egregious, saying that Black leaders were "the new racists"; following Reagan's reelection in 1984, he famously said,

I say to America's Black leadership, "Open the plantation gates and let us out." We refuse to be led into another political Jonestown as we were during the presidential campaign. No more Kool-Aid, Jesse, Vernon, and Ben.

The "Jesse" Pendleton was referring to was Jesse Jackson, who had mounted a vigorous campaign for the Democratic presidential nomination in 1984, campaigning explicitly against Reagan's destructive "revolution" and garnering more than three million primary votes. That campaign culminated with a powerful speech at the Democratic National Convention in San Francisco, not far from where Mami and I lived in San Rafael.

I taught myself to read that year. I was three years old. One day, sitting with my mom at the dining room table outside the small kitchen in our apartment, I read her a Help Wanted ad, a section of the newspaper Mami was known to frequent.

She stopped dead in her tracks and sat down next to me at the glass table, sticky with my fingerprints and my breakfast. "Do that again," she said breathlessly. "Read this one," she directed, pointing at another ad.

I read it to her—it was an ad for a used car dealership. She stared at me for a long time.

"Well," she said as she got up to get ready for work. "I suppose it's time to get you into school, huh? Take your plate in the kitchen and get ready."

During the Reagan era, Black children like me didn't fare so well. Reagan's cuts to social services meant cuts to school lunches, of which I was a recipient. The polarization of race relations, exacerbated by the racialized politics of the 1980s, created difficulties for my mother when she tried to get me into a public school early, much less into the gifted and talented programs reserved for advanced students. School after school would tell her that they couldn't take me. Many didn't believe that I could read, even when I'd do it in front of them. So my mother had to enroll me in a private school. And to do that, she had to find jobs that would pay enough but also offer a flexible schedule to allow her to take care of me. That wasn't easy.

Black single mothers of Black children, like my mom, also didn't fare well under the Reagan Revolution. Reagan's characterization of Black single mothers framed their use of government assistance as something close to a crime, a way of taking advantage of the system and cheating hardworking taxpayers out of millions of dollars. At the same time, under the guise of supporting self-reliance, he refused to raise the minimum wage. Then, like today, Black women were working hard—but hard work didn't pay.

Even with political and global revolutions going on around me, many of my memories from this period are filtered through pop culture—but pop culture was another political battleground. The culture wars of the 1980s were fought on our screens, and I was a little Black kid sitting right in front of them.

MTV debuted in 1981, the year I was born. MTV didn't just have music videos; it became an important source of news, targeting an audience of young people coming of age, frequently offering counterpoints to the ascendant conservative politics.

Watching MTV was how I first learned about sex and sexuality, gender, HIV and AIDS, the fall of the Berlin Wall, and struggles for racial justice. MTV was my babysitter. It took care of me when my mom was working.

Watching MTV raised my consciousness about issues happening inside the United States and outside it. I learned about the fall of the Berlin Wall from the Jesus Jones music video "Right Here, Right Now." I learned about famine in Africa and learned that Africa was a continent and not a country from MTV in 1985, when many of my favorite musicians performed the song "We Are the World" to raise money and social awareness about the famines in Ethiopia and Sudan. My mother was faced with a barrage of questions from me on all these issues: Why did they build a wall in Berlin? Why were people starving and dying in Africa? Her response was often "Look it up, baby girl," and look it up I did—not on the internet, but in the encyclopedia set I had, which was missing a volume or two. What I couldn't find in my encyclopedia I could often learn more about on MTV News.

It was MTV that first raised my awareness of AIDS and HIV, starting with their coverage of the story of Ryan White, who was diagnosed with AIDS in 1984 following a blood transfusion and died in 1990. A lack of information and government action on AIDS and HIV meant that the disease was grossly misunderstood. Ryan was bullied for contracting the disease, discouraged from going to school, and shunned in public places.

Reagan's tacit support for this kind of discrimination meant that not only did millions of people die unnecessarily of the disease, but many died alone, without the support of their families and loved ones, because of the belief that AIDS and HIV were contagious in ways that they were not—by sharing drinks or just sitting in the same classroom, as was the case in Ryan's story. MTV used its platform to raise awareness about the disease, to call for support for those who were living with HIV or AIDS, and to set the record straight about prevention, enlisting celebrities to do public service announcements.

I remember people talking about AIDS and HIV as if only poor people in Africa or gay men were susceptible to contracting the disease. And though it was troubling that it took the death of a child to gain sympathy from an unsympathetic audience, it was an important insight into the politics of that time. Groups like ACT UP (AIDS Coalition to Unleash Power), formed in 1987, wanted to ensure that there would be no more silence around the AIDS crisis and used bracing tactics of direct action and militant advocacy to call attention to the crisis plaguing America. For instance, at the New York Stock Exchange in 1989, five activists chained themselves to the VIP balcony, calling on Burroughs Wellcome—the pharmaceutical manufacturer of the only approved AIDS drug, AZT—to lower the price. Several days after the action, the company cut the price of the drug by 20 percent.

Part of the cruel ambivalence toward the mounting AIDS crisis came from the conservative movement's rejection of the countercultural revolution of the 1960s and 1970s in favor of "family values." With this turn toward a conservative Christian worldview came a series of high-profile controversies over whose definition of morality would rule the day. Few during this era provoked these skirmishes over public morality more than Madonna Louise Ciccone.

Along with Prince, Michael Jackson, and Whitney Houston, Madonna was one of my favorite artists as a kid in the 1980s. Madonna used her platform to push against traditional notions of sex, gender, and sexuality—and to resist conformity in ways that were both superficial and substantive. Her first movie, *Desperately Seeking Susan* (1985), explored the relationship between a bored suburban housewife and a "bohemian drifter," a portrait of a woman trapped within society's expectations, yearning for freedom.

The video for her song "Like a Prayer," which I watched on MTV a thousand times, ignited a firestorm. The video's story line depicts Madonna as a witness to the murder of a white woman, committed by white supremacists but pinned on a Black man. The white supremacists see her witness the crime, and she flees to a church, where she takes refuge and tries to find the courage to speak up about what she's seen. Her use of Catholic iconography in the video and song brought down criticism from the Vatican. For a kid like me, Madonna was a powerful figure, using her art to fight against the suffocating, murderous patriarchy.

Between my mother and Madonna, I was starting to see myself more clearly: I was going to be an independent woman and wanted nothing to do with being told by any man what to do, how to think, and how to feel.

The struggle wasn't just over music videos, of course. Reagan—who has been called "the most anti-woman president of the twentieth century"—supported a war on women that particularly targeted those who were poor and of color. He was a staunch opponent of the Equal Rights Amendment, a constitutional amendment designed to guarantee equal rights for women. Reagan made sure it disappeared from the GOP platform the year he was elected president. At the same time, he was a proponent of the Human Life Amendment, which would have banned abortion and even some kinds of birth control. He was an early pioneer of the George W. Bush–era "global gag rule" policies, which limit international funding for any family planning organization that even uses the word "abortion." His approach to pursuing an anti-woman agenda included cutting funding for agencies that monitored claims of gender discrimination. This meant that pay gaps, wage discrimination, and sexual harassment claims were rarely investigated, much less successfully litigated or settled. This was the result of Reagan's narrative about government being "the problem, not the solution": a government that did not actively intervene in support of a woman's right to live a dignified life. Gender discrimination didn't just impact cisgender women—women for whom the sex they were assigned at birth (female) matches how they identify (woman)—but transgender women and gender-nonconforming people didn't even get lip service from their government.

Reagan appointed Clarence Thomas to head the Equal Employment Opportunity Commission, which was responsible for policies regarding civil rights laws to prevent discrimination based on race, color, national origin, religion, sex, age, disability, gender identity, genetic information, and retaliation for reporting a crime or discriminatory practice. Thomas, a Black conservative not unlike those appointed to oversee other civil rights agencies, questioned the very existence of discrimination—so he was unlikely to enforce protections against it.

A refusal to monitor or enforce the law mattered for women like my mother, and for those who would eventually be women, like me. At risk were not only women who worked for private employers but women who were federal and government employees. That included Mami.

For more than three years, my mother worked inside the

California correctional system as a corrections officer. She'd met my biological father while she worked there; he too was a corrections officer. Her work as a prison guard paid at least twice the monthly salary she received at any of the other jobs she would hold, which involved secretarial, sales, or other administrative work. It was a job that paid her, as she wanted, "like a man." But as she was one of the few Black people and even fewer Black women on the job, conditions were particularly dangerous.

Mami remembers an uprising in her unit. As she and others went to respond, they were locked into a unit with guns that had no ammunition. Mami told me her superiors often made conditions even more unsafe as a way to seek additional funding for more personnel and other needs that had been slashed under Reagan's "small government" agenda. Even though the job paid better than most, conditions were dangerous enough that they forced her to seek other employment after she suffered an accident while on the job.

She was also vulnerable to the advances of her superiors. One of them, she said, took to paging her by name on the loudspeaker in the prison. When she arrived in his office, he would make sexual innuendos and offers. He was married, of course. This was dangerous, she said, because it signaled to other officers that she might be receiving special treatment or, at the very least, trying to secure such treatment. It made her less safe in a workplace where being a woman was already a liability. I asked her what she did to protect herself.

"Well, once when he called, I went into his office," she told me. "I cussed him out from top to bottom and told him that not only was I not attracted to him but that he couldn't afford me, because I don't share. That I knew that his wife was also very expensive and that he wouldn't be able to afford to keep us both.

I told him to quit calling me in his office, chasing a pipe dream. Wasn't gonna happen."

"Did that work?"

"It did work," she said. "I think he got scared that I was going to find a way to tell his wife. He definitely left me alone after that."

Stories like Mami's were not uncommon. Gender discrimination claims increased by 25 percent during Reagan's tenure, but the agencies tasked with investigating them were severely underfunded and headed by people who shared the same mindset—and protection—as the harassers.

Even as a corrections officer, my mother could not get support from the system she worked to uphold. When her relationship with my father ended and she tried to get child support from him, she had to confront a judicial system that did not adequately support mothers, much less the Black single mothers already demonized by Reagan as welfare queens. Before she settled out of court, the judge offered her one hundred dollars a month, to which she replied, "You can't keep a dog in a kennel for a hundred dollars a month, much less raise a child on that!"

And that's as good a summation as any of the rise of conservatism and the Reagan Revolution.

The 1990s were not only formative for my own politics and experiences but provided a foundation for many of the dynamics we see today in Black communities across the nation. I am part of a secret generation that isn't quite Generation X and not quite Millennial. Some refer to us as "Xennials," a subgeneration born between the late 1970s and early to mid 1980s—those who had an analog childhood and a digital adulthood.

The nineties were when the internet emerged to connect the

world digitally, but there were also less salutary shifts. It was the decade that ushered in a new regime of policing and incarceration for Black communities. To be sure, Black communities have always been policed and surveilled in this country, and with each new decade, the methods of control and containment become more sophisticated. Black communities and Black struggle are always shifting. The tactics, aspirations, and threats we face are in constant flux—from Black power in the late 1960s and early 1970s, to Black assimilation in the 1980s, to a program of Black annihilation in the 1990s.

By the 1980s, the War on Drugs had become a response to an earlier program, the War on Poverty, ushered in by President Lyndon B. Johnson in the late 1960s. The War on Drugs began to consolidate government resources around increased enforcement of drug crimes in the 1970s. Reagan took it all the way in the eighties, allocating almost $2 billion to fight the so-called war.

Then, in the nineties, states began to pass harsher penalties for drug use, drug possession, and drug sales, with policies like "stop and frisk" in New York and "three strikes" in California.

The impacts of the drug war were and are devastating on Black communities. Drug use became synonymous with Black communities, even though our communities use drugs at roughly the same rate as white communities. For an impoverished Black America, the War on Drugs was a war on Black communities and Black families.

I did not grow up in an impoverished neighborhood in Black America, but I was not exempt from the drug war's effects. In the late 1980s, my mother married my stepdad, a white Jewish man who was a fourth-generation San Franciscan and who'd been a part of my life from the time I was four years old. They married when I was eight, in the backyard of the house we'd moved to a year or two prior. That was also the year my baby brother, Joey, was born.

From the time I was born to the time I was four or five years old, my mom, her twin brother, and I lived in a two-bedroom apartment in San Rafael, California, in what was called the Canal District. The Canal was home to working-class and middle-class families, and at the time, it was predominantly Black and Latino. When my mom and stepdad moved in together, we lived in a one-bedroom apartment near Lincoln Avenue in San Rafael, right next to the 101 freeway and also home to working-class Black, Latino, and white families. I was around seven years old when we moved to a single-family home near Gerstle Park. The families who lived near us were middle to upper-middle class and no longer predominantly Black and Latino. I was in seventh grade when we moved to Tiburon, California—a wealthy, mostly white enclave on the other side of the Golden Gate Bridge from San Francisco.

To be Black in the 1990s in an overwhelmingly white community meant that I was subject to the stereotypes about Black people that were being driven by a conservative administration, now led by George Herbert Walker Bush, another Republican, who was in office from 1989, the year my brother was born and my parents were married, until 1993.

Being a preteen with very little choice about where I was living, I was admittedly embarrassed by this. I wasn't embarrassed to be Black—I was embarrassed to stand out as much as I did. Being new to the community, poorer than my peers, Black, and an angsty preteen was certainly an interesting combination. My white peers, many of whom were from wealthy families, idolized so-called gangsta rappers and emulated what they believed was the stylishly nihilistic lifestyle of impoverished Black people. Their blond hair sticking out of flat-billed baseball caps, they wore baggy clothes with expensive underwear peeking out from sagging pants. For them, Black culture was defiant, edgy, and rough—the complete opposite of the lives that many of them lived.

I was always mindful that I was Black, subject to the same stereotypes as all Black people but even more so as an isolated Black person in a sea of white people. I was given the same admonishments that other Black children were given: to be twice as good and work twice as hard because white people would always assume you were half as good. As a young Black girl, I was told to keep my wits about me and to always behave as if my mother was watching.

Of course, none of these admonishments prevented the inevitable. I was still subject to my white teachers believing that I was only half as good as my classmates, still subject to being suspected of things that I wasn't doing yet.

One day I came home from school and my parents were furious. They'd gotten a call from my middle school saying that I'd been reported to be smoking weed in the bathroom after school. I'd never smoked marijuana, much less dared to smoke it in a bathroom at school, an environment that I knew was highly surveilled, particularly for me, one of only ten Black students in the whole school. I explained to my parents that I'd never even smoked weed, which resulted in an investigation of my face, my eyes, my hands to see if they could detect a smell. Curiously, the subject was never broached again, but I never forgot it. My white peers were already having sex, sneaking out of their houses, drinking forty-ouncers in large lavish homes under the not-so-watchful eyes of au pairs and live-in nannies, and yet here I was, being accused of doing drugs when I'd never gotten so much as a B- on a report card.

. . .

When I did begin to test boundaries, as most teenagers do, I was met with fierce resistance. I had a Black mother, and if you know—you know. My dad was much more lenient about certain things than my mom was—he wasn't much for rules, having been in trouble a lot as a kid himself. My dad seemed more interested in being my friend than being my parent. My mother, on the other hand, always reminded me that not only was she not "one of my little friends" but that those friends would not suffer the same outcomes as I would for taking the same risks. Interestingly, my mom took a complicated approach to raising a teenager. She preferred that I do at home what most teenagers did out of the sight of their parents and yet often in public. When I began to smoke cigarettes, my mother admonished me not to do this at school but instead to smoke at home, where she could control who was there to witness it and who was not. My dad smoked weed religiously, and though I never smoked with my parents until I was much, much older, it was always clearly understood that I'd better not ever ever ever be found smoking weed in public.

When I shoplifted from a local drugstore, I think my mother was angrier that I was caught, in public, than she was at the actual act of shoplifting. To be caught in illegal activities was dangerous for anyone, but it was especially dangerous for Black people, and it didn't matter that I was a Black child growing up in a wealthy white community—I was still Black and I was old enough for my Blackness to be a liability. I was a teenager and I was rebelling, but my mother knew, I believe, that I was also giving in to what others already thought about me—that it was safe for me to break the law because that's just what Black people did. That it was safe to do drugs because that's just what Black people did. My mother made sure I knew that wasn't just what Black people did. And it was my mother who made sure that I didn't valorize "being a criminal."

This too was an impact of the War on Drugs: a fetishization of Black culture as outlaw, as rebel, as renegade, while criminalizing Black people whether we were outlaw, rebel, renegade, or not.

In 1991, Supreme Court Justice Thurgood Marshall decided to retire from the court. Marshall was a longtime advocate for civil and human rights, having risen to prominence in the infamous *Brown v. Board of Education* case, which aimed to desegregate public schools. George H. W. Bush, Reagan's former vice president, had become president. Bush selected forty-three-year-old Clarence Thomas, the former head of the Equal Employment Opportunity Commission (EEOC) and now a federal judge, as his nominee. Appointing Thomas to the court would maintain its racial makeup while also building toward a conservative majority to support a judicial agenda that included the overturning of affirmative action and abortion.

It was all but assured that Thomas would be confirmed, despite opposition from key civil rights groups, including the NAACP, the Urban League, and the National Organization for Women. That quickly changed when Anita Hill, a law professor from the University of Oklahoma, alleged that Thomas had sexually harassed her when she worked for him at the EEOC. She claimed that Thomas made inappropriate sexual comments and references to pornographic films when she refused invitations to go on a date with him.

Much has been written about the controversy that ensued. Needless to say, Thomas was confirmed, but not until after a highly publicized Senate hearing where segments of the Black community very publicly fought one another. Thomas described the event as a high-tech lynching, galvanizing some Black people to support him, alleging that Hill was part of a conspiracy to take down successful Black men. But in the main, Black women rallied around Anita Hill.

I remember the campaign to declare "I Believe You, Anita." There were bumper stickers and T-shirts with the declaration; 1,600 Black women took out an ad in *The New York Times* declaring their support. And I remember my mother talking to me about the case, sharing her support for Anita Hill and stories of being harassed and ridiculed in her workplaces.

Hill's case was an excellent illustration of the recently defined concept of "intersectionality."

Just two years before, Dr. Kimberlé Crenshaw had coined the term to describe the way different forms of discrimination overlap. In a paper she wrote for the University of Chicago Legal Forum titled "Demarginalizing the Intersection of Race and Sex," Crenshaw detailed legal cases in which courts were unable to protect Black women as Black women because they were (a) unable to represent the experiences of all Black people and (b) unable to represent the experiences of all women, and (c) because the courts could not fathom that discrimination could happen based on race and sex at the same time.

It was fitting, then, that Crenshaw assisted Professor Hill's legal team just two short years later. But even as Thomas was confirmed, the transformational idea of intersectionality began its slow climb to public awareness.

Earlier that year, on the evening of March 3, 1991, a young Black man named Rodney King was pulled over for a traffic stop in Los Angeles, California. After King exited his car, four Los Angeles Police Department officers—Sergeant Stacey Koon and officers Laurence Powell, Theodore Briseno, and Timothy Wind—struck him more than fifty times with nightsticks while also kicking him.

The incident was videotaped by a bystander, George Holliday, and the video was broadcast on every major television station into homes across America. The video captured what Black communities had known and protested for years prior to this event—an epidemic of police using excessive force against Black people.

The officers in the case were indicted, and a jury was assembled that included ten whites, one Latino, and one Filipino American. But it included no Black people, by design. A year later, the jury acquitted the officers on all charges.

In response, South Central Los Angeles rose up in a spasm of anger.

Over a six-day period, the uprising resulted in sixty-three deaths, more than 2,300 people injured, and nearly 12,000 arrests, along with nearly $1 billion in financial losses. The uprisings exposed a complex web of racial tensions that had been bubbling under the surface in Los Angeles—and around the country—for more than a decade.

I watched coverage of the L.A. uprising on television. Even as a kid, I felt I understood what the newscasters didn't seem to: Black people were enraged by a persistent dynamic of racism that rendered our lives less valuable. The aftermath of the uprisings sparked a national discussion on the enduring legacy of racism and police violence against Black communities and spurred an attempt to explain how race relations could improve. It also exposed, very clearly, that the dynamics of segregation and discrimination from the era of Jim Crow had not disappeared but only transformed. Racism was being discussed overtly, but that was as far as it ever seemed to go: talk.

In the meantime, I was being taught about race using the same kinds of euphemisms that Ronald Reagan became so famous for. In my liberal community, we were told that the United States was a "melting pot" of different cultures and communities, coming together to form one country. The metaphors would change each year—from melting pot to salad bowl, until eventually, there were no more lessons about how we all got along. All of that changed, I believe, when South Central Los Angeles burned to the ground.

In 1993, Bill Clinton was inaugurated as president of the United States. His election ended twelve years of Republican control of the White House. Clinton was a charismatic southerner who played the saxophone and appealed to Black communities that had experienced hell under those twelve years of conservative Republican rule.

Though he was a Democrat, Bill Clinton was a conservative one. His policies made him appealing to Republicans, and along with his charisma, he had a tough-on-crime stance that would come to greatly exacerbate mass incarceration. In 1994, Clinton ushered in the Violent Crime Control and Law Enforcement Act—an infamous bill that included the Violence Against Women Act and an assault-weapons ban, along with $9 billion for prison construction and funding for 100,000 new police officers. The bill expanded the federal death penalty, included mandatory minimum sentencing, and encouraged states to adopt harsh punishments and limit parole. Bill Clinton used the fear that Black and white leaders alike expressed about how communities were changing, changes that most of them attributed to personal choices rather than policy impacts. Bill Clinton believed in that personal responsibility narrative—particularly when it came to Black communities. And as Michelle Alexander has beautifully and pointedly written about, Hillary Clinton wasn't just sitting in the Oval Office sipping tea—she joined her husband in championing legislation that would devastate Black communities for decades to come.

The War on Drugs had begun to morph into the War on

Gangs. Economic policy shifts meant that white families moved out of the cities and into the suburbs. Television news programs and newspapers were swelling with stories of crime and poverty in the inner cities. Since there was little discussion of the policies that had created such conditions, the popular narrative of the conservative movement within both parties blamed Black communities for the conditions we were trying to survive. More and more pieces of legislation, written under the blueprint of the conservative movement but extending across political party lines, targeted Black communities with increased surveillance and enforcement, along with harsher penalties. None of these legislative accomplishments included actually fighting the problems, because this movement had created those problems in the first place.

"We also have to have an organized effort against gangs," Hillary Clinton said during an interview on C-SPAN in 1996, "just as in a previous generation we had an organized effort against the mob. We need to take these people on. They are often connected to big drug cartels; they are not just gangs of kids anymore. They are often the kinds of kids that are called super-predators—no conscience, no empathy. We can talk about why they ended up that way, but first we have to bring them to heel."

During this era, attacks on Black communities came from nearly every direction. Hollowed out by the public health crisis of crack cocaine, our communities were also broadly criminalized by our government.

Pop culture in the 1990s was once again a battlefield. I grew up during the era of gangsta rap, a hardcore form of music that graphically detailed the experiences of inner-city Black communities. I am far from a rap connoisseur, but I do have fond memories of convincing my parents to take me to the Warehouse to purchase my first album with explicit lyrics, which I am proud to say was from Yo-Yo, a protégé of Ice Cube from Niggaz wit Attitudes (N.W.A).

Of course, none of the lyrics that I was listening to mirrored my current life. I was being raised in a predominantly white suburban community where there weren't many Black people to begin with. But I distinctly remember watching televised hearings in Congress over gangsta rap in 1994 and laughing at the idea that somehow the music someone listened to made them want to emulate the behavior described in it. It took the testimony of notable rappers to explain to a panel of congresspeople that there should be more attention paid to what was happening in Black communities ravaged by drugs and violence than outrage over the music that reflected those realities. It was true— the white kids I went to school with listened to the same music, and it didn't mean there were drive-by shootings in Marin County, therefore it was bullshit to claim that somehow listening to music would make you emulate the behavior that critics claimed the music glorified. Again, it was much easier to address unsavory individual behavior than it was to address the movements and policies that had created those conditions in the first place.

There were congressional hearings about gangsta rap but no hearings on poverty in Black communities, no hearings to determine why the most salient avenue for economic progress was dealing drugs, no hearings to define the role that street organizations played in urban communities or how they provided family for kids in areas where families had been decimated by drug addiction, poverty, incarceration, or violence.

Black communities were being demonized for adapting to survive under some of the most dehumanizing conditions possible. Some of the loudest voices denouncing gangsta rap were from our own Black community. These voices were not a new phenomenon but represented an ongoing tension in Black communities. To some, crime, violence, and other kinds of dysfunction were best addressed by imparting "good" morals and values, by advocating for personal responsibility, and by increasing the presence of law enforcement in Black communities. Others thought that those problems could only be combated by first identifying and reforming racist policies and institutions.

In 1996, Clinton signed the Personal Responsibility and Work Opportunity Act, a bill that gave states control of welfare and ended nearly six decades of federal government control of the programs. In dismantling the federal welfare program, Clinton created the Temporary Assistance for Needy Families program (TANF), which changed the structure and financing of cash assistance programs. Welfare was now funded by federal block grants to states, along with requirements that states match some of the federal dollars.

Although the majority of welfare recipients were white women, Clinton implicitly furthered the notion, made popular by Ronald Reagan, of the "welfare queen." That's why TANF also included work requirements for aid—colloquially known as welfare-to-work programs—which shrank the number of people who could access aid and created caps for how long and how much aid a person could receive, while also instituting harsh punishments for recipients who did not comply with the rules.

When Clinton ushered in these two landmark pieces of legislation—one that put the criminalization of poor people and Black people on steroids, another that limited government support for poor communities assumed to be predominantly Black—it further advanced the agenda of the right, although it was done by a Democratic president. This agenda identified

Black people as a threat to the American way of life, people who took advantage of wasteful government programs that encouraged their beneficiaries to be lazy and live off the public dole. Attempts to control and contain Black communities and Black people—whether gangsta rappers or welfare abusers, drug dealers, super-predators, or gang members—were identified as the solution to that threat.

Fundamental to the ideology of the right is that there are people who are literally siphoning off the hard work of others, who want rights and protections that are unnecessary and undeserved and who do not contribute in any productive way to society. Importantly, this ideology is not limited to political party—as demonstrated by President Clinton and his instinctive desire to put Black people in our place.

Bill Clinton made a political career of being an overseer in Black communities while at the same time claiming to be a rare friend of those same communities. When faced with criticisms about the impacts of the 1994 crime bill or the bill severely curtailing welfare, he argued that they weren't racist, because Black communities pushed him to pass this legislation. As disingenuous as that defense is, it's not totally wrong.

There were Black advocates who supported those bills, often driven by desperation. Some believed that my generation had lost its moral compass—that we were the main impediment to our own progress. Others believed that government intervention, along with better behavior, would be the thing that saved Black communities from ourselves. All believed that there was something inherently wrong with us.

During the 1990s, Black leadership was fractured, still reeling from the turmoil of the last period of civil rights and Black power. Malcolm X was assassinated in 1965. The Reverend Dr.

Martin Luther King, Jr., was assassinated in 1968. Chairman Fred Hampton of the Black Panthers was assassinated in 1969, and Huey Newton was killed in 1989. Visible leadership in Black communities during the midcentury civil rights era was largely composed of male faith leaders. When the fight for civil rights transformed into a movement for Black Power and self-determination in the late 1960s and the 1970s, Black men still largely comprised that leadership, with Black women pushed to the sides and to the back. The Black Power movement collapsed—its leaders killed or marginalized or assimilated into conventional politics.

In the 1980s and 1990s, leaders like Jesse Jackson and Al Sharpton took the place of leaders like King and Newton. Politically, they were complicated figures. Jackson began his career working for Dr. King in the Southern Christian Leadership Conference (SCLC). He oversaw the Chicago chapter of Operation Breadbasket, an initiative designed to increase Black employment by placing pressure on white-owned businesses to hire Black people and use Black-owned suppliers. In 1971, Jackson split from the SCLC and went on to form the Rainbow PUSH Coalition (initially Operation People United to Save Humanity, later changed to People United to Serve Humanity). Jackson ran for president of the United States in 1984 and 1988, coming in third in the Democratic primaries in 1984 and securing even more votes in 1988 as only the second African American to run for president of the United States (after Shirley Chisholm).

Al Sharpton was the head of the Youth League of New York's Operation Breadbasket and later started the National Action Network, which led protests against racist violence throughout the 1990s.

As in previous generations, Black leadership as embodied by these two men was centered on charismatic male figures—and, in this case, figures also plagued by charges of corruption.

In some ways, the nineties were the era of patronage politics, and Jackson and Sharpton played that game. To be seen as a friend to Black people came at a price, whether it be a commitment to hiring Black people, supplying from Black businesses, or contributing to the organizations that were led by Black leaders. In some ways, this trivialized the issues affecting Black people by turning every crisis or crime against the community into an opportunity for a payout or leverage for a deal. Allowing for any crime, any injustice, any protest, to disappear with a well-placed check, helped keep policymakers from ever being truly accountable to Black communities.

While each man is known as a strong advocate for the rights of Black people, neither could consistently claim the moral high ground. Both Sharpton and Jackson are rumored to have been involved in business deals and other activities that undermined their moral authority. Jackson was trained under King, and King himself expressed concerns about what he considered Jackson's self-serving behavior (to be clear, King was no angel and had self-serving behaviors of his own). Sharpton admits to cooperating with the FBI, though he asserted in 2014, "I was not and am not a rat, because I was not with the rats. I'm a cat. I chase rats," claiming that he was not an informant but that he worked to help the FBI to capture notorious mob figures and associates in the music business, including boxing and music promoter Don King, who had threatened him because of his own music industry activities. "If you're the victim of a threat, you're not an informant—you're a victim trying to protect yourself. . . . I encourage kids all the time to work with law enforcement—you're acting like it's a scandal for me to do that?"

Indeed, working with the FBI *is* controversial. Many of the Black liberation movements were targeted by the FBI for their political activity through government programs such as COINTELPRO. Sharpton's remarks gloss over the historic role of the state in surveilling and disrupting Black social movements of all types—liberal and radical ones alike.

Jackson and Sharpton's leadership raised questions about what vision they were leading Black America toward. Are the conditions that existed in Black America—racial antagonism, high unemployment and underemployment, disparities in health and educational achievement, and so on—resolved by Black capitalism, traditional charismatic male leadership, and leaders with opaque motivations and objectives?

Movements shape us, and we shape them—sometimes consciously, other times unconsciously. My generation was and is still being shaped by the conservative consensus and the right's rise to power. The entrenchment of conservative values, ideologies, stories, and policies in every structure, every system that organizes our lives has had profound consequences on the way we live and who we are.

In the fractured and regressive political environment I have described above, my story as an organizer began. There was a lot of work to do and a lot to learn—and unlearn, as the case would be.

PART II

A NEW GENERATION EMERGES

CHAPTER THREE

FIRST LESSONS

ORGANIZING IS THE PROCESS OF COMING TOGETHER WITH other people who share your concerns and values to work toward a change in some kind of policy, usually of the government, but also of universities, private companies, and other institutions whose policies affect and shape our lives. Organizing has been a part of who I am ever since I can remember, although for a long time I didn't call it by that name—I thought I was just working with other people to solve the problems that impacted our lives. For me, organizing is as much about human connection and building relationships as it is about achieving a political goal. The work feeds me. It's embedded in who I am. But the idea of building relationships with our neighbors and others in order to accomplish things in the world is embedded in all of our lives: It's part of all the things we do every day to survive, to feed ourselves, to express ourselves, to restore ourselves. Humans are social creatures; connection is at the core of who we are. And organizing is connecting with a purpose. When we connect to others, we learn about them and about ourselves. And that understanding is the beginning of real political change.

Part of my motivation for organizing was a desire not to feel alone in the world. To know that there are people out there who are experiencing similar things, are facing similar questions and contradictions, and who know deep inside that the way things are isn't the way they have to be. Everyone finds that primary point of connection in different places. For some activists and organizers, that connection is found in a shared concern or problem. For others, it is found in a shared vision for what's possible. For me, it's a little bit of both: the process of getting from a connection found in a shared problem or concern to a connection about a shared vision for what is possible—from a shared problem to a shared future.

That's a journey you can't make alone. Growing up as a Black girl in Marin County, a predominantly white suburb of San Francisco, I regularly experienced what it was like to be the "only one" and what being the only one meant for the prospects of my survival. I was an only child until I was eight. I was often the only or one of the only Black children in my schools, in my neighborhood, in my family. I lived in a world that rewarded conformity, but I never felt the same as most of the people I grew up with and around. I knew how it felt to be treated differently, but I had a sense that it wasn't something you could do much about.

Being Black in a predominantly white environment, I experienced all the ways that Blackness was penalized: I had to deal with beauty standards that excluded me, unfair racialized accusations and microaggressions from authority figures, and teachers who assumed I wasn't smart or capable, policed my relationships with my classmates—in particular when it came to gender and sexuality—and affixed racist stereotypes and ignorance to my very existence. I had a teacher in fifth grade who asked me if the bottoms of my feet were as light as the palms of my hands.

But it was more complicated than that. My Blackness was both demonized and romanticized. I was often the only Black person my friends knew, and I wasn't like the Black people they saw on television or whose music they listened to—this confused them. I knew that the things that gave me currency among white students—my straightened hair, my proximity to white wealth and privilege, the resources that allowed me to excel academically—were not always accessible to my few Black peers. I saw how some forms of social currency changed how people perceived my Blackness; I also saw how my Blackness changed how much value that social currency gave me. This introduced me to the truth that while each of us carries the particular privileges and burdens of our individual lives, those burdens are dramatically shaped by race, gender, class, citizenship, sexuality, disability, and other features of our identity.

Once I started college, at the University of California, San Diego, I experienced for the first time what being different meant on a much more intimate level—what it meant for my own survival. I moved from a small, polite environment where everyone sort of knew one another to an environment that was bigger, much less connected, and more socially diverse. For the first time, I was seeing myself in my environment while at the same time feeling very alienated from it. There were still only a small number of Black people in my university but enough that being different wasn't such a lonely burden to bear.

The strange reality that I was living in began to make sense when I was introduced to Black feminist thought. I learned that I wasn't the only one who felt this alienated. Black feminists had been writing about Black women and belonging in a world that was mostly shaped around the preferences, tastes, and other norms of white people and whiteness—a world that included that very college I was attending. It was there that I was exposed to different ways of thinking about why the world functions the way it does and different methods for achieving change. I learned from queer Black women and other queer women of color—my peers and teachers and creators of the art and literature I devoured. I read everything I could get my hands on by Audre Lorde, bell hooks, Cherríe Moraga, and Patricia Hill Collins. For the first time, I had Black teachers, some of whom were queer. I began to understand that difference was a source of strength and power, that being on the outside provided a different vantage point—one with potentially more range and insight. The world revealed itself in fresh ways, and I wanted to know more. I decided to major in anthropology and sociology—I wanted to immerse myself in people and culture.

I also learned about how relationships of power were shaped by race, class, gender, and sexuality. I worked at the student health center on campus, doing HIV testing and counseling as well as pregnancy prevention; I joined a student organization that was connected to Planned Parenthood; and I sat on the board of an organization designed to support gay, lesbian, bisexual, and transgender people. I was also learning about Margaret Sanger, who pushed eugenics as a way to build support for the birth control pill. When our local office of Planned Parenthood celebrated Margaret Sanger Day, I not only refused to participate but understood more clearly that everything in our lives is shaped by these factors, and my life was no different.

When I graduated from college, I wasn't sure what I wanted to do next. I felt like I was still learning about the world and wasn't quite ready to make a decision on what I would be doing with the rest of my life. I wanted to move back home to the Bay Area. I'd had enough of Southern California. I was in a relationship with someone who still had another year to go at UC Santa Cruz and I wanted to be closer to them. I applied to a number of programs that focused on youth, including Teach For America and AmeriCorps. I was accepted to both, but the AmeriCorps job was in Daly City in the Bay Area, doing what I most wanted to do, working with youth of color.

The novelty wore off pretty quickly. The program paid a mere $12,000 a year for full-time employment, with the promise of a $25,000 tuition award at the end of a year. After getting oriented to the program, we were promptly taken to the welfare office to sign up for food stamps. I worked for my parents at their antiques store and took a contract teaching job at a middle school in Oakland to supplement my income. Still, I was always broke. My roommate, a friend from Marin County, had wealthy parents whose money helped subsidize us both.

For a year, through AmeriCorps, I worked at a health clinic providing HIV/AIDS and pregnancy testing and counseling to young people in Daly City. I also helped support a related violence-prevention program. I volunteered at an organization to end sexual violence called San Francisco Women Against Rape (SFWAR) and participated as a peer counselor, facilitator, hotline volunteer, and medical advocate for people who'd experienced violence. As I did these jobs, I once again became aware of the contradictions within many of these efforts. I was getting to work directly with youth of color, in an organization that was mostly staffed by people of color, and yet most of the teachers and administrators were white. Some of the frameworks that we used seemed to perpetuate a "savior complex" as opposed to enabling and empowering young people to make the decisions that were best for them. Some people in the organization would describe issues like young girls dating men at least ten years their senior as "cultural norms," sounding more like tourists or anthropologists than members of these communities.

My volunteer duties at SFWAR felt more aligned with my emerging sense of politics, but they also helped shape my understanding of my own identity: Most of the staff was queer and of color. Being in that environment helped me explore my own sexuality, as I found myself attracted to and attractive to dykes and butches and trans people. During our training as volunteers, we learned about various systems of oppression—much as I had in college—but this learning was not academic; it wasn't detached from our own experiences. We were seeing how those systems functioned on the ground, in people's real lives—in our lives.

SFWAR was going through a transition: It was trying to move from a one-way organization that simply provided services in response to a pressing need to one that had a two-way relationship with the people who received them—both providing services and learning from, adapting to, and integrating the recipients into the process. This shift brought with it some upheaval, internally and externally. There wasn't a clear agreement internally about which direction to head in. Having taken on a more explicitly political stance, SFWAR was being attacked from the outside—and the work itself was hard enough without the added stress of death threats coming through our switchboard or funders threatening to withdraw.

The more I looked, the harder it was to ignore that many of the organizations and efforts I'd become a part of and invested my time and passion into had never intended to include people like me in the first place—or only allowed our entry on terms that were not dignified. I became disillusioned about change and activism; I felt isolated and unsure. Before, the loneliness was comforting to me—in some ways, it was self-righteous. Now the loneliness was different.

. . .

My time at SFWAR was coming to a close, and one day I received a notice on a listserv I belonged to advertising a training program for developing organizers. They were looking for young people, ages eighteen to thirty, to apply to participate in an eight-week program that promised "political education trainings" and "organizing intensives." Each person selected would be placed in a community-based organization for training, and many organizations were inclined to hire the interns if their time during the summer proved successful. I wasn't sure what my next steps were after AmeriCorps and SFWAR, and the program sounded interesting to me, so I decided to apply. I was accepted.

The program had a rigor that I craved. Each day we were expected to show up on time and prepared. The political education trainings were engaging yet challenging. Two days a week, we read political theorists and explored topics like capitalism and imperialism, patriarchy and homophobia, and the history of social movements. The other days, we would work in community-based grassroots organizations. We were given a small stipend to live off during those eight weeks, while putting in what would sometimes be ten-to-twelve-hour days. We would also have weekly check-ins with the lead trainers to review what we were learning and troubleshoot any challenges.

Many of us were paired with another participant in the program; I was paired with a young Afro Puerto Rican gay man from Chicago who'd just done a six-month stint living in a tree in order to protect it from developers. His father was a police officer, but he was a free spirit who smoked a lot of weed, didn't wear underwear, and ate garlic rather than wearing deodorant. Each day we would go to the storefront where the organization was located, do role-plays on organizing with the staff, and then head out to West Oakland to knock on doors.

We were looking for people who wanted to get organized in response to a plan announced by the mayor to move 10,000 new residents into downtown Oakland in ten years. West Oakland is adjacent to downtown, so moving new residents into downtown really meant increased development and real estate speculation in West Oakland. Many of the residents of West Oakland at that time were poor or working middle class. Scores of elderly residents had been in those communities for decades, ever since the wartime boom encouraged them to move west from Louisiana, Mississippi, and other southern states. It was our goal to recruit one hundred West Oakland residents to participate in a community meeting to talk about the plans and their impact on the community and to build strategies to bring the community's influence to bear.

That summer, we talked to more than a thousand people. Our method was simply going door to door. My internship partner wasn't big on door knocking. As I would knock on each door and talk with residents, he could often be found smoking a cigarette outside or sitting on the curb, picking weeds and wildflowers and turning them into jewelry. But I loved it.

I started to feel fed again. Each door I knocked on reminded me of a family member, and each conversation taught me that much more about myself and the world around me. I learned how to really listen for what was underneath "No, I don't think I can make it" or "I need to give my kids a bath that night" or "Sure, I'll try to stop by." Everything that was not "Yes, I will definitely be there" was an opportunity to get them there eventually. We would learn about each other's families, our experiences in politics and activism, and each other. I spent countless hours in kitchens and living rooms, on crowded couches and porches, and in backyards. I learned how to engage other people in the slow process of changing the world.

Before the summer was out, I was offered a job, which I gladly accepted. I'd become hooked on organizing, obsessed with political theory, and committed to the work. I threw myself headfirst into it and moved from my much-too-expensive apartment in San Francisco to Oakland.

CHAPTER FOUR

THE FIRST FIGHT

MUCH OF WHAT I KNOW ABOUT MOVEMENT BUILDING, I learned by organizing in Black communities. And Bayview Hunters Point is where I learned to organize—the site of some of my most cherished moments of human connection and my most painful lessons about how power really operates. It was in Bayview Hunters Point where I learned to love the hardest, and it is where my heart was broken over and over again.

Organizing is about building relationships and using those relationships to accomplish together what we cannot accomplish on our own—but there's more to it than that. The mission and purpose of organizing is to build power. Without power, we are unable to change conditions in our communities that hurt us. A movement is successful if it transforms the dynamics and relationships of power—from power being concentrated in the hands of a few to power being held by many.

Most people, when they think about power, are actually envisioning empowerment. I think those things are related, but different. Power is the ability to impact and affect the conditions of your own life and the lives of others. Empowerment, on the other hand, is feeling good about yourself, akin to having high self-esteem. Empowerment is what happens when people come together and don't feel alone anymore and don't feel like they're the only ones who experience what they do. Unless empowerment is transformed into power, not much will change about our environments. It's power that determines whether or not a community will be gentrified, a school district funded, a family provided with quality healthcare that is affordable on any budget.

Organizing in Bayview Hunters Point taught me a lot about power—what it is, what it isn't, how it operates, how it can be challenged, and how it can be transformed. Through a decade of organizing in this small but mighty community, I learned lessons that were valuable not just to the project of building power in San Francisco but to the larger project of building movements across the nation.

Community organizing is often romanticized, but the actual work is about tenacity, perseverance, and commitment. It's not the same as being a pundit, declaring your opinions and commentary about the world's events on your social media platforms. Community organizing is the messy work of bringing people together, from different backgrounds and experiences, to change the conditions they are living in. It is the work of building relationships among people who may believe they have nothing in common so that together they can achieve a common goal. That means that as an organizer, you help different parts of the community learn about one another's histories and embrace one another's humanity as an incentive to fight together. An organizer challenges their own faults and deficiencies while encouraging others to challenge theirs. An organizer works well in groups and alone. Organizers are engaged in solving the ongoing puzzle of how to build enough power to change the conditions that keep people in misery.

An organizer is simultaneously selfless and selfish. They are selfless because they know that sparking a desire for justice requires they do more listening than talking, more stepping back so others may step forward. They are selfish because, in doing for others, they are feeding themselves. Unlocking a hunger for social change inside someone else is strangely rewarding. It is a confirmation that the countless hours you spend trying to untangle that knot are worthwhile. An organizer gets high off motivating others to take action.

In 2005, I joined a small grassroots organization called People Organized to Win Employment Rights (POWER) to help start a new organizing project focused on improving the lives of Black residents in the largest remaining Black community in San Francisco.

I'd been following POWER for a long time. It was founded in 1997 with the mission to "end poverty and oppression once and for all." POWER was best known for its work to raise the minimum wage in San Francisco to what was, at the time, the highest in the country, and for its resistance to so-called welfare reform, which it dubbed "welfare deform." POWER was unique among grassroots organizations in San Francisco because of its explicit focus on Black communities. That was one of the aspects that attracted me to the organization's work. POWER was everything I was looking for in an organization at that point in my life—a place where I could learn, a place where I would be trained in the craft of organizing and in the science of politics, and a place where I didn't have to leave my beliefs, my values, and my politics at the door each day when I went to work.

Joining POWER would change how I thought about organizing forever.

I had very little understanding of how to start a campaign when I joined the staff at POWER—but I didn't have to figure it out on my own. Soon after I started, a co-worker broke it down for me: "Starting a campaign is like starting a fistfight. Sometimes you just need to punch someone in the face, step back, and see what happens." Well, I'd never been in a fistfight, but I could understand the approach, theoretically.

We were looking for Black people who wanted to organize to make San Francisco a better place for our communities—but the problem was, the Black community in San Francisco was diminishing at a rapid pace. In 1970, the Black population in San Francisco was 13.4 percent; by the time I'd started at POWER in 2005, the Black population had dropped by more than half, to 6.5 percent. Redevelopment activities, sometimes called urban renewal (or "Negro removal," as some Black folks had dubbed it), had transformed San Francisco's once bustling and thriving Black district called the Fillmore into a playground for young, wealthy white professionals with families. Many who were displaced from the Fillmore District relocated to Bayview Hunters Point, a small community in the southeastern section of the city.

Bayview Hunters Point didn't exist on tourist maps; it was often a shaded-out section, stretched wide along the southern edge of the city like an extended hand. Bayview Hunters Point contained most of the Black people who remained in San Francisco, with a few remaining in the Tenderloin, Lakeview, and scattered Fillmore neighborhoods.

As a teenager, I'd made a few clandestine excursions to the neighborhood, but I'd never spent much time there as an adult.

It struck me as relatively isolated. It had once been home to a commercial shipyard, which was later taken over by the U.S. Navy, a power plant, and shrimping businesses. Large, nondescript rectangular buildings with few windows characterized a significant portion of the community, surrounding an inner core of Victorian-style single-family homes. The best views were reserved for the public housing residents, perched on top of a hill overlooking the San Francisco Bay on one side and the rest of the city, from the Mission District to downtown, on the other. The Hill was home to the highest concentration of public housing in the entire city, above the infamous Hunters Point Naval Shipyard. The community was relatively small, the sort of place where everyone seemed to know everyone. When I traveled around the area, it wasn't uncommon for me to be stopped by someone asking what part of the neighborhood I was from—it would happen when I was walking down the street or if I was in a car, stopped at a traffic light.

Years of disinvestment and neglect had left this neighborhood fundamentally ravaged, but it was sitting on some of the best land in the city, along with some of the best weather. While San Francisco was known for its fog, Bayview Hunters Point got sunshine, thanks to the microclimates that characterize the Bay Area.

Quietly, developers and city officials began discussing and planning for a massive redevelopment project with Bayview Hunters Point as its epicenter. It was to become the largest redevelopment project in the history of San Francisco.

Gentrification had become synonymous with development in our city. Coffee shops, beer gardens, high-end boutiques, and specialty grocery stores often came with eviction notices, "right to return" vouchers that somehow were never redeemed, increased police presence, and the flight of poor and working-class families, mostly Black and brown, who could not afford the amenities that came with the new residents seeking San Francisco's hottest new neighborhood.

Our work to build an organizing project to improve life for the city's Black communities began with learning more about how people in the community were experiencing the silent but persistent efforts by the city and developers to transform their neighborhood. We went from house to house and attended city-sponsored community meetings on the redevelopment activities. But we also joined meetings with organizations working on other issues, from fighting to clean up the toxic environment of the Hunters Point Naval Shipyard, created by industries that flouted regulations and improperly disposed of hazardous materials, to groups working to empower youth to be change makers. As a group coming from outside the neighborhood, we realized we had to gain the approval of the community. We needed to hear that the residents wanted us to be there and saw some value in our presence.

We certainly weren't the first organization of our kind in Bayview Hunters Point. Plenty of people had been involved in community organizations of some sort, whether it was church groups that supported the poor or groups devoted to racial empowerment like the Nation of Islam. What the community didn't have was power. While organizations were plentiful, none could change what was happening to their community, at least not on their own.

I would spend my afternoons going from house to house, sitting with folks at a kitchen table or leaning on a porch, talking with a resident as they peered through a thick screen door at me. I would run through a set of questions designed to get to know them better and learn more about what they cared about.

How long have you lived in this community? What do you like about it?

Have you noticed any changes? What are you seeing?

Did you know that Bayview Hunters Point is now a redevelopment project? How do you feel about the changes happening in the community?

What kinds of changes do you think need to happen in this community? Do you think the city wants the same changes?

Why do you think the city wants to make changes here now?

Who do you think these changes are for?

What do you think it would take to get the changes here that the community wants?

Do you want to be a part of an organization that is fighting to make sure all of the changes that happen in this community are for the benefit of this community?

Over the course of a few months, I had a couple hundred of these conversations with residents throughout the community. I talked to middle-class families trying to stay in the neighborhood. I talked to people who'd grown up in the neighborhood and had inherited their homes from their parents or grandparents but were struggling to hold on to them. I talked to families living in public housing and young people who were gang-affiliated. I talked with pastors and I talked with elders. I talked with people who worked at local service agencies, clinics, and libraries. I talked with business owners and workers. I got to know the names of grandchildren and pets, and eventually I started to be invited off the porch and into the home. Soon, the people behind those doors we knocked on became familiar faces who would attend and plan neighborhood meetings to address their concerns.

San Francisco has never been a city that is friendly to Black people, but that hasn't stopped individual Black people from having and wielding power there—some on behalf of the most vulnerable residents, and others on behalf of the powerful interests that preyed on the most vulnerable. It was as if some had adopted the notion of eat or be eaten when it came to that community. Some leaders could deliver a good talk, laced with grandeur about Black power, and as soon as the applause died down, turn around and take a payment from a corporation to advocate for something damaging to the community.

I realized there were two kinds of leaders, and I started to identify them by name and reputation. Some, like Elouise Westbrook, Espanola Jackson, and Enola Maxwell, were considered the mothers of the community. They worked on behalf of and with the Black women who lived in public housing and were recipients of general assistance to bring more resources to the residents in the form of childcare, affordable housing, and jobs.

And then there were those who sought to wield influence through their relationships with corporations and developers. Under the administration of then-mayor Willie Brown, Jr., a powerful figure in both municipal and state politics, many Black people were given patronage jobs in exchange for support of projects that often benefited powerful interests. After Brown completed his second term as mayor, some of these same people became "community consultants" for companies like Pacific Gas and Electric, while others headed city departments like the Department of Sanitation or occupied posts on boards and commissions like the Redevelopment Agency. It was this crew that greased the wheels for the major redevelopment programs that would displace the Black voters these same people had entered politics to represent.

When I talked to people from other parts of San Francisco about Bayview, I'd hear all kinds of stories—you would think the neighborhood was simply full of guns, drugs, and gangs. But there was nothing simple about the Bayview I discovered. There were Black families, Southeast Asian families, Latino families, and white families. There were young people and elders, and no one fit a stereotype. Someone who might be labeled a drug dealer went to church each and every Sunday, and even if they did sell drugs, they also helped elderly women with their groceries. An older woman could be dressed to the nines every day and yet have no food in her refrigerator and no one to visit her. You could walk past a crew of young men shooting dice and find out they were discussing a new policy the mayor was pushing. I would find out more and more about this community each day I walked the streets and knocked on doors, sometimes until it was dark. I knocked on thousands of doors, and never did I feel unsafe.

The first campaign we worked on involved a community beautification project called underground wiring, which required each residential property to pay up to $1,400 to place the utility wires that crisscrossed the area above their homes beneath the streets instead. Residents who were unable to pay could be subject to having a lien placed on their home. The City and County of San Francisco sent letters to each homeowner in Bayview Hunters Point giving instructions on how to complete the work. Households that didn't comply received increasingly threatening letters. At some homes I visited, householders would come to the door with the opened envelope in their hand, confused about why they were being required to pay for something that was billed as a city beautification project. To make matters worse, the median income in the neighborhood at that time was approximately $40,000, half the citywide median income. For many who were just barely making it, $1,400 was a steep bill to pay.

The city had a program that would help residents in need to pay for the "undergrounding"—but the program only had enough money for a few residents to take advantage of it. Most residents had no idea that the program existed, and the city didn't do much to publicize it. We immediately went to work making sure each resident knew there was a program that would pay for the underground wiring, and we began organizing residents around the project.

Most of the people we talked to were angry that the city was threatening residents with a lien on their homes. Longtime residents were able to draw parallels between the Negro removal of the 1950s and the new redevelopment projects that were coming to their neighborhood. Our community meetings quickly grew from a dozen or so participants to between seventy-five and one hundred residents per meeting.

Meetings always included food, childcare, and translation, and at that time most were held in the community room of the local library. Miss Linda, the librarian, was appreciative of the efforts being made to organize the community to fight back effectively against an onslaught of corporate-led development. She ensured that the community room was available on the third Saturday of each month.

Our physical office was located in the Mid-Market area of San Francisco, next to an old Greyhound station that was eventually converted into the city's Department of Homeland Security office, above a methadone clinic that served the many addicts who populated the streets, and just a few short blocks from City Hall. From our offices, Bayview Hunters Point was a twenty-three-minute drive by car and approximately an hour by bus—a distance of four and a half miles. The city's subway system didn't serve Bayview, so transportation was a big part of what cut residents off from jobs and other opportunities.

To set up our community meetings, I'd have to get up early on a Saturday and commute from my apartment in East Oakland to our office in San Francisco for the meeting supplies and materials, picking up two to three members along the way; we'd arrive at the library about an hour before the meeting to set up. We often put together the agenda for the meeting with our members, most of whom were seniors in the community, people on fixed incomes, and those who couldn't afford to pay for the project and were now faced with eviction because of a lien. Together, we'd figure out what we needed to accomplish and strategize an approach to tackle our problem.

In time, we developed a set of demands for the city related to the underground-wiring project. We called them "demands" because we wanted to be clear that we wouldn't give up on them without a fight. We demanded that the city pay the wiring cost for every resident who could prove they made at or below the neighborhood median income of $40,000 per year; we demanded the city hold community meetings to inform people of the program; and we demanded that they remove the threat of placing a lien on someone's home for not being able to pay the cost of the underground wiring.

We next set up meetings with city administrators, many of whom weren't sympathetic at first—they'd hear us out but then respond with a shrug: "Sorry, there's not much we can do." One day, we decided to perform a direct action: We brought approximately fifteen seniors to the office overseeing the project and chanted in the waiting room about the racism of the program, demanding to see the head of the department. We left within two hours—victorious. The city had agreed to our conditions. They would accept every application for the subsidy program, as long as the applicant could prove that their income was at or below $40,000 per year.

Immediately, we got to work setting up community clinics where people could come to get support on their subsidy applications. All in all, we convinced the city to increase the program budget by $750,000 to cover every resident who wanted to take advantage of it. It was our first big win, and now we were making waves in the community—including among some of the neighborhood's longtime power brokers.

At POWER, we'd accomplished our goal of getting the city to pay for the improvements that it sought to impose on residents. It wasn't freedom, but it was something that was widely and deeply felt, particularly by low-income seniors in the neighborhood. The way we accomplished it was also important: The campaign was a good example of how to use escalating tactics to put pressure on people with power. We used direct action when meetings alone proved ineffective. Bringing the people who were affected face-to-face with the people who were making decisions over their lives also helped make visible who made those decisions and why they made decisions the way they did— without community input or consultation, and without concern for how their decisions would impact the people they were making decisions about. It helped clarify what was at stake—if the people in the community who were most vulnerable to the negative impacts of redeveloping their neighborhood were not involved in shaping those decisions or how they were implemented, the people who needed that development the most would not benefit from it. Together, the informational meetings and the confrontations politicized the community members who were involved. The city called the project a beautification program that would improve the quality of life in the neighborhood—but through meetings and pressure we exposed its real agenda, which was to improve the quality of life for prospective residents at the expense of existing residents.

By 2007, POWER joined a neighborhood coalition that had come together to organize residents of the community to ensure that the development project slated for the neighborhood would benefit people currently living there, not just the residents the city was trying to attract. Our coalition was approached by a progressive member of the Board of Supervisors about a campaign idea he had that would win guaranteed benefits for Bayview residents. By then we'd built a relatively strong base of community members who were now active in the fight to take back their neighborhood. Our community meetings were robust and consistent, averaging about fifty people each month.

Chris Daly was a controversial figure on the board, to say the least. Daly was a white, Duke-educated cisgender male who was unconcerned with convention or compromise. Daly had entered San Francisco city politics through his work with people who were homeless and those who received some sort of government assistance. His election to the board set the stage for the election of several other progressive supervisors; as a relatively senior member, Daly was an important, if volatile, part of a progressive majority. He had developers and corporations who were bad actors in his sights—and he was more than happy not just to be vocal about that but to try to maneuver policy so that developers and corporations had to pay their fair share.

When we met, he pitched the idea of creating a ballot measure to require that half of all new housing built in the redevelopment zone be made affordable to people in the community at or below the neighborhood median income, which was still hovering around $40,000 a year. For context, that year the median income for the region was a little bit above $100,000 a year. This approach would force the redevelopment project to increase affordable housing units to more than the 15 percent required by state law, and even higher than the 25 percent that had become the norm in other municipalities. It would have been a lifesaver for San Franciscans, many of whom, like me, were being priced out of the city or were close to being unable to afford housing.

There was a catch, however: To move forward, we had to gather signatures to qualify the measure for the upcoming election, which would be held in June of the following year. That meant we needed 8,000 signatures by the deadline, in less than three weeks. Anyone who signed our measure had to already be registered to vote. And if we got the signatures we needed and qualified to be on the ballot, we still had to campaign for the measure to pass in the general election. To win, we would need about five times more votes than signatures—40,000, give or take.

Our coalition loved the idea of the initiative but was skeptical about our ability to pull it off. POWER hadn't done much electoral organizing on its own, much less led and anchored that kind of campaign. Would we be able to collect that many signatures? Was what we were proposing with the measure even possible—could you make it a rule that the housing built in the largest development project the city had ever seen be made affordable to people who were low-income? How would we get the resources to run such a campaign? We were a small, underfunded grassroots organization with explicitly radical politics, and much of our work with elected officials was confrontational, which some elected officials were turned off by—especially if they were the target of it. From a certain perspective, you could say our electoral work was mostly making the mayor and other city officials angry and vengeful when we targeted them and exposed their unholy alliance with the rich and powerful. Not quite the same kind of project as building a coalition for a citywide campaign with groups and individuals who didn't share our politics and didn't all agree with our strategies.

But we still thought it was a great idea—and could see a

fuzzy path to success. Daly had relationships with people who had resources they were willing to contribute to help us get the campaign started. One person he knew was willing to give us a free version of the voter database created by NGP VAN, a technology provider to Democratic and progressive campaigns and organizations, to make sure every signer was a registered voter. We had a robust network of volunteers who would be willing to help gather the signatures needed. We'd begun working closely with the Nation of Islam, environmental justice organizations like Greenaction for Health and Environmental Justice and the Sierra Club, and other faith-based organizers who would lend their support. After talking with our coalition partners, as well as the membership that POWER had built in the neighborhood, and debating the best approach, we decided to give it a shot.

Quickly, we calculated what it would take to get to 8,000 valid signatures, breaking it down by number of shifts, people required to fill those shifts, and signatures per hour needed to reach our goal. We mapped out locations across the city where we thought we'd have the best chance of success. And we set up daily shifts of volunteers who would use the few computers in our office to check each signature as it came in. I drew a thermometer on a large piece of butcher paper to track our progress. If we exceeded 8,000 by a margin of error that could account for invalid signatures, we would be in business. So we set out to collect 10,000 signatures—and we had two weeks to do it.

Weekdays were slow, and at first the signatures trickled in. But when we hit the weekend, things started to move. We set up petition stations at grocery stores around the city, with a focus on working-class neighborhoods. We knocked on doors throughout Bayview Hunters Point. Even though we knew this was a slower and less effective way to collect the signatures than street canvassing, we thought it was important to deeply engage community residents with the most at stake—they, of all people, would be motivated by the idea that half of all new housing built in the zone would be affordable to people who lived in the community.

Each day, we gave four-hour shifts to our volunteers. When they came to the office, they picked up materials—a clipboard, a few sheets of the petition, and information on the next membership meeting. For those who weren't familiar with canvassing, we conducted an orientation that covered the goals and objectives of the organization, the goals and objectives of the campaign, and things to look out for while gathering signatures. If a petition sheet came back completed, the signatures were checked immediately to ensure that the people who signed were registered voters in the City and County of San Francisco. We were assisted by members of the Nation of Islam, who, I noticed, mobilized quickly and efficiently.

At the end of ten days, we had collected 11,414 signatures. Now there was another step—having the city attorney certify the results. Just as we'd done with the signature collection, we set up shifts of volunteers, this time to observe employees in the city attorney's office as they checked each signature for validity. We weren't ready to let all that hard work get swept under the rug by political calculations behind the scenes. And just like that, the first improbable step was completed: In November 2007, we qualified the measure for the ballot. The general election would be held in June 2008. A combination of faith, hard work, and extended networks had brought us the initial victory—but how were we going to pull off the rest? There was no time to celebrate. Our coalition had six months to convince voters in San Francisco to pass the measure.

Our measure had been assigned the letter "F," and thus the Proposition F campaign had begun. We decided the "F" stood for Families, Fairness, and the Future.

. . .

Of course, there were people working just as hard—and with vastly greater resources—on the other side of the question. Our ballot measure was set to throw a serious wrench into the plans of a multibillion-dollar developer that had its eyes on Bayview Hunters Point: the Lennar Corporation.

Lennar was carefully working through a plan to take Bayview Hunters Point and turn it into San Francisco's hottest new neighborhood. The first step in its plan was to acquire the land for next to nothing and have the city roll out a red carpet of benefits and tax breaks in exchange for Lennar's work to develop and sell a neighborhood that was seen as undesirable. The city came through on that part: It sold eight hundred acres of waterfront land to the Lennar Corporation for one dollar. Why so cheap? Some of the land was contaminated with toxins.

Bayview Hunters Point was formerly home to the Hunters Point Naval Shipyard, one of the only dry docks on the west coast. The shipyard was built in 1870, purchased by the United States Navy in 1940, and permanently closed in 1994. For years it had been the main economic engine for the community. During the 1940s, many Black people migrating from the south found decent work and decent pay at the shipyard. During wartime, it was used to decontaminate ships that carried components for the first atomic bomb. After World War II, the Naval Radiological Defense Laboratory occupied part of the area, where it decontaminated ships employed in nuclear testing in the Pacific and studied the effects of radiation on laboratory animals and human beings.

Many residents whose families had lived in the community for generations had stories about that shipyard, and it was hard to distinguish legend from fact. The lab conducted tests on both human and animal subjects, and some people believed that those who did not survive were buried on the site. Others remembered vividly when a fire burned underground on the shipyard for nearly thirty days before someone came to do something about it. The stories were retold many times and passed down through generations, so that the details had gotten blurry and urban legends began to weave in with the truth.

What was unmistakably true, however, was that Bayview Hunters Point was a community that was neglected, ignored, and ridiculed. When the navy closed the shipyard, it clipped the community's economic lifeline. The many businesses that supported the shipyard shut down. Older residents told me stories about how the neighborhood thrived before the bottom fell out. Their stories were funny and, considering how neglected the neighborhood currently was, seemed almost absurd—the storyteller would paint a picture of roller-skating rinks and Black-owned banks and doctor's offices and grocery stores. It was hard to imagine when I looked around at what surrounded us.

Bayview Hunters Point didn't have a single full-service grocery store. Instead, its residents shopped at dollar stores with packaged processed food beneath the standards of regular grocery stores, discounted because it was not grocery store quality. Liquor stores and discount stores seemed to hold down the corners of every block. A few family-owned businesses with irregular hours dotted the main street; even when they were open, they looked closed.

But it was a community that, despite it all, had no shortage of heart, determination, and resilience. Even when people lowered their voices and cast their eyes downward when talking about the current state of things, I could sense a community where people looked out for one another, cared about what happened to their neighborhood, and deeply wanted the community to thrive once again. I'd never felt more safe than I did in Bayview. Behind the windows with slate-gray grates covering them were people watching what was going on. Behind the double-locked front doors were families who loved and laughed, families who took care of one another and their neighbors. The neighborhood had a radical Black newspaper called *The Bay View;* the editors, Willie and Mary Ratcliff, actively recruited community members to write about issues impacting the neighborhood and Black people throughout the world. They circulated the newspaper to people in prisons and jails—to the degree that the warden would allow it. To me, they were one of many signs of fierce life, community spirit, and resistance in the neighborhood.

It was also indicative of the area's core identity: While a wide range of ethnicities lived there, Bayview was fundamentally a Black community.

Even Lennar knew that Bayview Hunters Point was a Black community, and it was intent on figuring out how to use that information for its campaign. This turned into a fascinating sociological study for me—observing the behaviors Lennar adopted in order to fit in as a means of accomplishing its agenda. The company spent considerable capital brokering relationships with Black people. When Lennar presented redevelopment plans at community meetings, it made sure to send Black representatives to present those plans. The community meetings were catered with soul food, with the usual spread of fried chicken, greens, and macaroni and cheese.

Bayview Hunters Point was the first place where I was forced to grapple with the contradictions Black people engage in to survive—whatever survival means for them. It also forced me to grapple with a brutal reality: Not all Black people want the best for Black people. In fact, some will knowingly harm Black people for their own benefit, everyone else be damned.

Patronage and "pay to play" politics had become commonplace in San Francisco. This kind of practice was routine under

the administration of then-mayor Willie Brown, Jr., but patronage politics were commonplace under white mayors too. "Community consultants"—people who were paid by the developer
or other corporations to help win favor for proposed projects—
were regular fixtures in most public meetings I attended about
the redevelopment project. They were familiar faces: Mostly cisgender men, they'd arrive in suits that were ill-tailored, with
gold rings and watches. They would enter the hearing, wait for
the public comment period, say a few sentences about how
Black people had been ignored for too long and we needed this
project to bring jobs to the community, and then they would
leave. I would watch this theater and get annoyed and angry but
also sometimes amused. It was fascinating to me that these people were being paid by the company to deliver rubber-stamp
statements about support or opposition to this or that project
but would never have been directly hired into the company
through regular channels had they tried it. They had a place and
they stayed in it.

We started to discover that this sort of patronage politics could work against us but could sometimes work for us.
The downside, of course, was when the community consultants would publicly attack and try to delegitimize us. They
would frame us as "outsiders who were experimenting on a
poor Black community that deserved so much more than it
was getting." We would be accused of wanting to take food
out of mouths and money out of pockets. Their argument was
bluntly material: First they would say that development brings
jobs to communities that need them. Next they would say that
development was happening all over the city, so why should the
Black community miss out on an opportunity to have the same
advantages as other neighborhoods in San Francisco? And finally they would say that it was time to clean up the community
and make a path for luxury development. "Public housing was

never meant to be permanent housing," they would say when addressing concerns about public housing units being lost in the transition to mixed-income housing. "It's time for some of those families to stand on their own two feet."

However, when patronage politics worked in our favor, we had to be savvy about it. It was best when we found the places where our short-term interests aligned with Black people who worked within the city's bureaucracies. There were always people in the city government who wanted to do the right thing and saw cooperation with us as a way of creating positive change from the inside. The cooperation they offered was always quiet but could be consistent. These were allies inside departments like the Redevelopment Agency who would give us information that had been otherwise difficult to obtain. Someone would let it slip that if you read the project's fine print, you'd notice that there would be community oversight for only ten years, or that despite its promises, the Redevelopment Agency had neglected to ban the use of eminent domain on household properties—which meant that there was a danger of the city being able to take a home in order to build something else. There were times when the developer had intentions so nefarious that even the consultants and Black administrators and bureaucrats could not help but object. They did, after all, still have to live in the community.

At the same time, the more we talked with residents, the more we started to see that the support for redevelopment wasn't entirely driven by corporate interests. Sometimes, older residents—the ones who'd seen the decline of the community most clearly—were the largest champions of redevelopment and associated initiatives. They wanted to see the community restored to its old grandeur, so they were proponents of more police in the neighborhood and turning housing projects into mixed-income housing that would attract wealthier residents.

Some would decry the ways in which they felt the "younger generation" had run down the community, as if it were purely a matter of choice and not deliberate economic starvation that had stopped others from reaching the low rung of the middle class they'd managed to attain. And even though some of the residents had been displaced by an earlier redevelopment project in the city's other Black neighborhood, the Fillmore District, they saw that project as more clearly driven by racism and corporate greed, not by residents who wanted to see their community change for the better.

Redevelopment was never a simple question when it came to Black communities in San Francisco. It was true that residents locked out of the economy by racism—in a community abandoned by the navy, left with little more than toxic hot spots and derelict buildings—deserved improvements that could provide people with what they needed to live good lives. But it was also true that the city had long planned to remake the neighborhood for wealthier and whiter residents who were renewing their interest in the City by the Bay, and they planned to do it with or without the consent of the people who lived there.

The story of Bayview Hunters Point isn't markedly different from the stories of many Black communities across the nation. There are those who remember when Black families had a shot at creating a better life for themselves, when there was some relative safety in segregation, back when people *knew* one another and depended on one another to survive. Often, the turning point in this narrative—the point where things "went wrong"— is when drugs and guns flooded the community, leading to violence and flight, abandonment and disinvestment. So, when it came to gentrification, there were people who saw it as a positive, who felt strongly that any change was a good change in a community where it seemed like there were no other options and no other avenues. If an important component of organizing is knowing what moves people to take action and what keeps them from getting active, in Bayview—and other Black communities—we saw how important it was to understand the specific historical dynamics that shaped the community's understanding of how the world functions and why.

Black communities are not a monolith. Not only do we defy stereotypes of who we are and who we can be, but we also defy stereotypes of what we believe politically. In progressive circles, many people—mostly not Black—are surprised to learn that Black people can be quite conservative when it comes to social policy, perhaps falsely believing that all Black people inherently prioritize freedom and equality for everyone. This misperception is actually quite dangerous. While it may be safe to say that Black communities want to see a better world for themselves and their families, it isn't accurate to assume that Black people believe that *all* Black people will make it there or deserve to. While some of us deeply understand the ways in which systems operate to determine our life chances, others believe deeply in a narrative that says we are responsible for our own suffering—because of the choices we make or the opportunities we fail to seize. Some Black people think we are our own worst enemy.

Shortly after we qualified for the ballot measure, our coalition started hearing whispers about a competing measure orchestrated by a coalition of community organizations: a group named Alliance of Californians for Community Empowerment (formed from a defunct chapter of the Association of Community Organizations for Reform Now), the San Francisco Labor Council (comprising labor organizations throughout the city), and the San Francisco Organizing Project (an affiliate of the PICO network, a coalition of faith-based organizations). Their measure, later named Proposition G, would have undercut Proposition F, mandating that the city move forward with transferring the land at the Hunters Point Naval Shipyard to the master developer, the Lennar Corporation; rebuilding the Alice Griffith Housing Development, a public housing development located near the stadium in the community that was badly in need of repair; and authorizing a new stadium to be built to help keep the 49ers in San Francisco. Their measure made no provisions for ensuring that the housing being built would be affordable, though press releases from the developer tried to assure residents that 20 percent of the housing built in the project would be made affordable.

The developer moved to sign a "community benefits agreement" with the newly formed coalition, which called itself the Committee for Jobs and Housing in Bayview. The aim was to ensure that the project would proceed as is, under the guise of having support from the community for the plan. That community benefits agreement was then used to assuage concerns about the progress of the cleanup efforts at the shipyard, distract from murky commitments for local hiring, and get people to overlook the fact that handing the land over to the developer for the price of one dollar was a major giveaway that shouldn't have passed muster.

Despite the fact that all of the organizations comprising the committee were led by white people with little to no relationship to the community itself, the developer touted the agreement as a sign of massive community support. In one op-ed in the local paper, the then–vice chair of the San Francisco Labor Council, a white woman, wrote in support of the project, citing her opinion that Black people were leaving San Francisco en masse because we were killing one another—not anything to do with displacement driven by corporate development, making housing unaffordable, and unequally distributing resources. The agreement was successful in undercutting the campaign to win affordable housing for the community, particularly in the areas most vulnerable to displacement due to additional market-rate development. When Election Day came, our proposition failed.

Black people were not a robust component of San Francisco's progressive community. I was often one of a very few in coalitions and meetings. And while I thought that perhaps this was just a phenomenon in San Francisco, I would later learn that Black people are not a huge force—at least in numbers—in any progressive political community. This is a problem. Black communities are on the losing end of the spectrum when it comes to anything that progressives care about, whether it be affordable housing, affordable and quality education, democracy, maternal health, police violence, incarceration and criminalization, or environmental concerns, to name a few. Without Black people, there is no such thing as "progressive" anything.

Most important, the underrepresentation of Black communities in progressive coalitions can lead to at least two tragic outcomes. One, the concerns of Black communities never quite make it into their agendas to change the country and change the world. If progressive movements are largely envisioned and created in the image of white people and the concerns of white communities, Black communities will continue to suffer from disparities brought on by rigged rules that are designed to keep Black communities away from resources and power. If the agendas we adopt are largely designed to maintain the well-being of white communities and white families, that is what will be achieved.

The other tragic outcome is that without Black communities, a progressive agenda can never be truly achieved. Any progressive agenda that does not include the well-being and dignity of Black communities as a fundamental pillar is not really progressive at all. It will, at best, win big changes for some while still excluding others.

What can Black communities do under these circumstances? There's no single answer.

Some are willing to take what we can get and try to make the best out of what should be better. The community benefits agreement, for instance, was negotiated in exchange for an agreement not to contest the project for the duration of the project—one hundred years. Meanwhile, many of the benefits promised to Bayview Hunters Point have still not come to fruition, more than a decade later. But the people who supported it—including some of the Black people in the community—decided to just take what they could.

For others, the answer is to turn their backs on progressive movements. This is a dangerous place for Black communities to occupy and may further isolate us from accessing and building political power.

Twelve years after the battle of Proposition F and Proposition G, the same questions remain. Recently, it was discovered that contractors falsified records of cleanup activities on the Hunters Point Naval Shipyard, for instance—but many of those who negotiated that community benefits agreement have moved on, leaving residents with little recourse to hold anyone accountable for the deal and its aftermath. They certainly can't get help from the developer, which, despite being given a sweetheart deal, has little to no accountability to the community whose neighborhood was sold out from underneath them.

Bayview Hunters Point was a community that no progressives in San Francisco would touch. It was once said that it was impossible to organize there. Today, Bayview is officially a part of the story of gentrification in San Francisco and thus regarded as a community worth fighting for—even if the leverage points to best fight the process have long since passed.

For weeks after losing that campaign, I thought long and hard about what we could have done differently. That campaign stretched our organization and our coalition in ways that were difficult but important. My organization, POWER, had always appealed to me because of its unapologetically radical politics and vision—and yet it wasn't our radical politics that could have won the campaign, given the deep-seated beliefs community members had about how change happened and what kind of change was possible. Winning simply required us to get as many people to our side as possible—a simple math equation in which whoever had the most votes won. I wished we'd gotten to work earlier to build as broad a coalition as possible in order to win. If we'd had more partnerships to draw from, we might have been able to access more of the resources we needed to win. As it was, we came close, and we did it through broadening our coalition and building support for our proposal among people who couldn't have been more different. The way we made inroads in our fight to stop the gentrification of Bayview wasn't just by building with organizations and groups that already agreed with us: It was by building with the Black woman who worked for the city, who would never come to a meeting but perhaps had relatives or friends who lived in the community. It was that Black woman who would slip us information about when meetings previously unannounced would occur, or who would inform us discreetly about the next move the developer planned to make. We came close to winning by agreeing to build with organizations that we did not consider to be radical and some that we didn't even consider to be progressive. We brought the campaign to those we did not believe would join us, and we allowed ourselves to be surprised—and we often were.

Building broad support did not mean we had to water down

our politics. It didn't mean we had to be less radical. It meant that being radical and having radical politics were not a litmus test for whether or not one could join our movement. It meant that we created within our campaign an opportunity for more people to be part of the fight to save what was left of Black San Francisco and to see that fight as their own.

Organizing in Bayview forever shifted my orientation toward politics. It's where I came to understand that winning is about more than being right—it is also about how you invite others to be a part of change they may not have even realized they needed.

CHAPTER FIVE

UNITE TO FIGHT

I LEARNED SO MUCH ABOUT ORGANIZING BLACK COMMUNITIES through my work in Bayview, but the Bay Area has also—for generations—been a crucible for radical multiracial political movements. That was the world I'd joined in the early 2000s, before I started organizing in Bayview Hunters Point.

The truth is we depend on one another to survive. In communities across America, people from different races, backgrounds, experiences, and ethnicities live together. We ride the bus together, work in the same industries, send our kids to the same schools, and, for the most part, desire the same things: We want to make sure that the people we care about have food in their stomachs and roofs over their heads. We want a better set of choices and chances than we had and a secure and bright future for those who come after us.

And yet, we don't all have what we need to live well. Interdependence sounds so beautiful, but often that dependence is predatory, rather than cooperative. For instance: If there were no

Black people, there would be no white people. Whiteness depends on Blackness to survive—whiteness as a valued identity would not exist if there wasn't Blackness, an identity that has been associated with violence, crime, and dysfunction.

During the Occupy movement in 2011–12, a helpful (though deceptively simple) equation emerged that told the tale of the economy in plain terms: There was the 99 percent, and then there was the 1 percent. The 99 percent are those of us living under a roof we don't own and can't own because we can't afford it; those of us trying to care for our aging parents at the same time we are caring for our own children and struggling to figure out how to afford it; those of us living in communities where there aren't any grocery stores but there are liquor stores on every corner. The 1 percent are those who own the companies that charge up to $5.70 for a fifteen-minute phone call from prison; those who buy housing for cheap in poor communities, renovate it or turn it into condominiums that the same people in that community could never afford. The 1 percent are the people who run insurance companies that gouge families for the cost of care.

Within the symbolic 99 percent we find most people of color, women, immigrants, people with disabilities, and some white men. And in the 1 percent, with few exceptions, you will find white men.

But this reality doesn't stop people in the 99 percent from believing that they will one day become a part of the 1 percent if they just work hard enough. And they blame other groups within the 99 percent for being the obstacle between them and a Bentley. Black folks and poor white people will say that immigrants are taking our jobs and that's the reason unemployment is so high in our communities. People of all races will say that Black people are the main abusers of social programs, turning temporary programs into lifelong dependency. Immigrants will say that Black people are lazy and don't want to work and that is the reason we are unable to achieve the American Dream.

As organizers, our goal was to get those in the 99 percent to put the blame where it actually belonged—with the people and institutions that profited from our misery. And so, "unite to fight" is a call to bring those of us stratified and segregated by race, class, gender, sexuality, ability and body, country of origin, and the like together to fight back against truly oppressive power and to resist attempts to drive wedges between us. More than a slogan, "the 99 percent" asserts that we are more similar than we are different and that unity among people affected by a predatory economy and a faulty democracy will help us to build an unstoppable social movement.

Many of the organizations that I helped to build between 2003 and today upheld the principle of "unite to fight" before "the 99 percent" was a popular phrase. This orientation is not just important for the potential of a new America; it is important for the potential of a globally interdependent world.

There are very practical reasons why multiracial movements are vital to building the world we deserve. Segregation by race and class has been used throughout history to maintain power relationships. Segregation, whether through redlining or denying citizenship, helps to create an other, which helps in turn to justify why some people have and other people don't. It reinforces the narratives that make unequal power relationships normal.

This is why it's so important—and difficult—to engage authentically in the complicated conversation about multiracial organizing as a theory of social change. When I say "theory of social change," I mean an organizing idea that helps us answer these simple questions: What sparks change? How do we inspire our communities to fight, and how do we keep our communities fighting for the long haul? What gets in the way of fighting back, and how do we address those challenges?

Without having a nuanced, authentic, and courageous conversation about multiracial organizing as a theory of change, we will leave our most critical work undone.

I have always worked in multiracial organizations. The first base-building organization I joined had a membership comprising Black Americans (Black people born in the United States), Chicanos (Mexican Americans), immigrant Latinos (born outside the United States), working-class white people, and a few Asian folks, some of whom were born in this country, some of whom were not. When I began working at POWER in 2005, our organization had an explicit strategy that involved building a base of African Americans and immigrant Latinos. In fact, our model of multiracial organizing was one that other organizations looked to for inspiration on how to build multiracial organizations. The National Domestic Workers Alliance, where I currently work, is a multiracial organization comprising Pacific Islanders, Black immigrants, U.S.-born Black people, South Asians and others from the Asian diaspora, immigrant Latinos, Chicanas, and working-class white people. My organizing practice and my life have been enriched by having built strong relationships with people of all races and ethnicities. I've had the opportunity to interrupt stereotypes and prejudices that I didn't even know I held about other people of color, and interrupting those prejudices helps me see us all as a part of the same effort.

Capitalism and racism have mostly forced people to live in segregated spaces. If I stayed in my neighborhood for a full day, I could go the entire time without seeing a white person. Similarly, in other neighborhoods, I could go a whole day without seeing a Black person or another person of color. This isn't by accident—restrictive covenants, redlining, gentrification, and other social and economic processes shape neighborhoods in such a way that they are segregated by class and race. Sometimes the racial makeup of a segregated neighborhood changes: It remains limited to communities of color, but the composition of that ethnic mix can shift. In my neighborhood in Oakland, there are families who are Chinese, Vietnamese and Laotian, Cambodian, African American, Eritrean, Chicano, and both longtime and recent immigrants from Mexico and Central America, among others.

There's a lot of beauty in this kind of diversity within Oakland neighborhoods. In many instances, families of different races have lived together in the same community for decades; they know one another's families and look out for one another. I'm lucky to have lived on the same block for nearly fifteen years, with families who have been there twice as long.

There are also challenges. People who live in the same neighborhood don't always get along just because they live in the same place. Anti-Black racism is a common experience in these neighborhoods, and it's not limited to Oakland. The Los Angeles uprisings in the 1990s revealed for outsiders the tensions that simmer among people of color and immigrant communities living in segregated neighborhoods.

Stereotypes and prejudices fly around from all sides as people try to make meaning out of their conditions and seeming powerlessness. When I was organizing in San Francisco, I would hear these accusations exchanged between people with no organized or systemic power to change their own conditions: "Damn Mexicans," Black people would mutter under their breath. "¡Pinches negros!" Latinos would exclaim.

These conversations rarely happened in the community meetings of the organizations I worked with. That didn't mean microaggressions wouldn't appear when we were together, but it did mean that people generally knew what was and what was not acceptable in that sort of space, like being on your best behavior at your grandmother's house and keeping those damn elbows off the table.

Typically, the most honest conversations would happen in spaces that felt safest—their homes. I would sometimes have the realest conversations when I was door knocking. "Look, I don't have nothing against nobody, but here's what I don't understand about these Mexicans," a conversation with a Black neighbor might begin. "How can so many of them live in one house? They got eighteen cars on one block—half of 'em don't work. They're loud, and the men be getting drunk and fighting on the weekends. I wish somebody would just deport they ass so I could finally have some peace and quiet." *Ouch,* I would think. *So much for not having nothing against nobody.* "And the Asians," they would continue, "at least the Asians got their stuff together. They live all up in one house, but that's because they're saving their money to buy another house. The Asians stick to their own. They help each other come up, unlike our people."

A co-worker and friend would describe similar conversations with Latina domestic workers she was organizing. "I don't understand why Black people are so lazy," they would say. "I just see these men standing around all day doing nothing. Hanging out. They don't even seem like they want to work. There was a movement in this country to get justice for Blacks," they'd proclaim, having experiences with social movements in their home countries. "But for what? What are they *doing* with that freedom they fought for?" I would grimace as she and I would exchange stories.

While these conversations most often occurred in private, sometimes they'd appear in our community meetings. Usually a newer member would say something disparaging of another race or ethnicity, and the room would go quiet. People would shift uncomfortably in their seats, and eyes would immediately be cast toward the floor. Inevitably, an organizer, flustered and trying to think on their feet, would go into a long diatribe that essentially amounted to "We need to be nice to each other."

Other times it would go toward a long and overly complicated explanation about how the system keeps us apart but we need to stick together because #BlackBrownUnity. The person would nod, embarrassed about the obvious slip, and the room would move on.

I've been on both sides of this, to be completely honest. I've been the person who needed to intervene but wasn't effective, and I've been the person who watched it all go down, thinking, *Nothing that you just said in that ten long minutes of talking changed one thing about how that person thinks or feels.* And often, it didn't. I have done countless one-on-ones after incidents like that and always felt like I was being told what I wanted to hear—because, in essence, I was.

My argument here is not that we shouldn't challenge racism, homophobia, patriarchy, ableism, and xenophobia anywhere and anytime they arise, because we absolutely should. My argument is that the way we tend to challenge aggressions that arise between and among oppressed communities is reflective of the same kind of systems we are trying to dismantle. Or, to make it plain, you can't tell people that they don't see what's happening right in front of their eyes. No matter how many times you tell someone that the sky is green, if they look at the sky and they see blue, they may nod and agree with you in the moment, but fundamentally they believe that the sky is blue. They know that when they're around you, they should nod and smile when you say that the sky is green, but when they are back in their environment, they will revert to seeing that blue sky.

And can you blame them? What they see in their communities is exactly what I see in mine. The only difference between us, honestly, is that I have a different story that describes why I see what I see and what that means for the possibility of changing our conditions.

I started using a different approach with the tough Black

women I was organizing to fight against environmental racism and police violence. Instead of saying, "Shh! Don't say that, it's not nice," or going into some academic or self-righteous diatribe about why we need to stick together, I decided to ask questions and help to place our experiences into context. When someone would make a disparaging remark about how many Latinos lived in one house, instead of saying, "That's not true," I would say, "Yes, I've seen that too. What do you think it's like to live in a house with so many people?" That would inevitably open up room for a conversation about why so many people lived in one house—what was driving so many Latinos to be crammed in? Was that the future they had imagined for themselves when they came to this country, or was something else going on? This would inevitably lead to a conversation about racist immigration policies and why so many people were being pushed out of their homelands and forced to travel to a strange land to try to fend for themselves and their families. Why was immigration policy not uniform across the board—why were Mexicans crossing a desert with nothing but the clothes on their backs but Europeans were arriving on planes with visas in hand? Why did a lack of affordable housing in San Francisco force people to live in cramped quarters?

And the same applied when I talked to our Latino members. Why were Black people standing outside during the workday, not working? It made no sense to respond to the inquiries of our Latino members by saying they didn't see what they were in fact seeing. I saw it too. Why were so many Black people, particularly Black men, unemployed? Why had there been several periods of successful resistance to racism and yet Black people were still living in deplorable conditions?

In 2007, I was still working with POWER. That June, we helped organize a delegation of thirty people for a trip to the United States Social Forum in Atlanta, Georgia. Half of our delegation was Black—some of whom were members of our Bayview Hunters Point Organizing Project—and the other half were immigrant Latina domestic workers. We tacked on a few extra days before the forum to tour Atlanta, and one of our stops was a museum that explored African American history. Inside, the museum takes its attendees through the history of slavery— beginning with the Ivory Coast communities in Africa that would become slave trading posts, then to a replica of a slave ship. As you stand in the hull of the replica, surrounded by wooden bodies packed in like sardines, you hear the sound of waves lapping against the boat, footsteps above your head, and men talking on the deck. Interwoven you hear groans, people speaking in different languages, trying to find anyone they know or who might know what home once looked like, sobs and whimpers. Once through the boat, you arrive in the colonies, where photos and replicas show Black people—men, women, and children—being auctioned off in the town square. The barren slave quarters, the songs of Black resistance inside cotton fields, stories of Black women killing their own children rather than have them born into one of the most horrific systems in history. Emancipation and Reconstruction, President Andrew Jackson and President Abraham Lincoln. Sharecropping and Jim Crow. The Great Depression. Separate and unequal. Segregation and the bus boycotts. Lunch counter sit-ins and violent responses from the Ku Klux Klan and the police. Four little girls murdered in a church in Birmingham, Alabama. Civil rights and Black power. Jesse Jackson and the Rainbow Coalition, Rodney King and the Los Angeles uprising.

As I walked through the museum that day, I cried—a lot. I cried at all that Black people have endured and continue to endure. Eyes red and puffy, I cried when I saw our Latina members—most of whom were domestic workers, wearing headsets for interpretation—learning in their native language the horrors that befell Black people in this country. Museum-goers stared at us, a motley crew of Black people, Latinas, and white people, communicating across language, culture, and experience. I saw our members soften toward one another. Though many had been in the organization together for years, this shared experience was different from being in a meeting planning campaigns or in a political-education session learning about capitalism. I cried for the potential of a world where this could be us every day—learning about one another, placing ourselves in one another's history, and caring for it with compassion, empathy, and commitment to never let ourselves be separated again.

Together, that day in June, we learned a lot about why so many Black people are unemployed, why there had been several periods of successful resistance to racism and yet Black people were still not free. I remember one of our members saying that she now better understood that Black people's fight for freedom, dignity, and a good life was still going on—that it was nowhere near complete. It reminded her of her own experiences in Oaxaca, Mexico, fighting corporations that were poisoning families and supporting corruption in the government. It reminded her of why, even though she had fought, she had to leave her homeland, because it was too dangerous for her to remain there. In that moment she was reminded of the deep humanity in all of us and what happens when our humanity is stripped from us. What she had learned about the United States was that Black people had fought for our rights and our freedom and had won. What she learned in coming to the United States was that the struggle for everyone's freedom was all of ours to fight for, that there was resistance and even joy inside miserable and dire conditions, and that we were a part of an ongoing resistance that we all hoped would bring back the dignity we all deserved.

And, as an organizer, it was my responsibility to keep telling the truth about what was happening in our communities. There were indeed too many people living in cramped conditions, too many people not working, and too many of us keeping to ourselves and worrying about our own. I would keep asking why I was seeing what I was seeing, and then I would ask myself what I could do to change it.

Asking questions is one of the most important tools we as organizers have at our disposal. Asking questions is how we get to know what's underneath and in between our experiences in communities. Knowing why something is happening can change behavior, in that it develops a practice in a person of doing the same—asking why they see what they see, what's behind what they see, and, most important, if they are motivated not to experience it anymore, what can be done about it.

CHAPTER SIX

TRAYVON, OBAMA, AND THE BIRTH OF BLACK LIVES MATTER

TRAYVON MARTIN WAS KILLED IN SANFORD, FLORIDA, ON February 26, 2012, just three weeks after his seventeenth birthday. Trayvon was visiting his father and his father's fiancée at her townhouse when he went to a local convenience store to get Skittles and an iced tea for his older brother, Jahvaris. On the way, he called his friend Rachel "Dee Dee" Jeantel. He walked into the store, purchased Skittles and a Snapple iced tea, and then left the store, still on the phone with Jeantel. It had started to rain, so Trayvon ducked under an awning—and that's when he noticed that there was a man watching him. That man was twenty-eight-year-old George Zimmerman. Still on the phone, Trayvon told Jeantel that some "creepy ass cracker" was watching him from a car, talking on a phone. She told Trayvon to run, and so he pulled his hoodie up over his head, ostensibly to stay somewhat dry, and began to run back toward his father's fiancée's house. Jeantel told Trayvon to keep running all the way to the house, but Trayvon thought he had lost the watcher and so he slowed down to a walk again. They continued talking until Trayvon said that the man was back. Jeantel heard Trayvon ask, "Why are you following me for?" and heard a man respond, "What are you doing around here?"

A few seconds later, there was a scuffle, and Jeantel heard Trayvon say, "Get off! Get off!" before the phone went dead. That was the last time she ever heard from Trayvon.

The first time I saw police violence that wasn't on television was in Washington, D.C., outside a reproductive justice conference. I'd never traveled alone to another state. I was in college, working with a reproductive justice student group on campus, and had been selected to attend the conference by a colleague. To be honest, I wasn't that excited about it. There was, however, a man I'd dated in college who had moved to Washington after he'd graduated, and after a sad and unavoidable breakup, we'd not seen each other in a few months. Though I wasn't totally ready to admit it, I missed him—and this trip was an opportunity to see him, which meant missing a lot of the conference.

After a fun and thoroughly confusing few days, I headed to the conference on the last day, both to check out what I had missed and also to get some breathing room from my decision to reunite with my ex. After the conference was over, I stood outside to smoke a cigarette. Within a few minutes, I saw a police car driving down the street outside the building where I was standing; I also saw a young Black man walking casually down the street. The car screeched to a halt, and a white officer jumped out to confront the man. After a brief interaction, the officer turned him around forcefully and slammed him up against the car. A young Black woman wearing round-framed eyeglasses was also standing nearby, and she suddenly sprang into action.

"Hey, why are you being so rough with him!" she yelled angrily at the officer. Unbothered, the officer continued to press the young man up against the car.

I looked over at the other woman. "This is really fucked up," I said to her. "He wasn't even doing anything—he was just walking down the street, minding his own business."

"Yeah," she said. "Cops are fucked up like that. Listen, write down everything you can—get the license plate number of the car, and write down a description of the officer and the kid. I'm going over there to see what's going on." She moved closer to the officer, and I frantically pulled out a piece of paper from the conference binder and began to write down everything I could.

I can't remember now what happened to the kid. I remember the Black woman returning to me, and I eagerly told her that I'd taken notes: Did she want them? What would she do with them? She wrote her email down. "Could you type those up and email them to me? I don't want to lose them." She walked away, and I stood there, dumbstruck. I'd never seen this kind of behavior up close—could police just treat people any kind of way?

Marin County was an aggregation of small unincorporated towns, each with its own city council, fire department, police department, and school district. When I lived and worked in Tiburon, California, it had its own police department and its own fire department. Growing up, we knew the police, and the police knew our families. When the police would eventually come to break up my friends' house parties, we often knew by name the officers who dispersed us. I was once pulled over in my town. I'd been driving over the speed limit—going about 50 in a 40-mph zone—because I was running late for work and I worked for my parents, who didn't play that. I explained to Officer Mike with the handlebar mustache that I was about to be late to work, and after I handed him my license, he recognized my address and my last name and asked me how my mother was. He knew my parents and how strict they were, so he empathized with me and let me go with a warning, with just enough time to make it to work.

One night, when I was a senior in high school, I'd taken my mother's car to "study" with a friend, which really meant we were meeting up to smoke weed. My friend was a girl in my honors English class—she was a bit of a prodigy, only fourteen but about to graduate with my class of seventeen-year-olds. She and I sat in my mother's car with the windows rolled up, passing a pipe back and forth while parked on top of a hill, staring out at the view of San Francisco and the Golden Gate Bridge. Occasionally, the car would be filled with the headlights of a car driving along the road. That's why I thought nothing of it when a pair of headlights again filled the car from behind us—until the headlights didn't pass. I looked in the rearview mirror to see red and blue lights. I was terrified.

I watched as the officer got out of his car, turned on his flashlight, placed his other hand on the holster of his gun, and walked toward the car on the driver's side. My friend and I sat in my mother's BMW 325i, barely breathing in a car full of weed smoke. When he got to the window, he rapped on it with two fingers. "Roll down the windows, please, ma'am." I shook my head. No way I was rolling those windows down—with a car full of weed smoke? No, thank you. I pictured coming home to my mother in handcuffs (again—two years earlier I was caught shoplifting from a local Longs drugstore. They only handcuffed me because I'd said I was emancipated and didn't have parents, thinking it would get me out of trouble. I was wrong, of course) and my dad going batshit crazy.

The officer knocked again, this time louder. "Ma'am, roll down these windows." His tone became more insistent, and I knew he meant business. I rolled down the window, and a huge cloud of smoke forced the officer to step back momentarily from the car. He looked at me, then at the small blond girl in the passenger seat. "License and registration, and proof of insurance." I opened the glove box and pulled out the car registration and insurance. My wallet was under the seat. "My wallet is under the seat. May I get it?" He nodded while shining his flashlight into the car. I handed him my license. He inspected it carefully. "Is this your address?" he said, pointing to my Tiburon address. I nodded. "Please step out of the car," he said. "Both of you."

We each slowly emerged from the car, terrified. He shone the flashlight around the interior. "That was a lot of smoke that came out of this car," he said. "Please open your trunk." I opened the car door, leaned down to the floor, and pulled the lever that opened the trunk, just as I remembered I had bottles of alcohol there from a party at a friend's house the previous weekend. *Shit,* I thought. *I'm dead.*

The officer walked to the back of the car, shining the light into the trunk. "Is this your alcohol?" he asked.

"No, sir," I said quickly. "It's my mom's, from a party we had."

"Hmph," he said. "And what would your mother do if she knew you were up here, smoking marijuana in her car?"

"Oh, man. She would kill me," I said quickly and definitively. She would. My mother is a sweet woman who smiles frequently and is generally lovely and slightly aloof. But she was not the person you wanted to mess with when she was mad. I had seen her angry only a few times in my life, and I knew from those few experiences that I didn't want to witness it again.

My heart pounded as I contemplated calling my parents from

jail. I was not from a household where you could act up and get away with it. When I was arrested for shoplifting, my grandmother had just arrived in California, a rare trip for a southern woman who now lived on her own in the midwest and didn't like anything about the west coast. My parents were livid, and my grandmother's presence meant they had to be on their best behavior, which made them even angrier. I was grounded for a year (no, seriously, 365 days), and that summer they made me do manual labor around the house every day for the eight weeks of vacation. I wasn't allowed to talk on the phone, so I wrote letters to my friends. If they wrote me back, I would receive them already opened. My dad had been so angry that he literally ripped my bedroom door off its hinges. Already defiant, I threatened to leave and move in with my best friend. After he'd demolished the door (and sort of halfway fixed it), he brought a trash bag into my bedroom, where I sat on the bed and sulked, and tore down nearly every photo I had on the wall—collages of teen heartthrobs from magazines, fortunes from fortune cookies, and pictures of my friends and me. He then removed the fluffy down comforter from my bed, leaving only a sheet, and took all but one of the eight puffy pillows I had on the bed. "You wanna be a criminal?" he yelled. "We're going to treat you like one!" He slammed the door and I sat, eyes round and body shocked. My parents did not play. I was more afraid of them than of the cop at that moment.

The officer had begun searching inside the car. He reached under the seats, first the driver's side, then the passenger side. He pulled out my velvet sack containing a metal pipe with a metal screen affixed over the hole, a lighter, half a pound of weed in a Ziploc bag, and a pack of cigarettes. Why did I have half a pound of weed, you ask? Well, I'd gotten it from a friend to sell in one-gram sacks, in order to make a little money that I didn't need to ask my parents for. Why I had the entire half pound with me, I don't know. But I knew I regretted it as soon as the cop pulled it from underneath my seat. I looked at my friend across the car, both of us imagining our lives behind bars as a seventeen-year-old and a fourteen-year-old.

The officer's voice broke my trance. "You ladies really shouldn't be up here doing this. It's late at night. Someone could have tried to harm you. You could have hurt someone else, driving under the influence of marijuana. You both are smarter than that," he reasoned. And then, looking at me, "How's your throwing arm?"

"It's great," I piped up quickly. "I used to play goalie in soccer."

"Fantastic. I want you to take this pipe and throw it as far as you can." Before he even finished his sentence, I picked up the pipe and hurled it down the grassy hill we'd been parked atop. Then I watched as he slowly returned each of the other items to the car where he'd found them. He slipped the weed back under my seat. "I want you ladies to sit up here for a minute and sober up. And then I want you to go home, and I don't want to see you up here again. Understood?" We nodded our heads vigorously. He closed my trunk and handed me back my license, registration, and proof of insurance. "You ladies have a good night. Be safe out here," he said, before getting back into his car and driving off.

A year or two later, I was home from college, visiting for the summer, and I'd gone to the local Starbucks to grab a coffee with a friend. While inside, I saw an officer and knew immediately who he was. I approached him, saying, "You gave me a chance a few years ago, and I just wanted to say thank you. I'm in college, studying sociology and anthropology. Thanks for not arresting me."

He smiled. "Sometimes people just need a chance to do something different. I'm happy to hear you're doing well."

My experiences were much different from those of many Black people across the country, and around the world for that matter, who have encountered police while underage with half a pound of weed. I was in a BMW with a little blond girl, and the address on my license said Tiburon and not Marin City. I'd grown up in Tiburon, and my mannerisms reflected that: I spoke "properly," according to that community's standards. I was also a woman.

But countless other Black people did not have all of those assets, nor were they afforded those chances. During my time organizing in Bayview, I became acutely aware of what police were capable of. One of our members lived in a housing project near the Hunters Point Naval Shipyard. I'd met her when she came to one of our community meetings, asking if we could help her organize a tenants' union, because the Housing Authority had stopped conducting maintenance in her complex. One day, I was hanging out with her at her home. Her unit had a front entrance and a back entrance. The front entrance faced the street she lived on, while the back entrance faced a courtyard surrounded by about four other units. As she and I sat out back, smoking cigarettes, suddenly there were fifteen men in different-colored fatigues swarming the courtyard. "We should go inside," she said. "That looks like the gang task force, and the guy that runs it is good for fucking with people." We watched as the officers went from unit to unit and then rushed into one. Inside, you could hear them kicking open doors. Outside, they laughed as the people of the complex—largely Black and Samoan—watched them in wary silence.

In 2011, San Francisco police officers shot and killed nineteen-year-old Kenneth Wade Harding on the corner of

Third Street and Oakdale Avenue, in the heart of the community. Officers were doing a fare check on the T train; the new train line had been constructed not to improve public transportation for the people who depended on it the most but, instead, to move professional workers from downtown San Francisco to Bayview Hunters Point, which by then was being remade into biotech research facilities and microbreweries. The T train had been the subject of significant controversy since its proposal. Neighborhood residents lamented the several years of construction that snarled traffic in the small community, making it difficult for the buses that many depended upon to pick up and drop off on time. To make matters worse, when the train line was finally built, it had more problems the farther out it traveled. Sometimes, the train just wouldn't come; other times, it would come but pause at stops for several minutes, forcing passengers to get out and find some other way to get where they were going.

Early in the line's life, the San Francisco Municipal Transportation Agency instituted fare enforcement on public transportation in the city. Uniformed police officers from the San Francisco Police Department (SFPD) began conducting fare inspections seemingly concentrated in particular neighborhoods, most of which were communities of color. Not having proof of payment could lead to a warning, a ticket that carried a $150 fine, or an arrest.

Fare enforcement was bad news for poor communities, Black communities, and immigrant communities. The police profiled passengers. To make matters worse, the paper slip you'd get upon paying the fare was easy to lose—a moment of absentmindedness could translate into a crippling fine or even arrest. Police officers would often ask for identification, terrifying for those who lacked documentation or had criminal records. Plus, receiving a ticket for $150 for not being able to prove that you paid a $2 fare was wildly disproportionate, and not being able to pay that ticket would make you liable for additional fees or other consequences, similar to getting a parking ticket.

On July 16, 2011, Kenneth Harding was riding the T train when SFPD boarded to do fare enforcement. His mother, Denicka, called him Kenny. Kenny, who had been living in Seattle, panicked when officers approached him for proof of fare, and he ran off the train. Witnesses describe Kenny jumping off the platform and running toward the Bayview Opera House, which was on Third Street between Oakdale and Newcomb. He was shot and killed on Oakdale Avenue, near Third Street, in broad daylight. As shrines to Kenny sprang up at the location where he was killed, SFPD released information to the press that Kenny had a gun and appeared to have shot himself. Police also released information about Kenny's criminal history, saying that he had been freed from jail earlier that year and was on parole in connection with charges that he tried to force a fourteen-year-old girl into prostitution in Seattle and that he was a person of interest in a shooting that killed nineteen-year-old Tanaya Gilbert and wounded three others. He hadn't been arrested for, much less convicted of, the killing—and was just a kid himself, too young to be executed in the street as a career criminal. And more to the point, none of this mattered: They killed him for evading a fare.

Two years prior, just a few blocks from my house in East Oakland, twenty-two-year-old Oscar Grant was killed on a platform at the Fruitvale BART (Bay Area Rapid Transit) station in the early-morning hours of January 1, 2009. Grant was coming back to Oakland from San Francisco, where he'd gone on New Year's Eve to join thousands of revelers ushering in a new year. On his way home on the BART with friends, a fight broke out in the car that Oscar was in. When the train arrived at Fruitvale station, BART police were waiting and removed Oscar and his two friends from the train and forced them to sit on the platform. Officer Anthony Pirone punched one of Oscar's friends several times in the face and then stood over Oscar and yelled, "Bitch ass nigga, right?" The partygoers on the train took out their cellphones and began to video what was happening. One of them was a student from San Francisco State University who had volunteered at my organization as an intern through the Black Student Union the previous year.

The train erupted with boos and profanity as BART officers held Oscar and his friends on the platform, facedown. Standing over Oscar was Officer Johannes Mehserle. Pirone knelt on Oscar's neck and told him he was under arrest for resisting an officer. Mehserle shouted, "I'm going to tase him, I'm going to tase him. . . . Tony, Tony, get away, back up, back up!" Pirone stood up, and, instead of unholstering his Taser, Mehserle unholstered his gun and fired a shot. The bullet entered Oscar's back, exited through his front, and ricocheted off the concrete platform, puncturing Oscar's lung. Witnesses say that upon being shot, Oscar yelled, "You shot me! I got a four-year-old daughter!" Seven hours later, Tatiana Grant, Oscar's daughter, would lose her father, and Wanda Johnson, Oscar's mother, would lose her son.

I remember coming home from a party with my partner and turning on the television to see the news. "Babe!" I yelled. "Check out what happened at Fruitvale—the police killed a kid in front of hella people!" We watched, in silence and despair, as the New Year began with the loss of a father, a son, and a friend.

Our community sprang into action. In the days following the murder, riders who were on the train released their cellphone footage to the media, and as a result, hundreds of thousands of people dismissed the BART police's version of the story and trusted what the footage showed them: that Oscar had been murdered in cold blood in front of hundreds of people. Demonstrations and protests ensued almost immediately and continued for weeks as District Attorney Tom Orloff took his time deciding whether or not to press charges. BART wrapped up its investigation in twelve days, ruling that the footage was inconclusive. At once, the spin campaign to demonize Grant began, until video was released showing he'd been punched in the face by Pirone before he was shot.

Oakland was now electric, not just with anger at the murder of Oscar Grant but also at the abuse that many had suffered at the hands of the police.

While BART police are a relatively new phenomenon in Oakland, the Oakland Police Department (OPD) has a long history of tense relationships with poor communities and communities of color. When I first started organizing in Oakland, I learned about the Riders case. The organization that hired me after my internship at SOUL Summer School in 2003 was called PUEBLO, People United for a Better Oakland. The founders of PUEBLO had lost loved ones to the OPD and built an organization to fight for police accountability, transparency, and other reforms. The Riders were a group of four Oakland police officers who were alleged to have kidnapped, beaten, and planted evidence on community members in Oakland for several years, while the department ignored it. The crew became public in 2000 when a rookie officer—fresh out of the police academy and on the job for just ten days—resigned and reported the actions of his former co-workers to the Internal Affairs Division. One hundred and nineteen people pursued civil rights lawsuits for unlawful beatings and detention and ultimately settled with OPD for $11 million and an agreement that OPD would implement significant reforms. All of the officers were fired, but three were acquitted of criminal charges, while one remains at large, having fled to Mexico to avoid being prosecuted. Since 2003, the OPD has been under federal oversight, and yet officials report that there has been little change inside the department. In total, Oakland paid $57 million between 2001 and 2011 to survivors of police violence—the largest sum by any city in California.

The Oscar Grant murder, in front of hundreds of witnesses, naturally struck a chord with Oakland residents, still reeling from the incomplete justice of the Riders case. Grassroots organizations and community leaders demanded the arrest of Mehserle after Orloff, who'd also prosecuted the Riders case unsuccessfully twice, failed to bring murder charges immediately against the officer involved.

I took to social media to help galvanize the protests.

. . . is Oscar Grant . . . be there today 4pm at Oakland City Hall! (Wednesday, January 14, 2009, 12:07pm)

. . . is sending strong spirit to Oscar Grant's family and friends . . . don't forget, pack the courthouse to demand justice for all those murdered by the police! All week long, 8am, Alameda County Courthouse on Fallon in Oakland (Monday, May 18, 2009, 4:40pm)

. . . says "It's about time." Ex-BART cop Mehserle to stand trial for the murder of an unarmed Black man. Murder, not manslaughter (Thursday, June 4, 2009, 9:21pm)

. . . about time: Officer Pirone, an officer who was present the night of Oscar Grant's murder, has been fired. Now, back to Mehserle . . . help build the fight to ensure JUSTICE FOR OSCAR GRANT! (Thursday, May 27, 2010, 2:32pm)

. . .

In the end, Mehserle was acquitted of second-degree murder and voluntary manslaughter in 2010; he would serve eleven months in prison for involuntary manslaughter. The light verdict—for such a brutal public execution—unsettled the community further.

Two years earlier, in 2008, the first Black person in history was elected as the president of the United States. Ron Dellums had been elected mayor of Oakland two years prior, in 2006, becoming only the third Black person Oakland would elect as mayor, the first one having been elected in 1977.

On May 16, 2010, seven-year-old Aiyana Stanley-Jones was shot in the head by police while she was sleeping during a raid of her apartment in Detroit, Michigan.

> . . . I am Aiyana Jones . . . 7 year olds should be breathing life, not bullets . . . (Monday, May 17, 2010, 3:17pm)

There were others over the next few years, but then came Saturday, July 13, 2013, when I sat with a friend at a bar, sipping cocktails and talking politics. It was announced earlier that day that the verdict in the George Zimmerman trial would likely be announced that evening. Trayvon had been killed in February 2012, but I don't remember hearing about the case until about April of 2013, when I ran across a news article on Facebook describing what had happened and saying the trial would soon commence. From that moment on, I was riveted by the story and the trial.

As my friend and I sat together, we discussed our assumptions about the likelihood of Zimmerman being convicted, in some form, as if it was inevitable. As much as I'd seen in the years I'd been organizing—the disappointments as mothers of slain children were forced to watch their children's character be questioned and denigrated—for some reason, unbeknownst to me then or now, I truly believed that Zimmerman would not walk free.

And so did my companion. For hours, we ran through various scenarios. It seemed likely that Zimmerman would be convicted of something: Perhaps the standard of murder in the second degree wasn't susceptible to the claim of overzealous prosecutors "overcharging" suspects, knowing that the burden of proof was too high? Was it possible that Zimmerman would be convicted of manslaughter, which the judge had instructed the jury was within their purview?

It seemed like something ominous hung in the air. It was a clear day—beautiful, in fact—which had transitioned into a balmy evening. By then we were joined by my partner and another friend, all speculating as to what would happen when the jury reached its verdict.

There was a game on that night, so more and more people started to arrive at the bar. Every so often, as I sat outside, roars and screams would erupt. And then, suddenly, there was silence.

"They're getting ready to announce the verdict," my friend said. The four of us got up and walked inside the doorway to get a look at the television. The station had interrupted the game to cut to the foreperson of the jury announcing the decision.

My stomach felt tight.

"We the jury, find the defendant, George Zimmerman, not guilty."

I couldn't breathe.

> I can't breathe. NOT GUILTY?!?!?!?!?! (Saturday, July 13, 2013, 7:04pm)

Not guilty?

At first I felt nothing. I stared at the television blankly, and the words and images became a blur. I remember turning around and walking outside, to get away from people, to try to find my breath again.

Not guilty?

Then I felt rage.

> Where those folks at saying we are in post-racial America? Where those folks at saying we have moved past race and that black folks in particular need to get over it? The sad part is, there's a section of America who is cheering and celebrating right now.

> And that makes me sick to my stomach. We GOTTA get it together y'all. Our lives are hanging in the balance. Young black boys in this country are not safe. Black men in this country are not safe. This verdict will create many more George Zimmermans. (Saturday, July 13, 2013, 7:14pm)

> #blacklivesmatter (Saturday, July, 13, 2013, 7:14pm)

I don't know why I had such a strong reaction. I wasn't even totally sure why I'd been so tuned in to the case itself. I know that something unnerved me about a child being killed by an adult. Something unnerved me about the way that Trayvon was being portrayed as a thug and a criminal; something unsettled me about the way that I was being asked to see him and many other Black men who were being murdered. A few years prior, it had been Oscar Grant, just a few blocks from my home.

> Black people. I love you. I love us. Our lives matter. (Saturday, July 13, 2013, 7:19pm)

Not guilty?

I talked with my friend Patrisse Cullors, a fellow community organizer, that night on the phone. She was in Soledad, California, visiting one of her mentees in prison. We talked briefly about the verdict; the shock of it was immense. There wasn't much to say, but there was everything to say. This, we saw, is how Black people die here. Here, in America, Black people die from someone else's fear of us.

Not guilty?

> Btw stop saying we are not surprised. That's a damn shame in itself. I continue to be surprised at how little Black lives matter. And I will continue that. Stop giving up on Black life. Black people, I will NEVER give up on us. NEVER. (Saturday, July 13, 2013, 7:42pm)

I have a brother. He's eight years younger than me. I used to be his idol growing up, I think because I was the one who mostly took care of him. He wanted to do everything I was doing and be everywhere I was, and with the age difference at that particular time in my life, I probably spent more time pushing him away than I did bringing him close. But I have a brother and he's eight years younger than me and he lives in Marin County—one of the wealthiest counties in the world. Marin County, while wealthier than Sanford, Florida, has some parallels to it—mainly that both are communities where a Black person could be killed for looking "suspicious."

My brother is six feet tall. For years, he refused to cut his hair and so he had a huge Afro. He's really the sweetest person you would ever meet, but sweet doesn't matter when you're Black.

Not guilty?

I was tired of blaming Black people for conditions that we didn't create.

We are the survivors of white supremacy. The survivors of whips and chains and failing schools and crumbling neighborhoods. I knew that surviving sometimes meant that even we would try to find the reason, some justification for why we are so hated, so despised, that we can be killed with impunity—to find a reason, if only for the sake of our own survival. But I was still infuriated by some of the responses to the verdict of the trial—people saying that it was tragic what happened to Trayvon, tragic that Zimmerman got away with it, but then pivoting to saying that this was why we needed to make sure our kids pulled their pants up, didn't wear hoodies, got an education, and the like.

In the aftermath of Trayvon's death, President Barack Obama commented during a press conference that if he had a son, he would look like Trayvon, making clear that he had a special, personal connection to the case. The president, however, was wary of commenting on the case after an earlier incident involving Henry Louis Gates, Jr., being arrested while trying to enter his home. Obama had commented that the police officer had "acted stupidly," and there was an uproar by law enforcement advocates across the country; Obama responded by bringing Gates and the officer who arrested him over to the White House for a beer. Never mind that it was completely asinine for a police officer to arrest a distinguished professor in front of his own home as if he were an intruder in the upscale neighborhood in which he lived—the uproar established firmly and clearly that questioning law enforcement in any way, or scrutinizing law enforcement and its effectiveness, was squarely and completely out of the question, especially in relation to Black people. It also firmly established racism not as systemic but instead as an interpersonal series of issues that can be dealt with by getting to know each other better and sharing a beer.

So when the verdict was announced that George Zimmerman, Trayvon Martin's killer, would be acquitted on all charges, President Obama again took a careful stance that avoided criticizing law enforcement, encouraged trust in a flawed system, and appealed to Black people to look at ourselves and solve the problem of dysfunction in our own communities so that, ostensibly, law enforcement wouldn't find occasion to kill us.

The problems with this approach, of course, are many.

George Zimmerman wasn't a member of law enforcement. He was a vigilante who took it upon himself to patrol the neighborhood—he *chose* to see Trayvon Martin as a threat rather than as a kid walking home from the store.

Our kids need to pull their pants up.

And as news outlets across the country announced the verdict in the "Trayvon Martin trial" (of which there was none: Trayvon Martin was not on trial—he was dead), President Obama had to make choices about how he would address the nation, knowing that Zimmerman's acquittal struck a deep blow to Black people in America.

Our communities need to make sure we vote.

One week after the verdict, President Obama announced that the White House would be developing an initiative to try to address the challenges being faced by Black men and boys. His reasoning was that even though the criminal justice system was racist and disproportionately targeted and punished Black people, the way forward was to invest in those who were more likely, "statistically," to be killed by a peer than by a member of law enforcement.

Our boys and our men need to stop wearing hoodies.

This dismissal of deaths by law enforcement didn't make sense— the problem was real. When taken together, the murders of

Black people at the hands of law enforcement, vigilantes, and security guards amount to a death every twenty-eight hours. Not all victims are unarmed, and not all killings are in cold blood. However, this many Black people dying in this fashion is troubling, to say the least. In 2015, 307 Black people in America were killed by law enforcement alone, according to *The Guardian*'s "The Counted" project, and 266 Black people were killed in 2016. This number does not include murders by vigilantes and security officers, and since police departments are not required to disclose this data in the first place, we really don't have an idea of how widespread the problem is.

Our kids need to get a better education.

But there is a bigger problem here, aside from the numbers. The bigger problem is the analysis that Black people who kill each other are somehow a bigger problem than Black people unnecessarily dying at the hands of law enforcement and vigilantes. This analysis is not limited to President Obama—it is in fact a reflection of a long-held belief within African American communities: that if Black people would just act right, then others would do right by us.

Intercommunal violence, as Huey Newton, co-founder of the Black Panther Party for Self Defense, would call it, is a problem, but it is not merely a Black problem. It is a problem that at its root is about an uneven distribution of resources and power and a very human—if still distressing and painful—response to not having what you need to live well. Statistically, white people kill white people at the same rates that Black people kill Black people. It's not Black dysfunction that leads to violence—it is proximity that leads to violence in a system that prioritizes the well-being of corporations over the well-being of people. *Not guilty.* And I knew that no amount of pants raising, voting, education, or removing hoodies would change the fact that a child was murdered by an adult who got away with it. Because in America, Black people are criminals whether we're eight years old or eighty years old, whether we have on a suit and tie (as my uncle did when he was stopped and arrested in San Francisco because he "fit the description") or whether we sag our pants, whether we have a PhD or a GED or no degree at all. In America and around the world, Black lives did not matter.

Instead, Black leaders, including President Obama, adopted right-wing talking points to describe why Trayvon Martin was killed. Obama acknowledged that there is a long history of racial disparities in our criminal justice system while making sure to state that you can't blame "the system" or "the man" for everything. In doing so, he capitulated to the same people who called him and his wife "monkeys" and "Muslim socialists." The narrative of personal responsibility for systemic failures has often been used by Black leaders to secure their seat at the table while making no tangible changes in the lives of Black communities.

It was absurd, and simultaneously infuriating, to watch President Obama encourage peace and calm and state that the protests needed to run their course, as if they were temper tantrums delivered by children who had otherwise gotten everything they wanted:

Now, the question for me at least, and I think for a lot of folks, is where do we take this? How do we learn some lessons from this and move in a positive direction? I think it's understandable that there have been demonstrations and vigils and protests, and some of that stuff is just going to have to work its way through, as long as it remains nonviolent. If I see any violence, then I will remind folks that that dishonors what happened to Trayvon Martin and his family. But beyond protests or vigils, the question is, are there some concrete things we might be able to do?

Equally absurd were some of the responses to the question President Obama posed with regard to concrete things we might be able to do. For example, in 2015, an Oklahoma Republican lawmaker drafted a bill that would ban the wearing of hoodies in public. The bill ultimately didn't make it through the state legislature, but efforts like this one were not isolated. Discussions of Black dysfunction began to permeate the aftermath of the Trayvon Martin murder and subsequent acquittal of George Zimmerman. Spurred by President Obama's call to invest in Black men and boys, the conversation also began to veer toward problematic notions of restoring the dignity of Black men, making Black men better fathers to Black boys, as opposed to investing in Black communities and Black families by addressing the many disparities that our communities experience.

That night, after the Zimmerman verdict was announced, I had a few more drinks, then left my friends at the bar and came home. I woke up in the middle of the night and cried. I cried for Trayvon's mother and all the other mothers who lost their children. I cried for the fear that something like this could happen to someone I loved, to my brother or my uncles.

But more than that, I cried for us. All of us. I cried for who we are, who America is, that we could let a child be murdered by an adult and let that adult get away with it. That we would make laws that justified being fearful of Black people, laws that allowed you to kill Black people and not face any consequences. I cried because this man, this obviously not white man, killed a Black child who was in Sanford visiting his dad, this Black child who went to the store to get candy, who never made it home that night because this man's fear of a Black child was greater than his reason. I cried because he got away with it.

Not guilty.

I sat up in bed and grabbed my phone.

> Can't sleep. Of course, woke up at 4:30am crying and howling with grief and rage. Wow. Reading about everything that did happen after I finally fell asleep last night. Lots to process. I just wanna be with my baby brother right now. I wanna hold him so tight and just pray. I want black people to be free. (Sunday, July 14, 2013, 5:04am)

I woke up the next day and found that everything was exploding. Protests were being called for across the country, including one in Oakland that day. My post had been shared and liked hundreds of times. The #BlackLivesMatter hashtag had begun to circulate all over Twitter and Facebook. The Dream Defenders, an organizing group in Florida, where Trayvon's case had been tried, were staging a takeover of the Florida State Capitol, demanding an end to the Stand Your Ground law that had allowed Zimmerman to walk away with no consequences. Hundreds of thousands of people across the country would take to the streets over the next weeks. In Los Angeles, they would take the protests to Beverly Hills. In New York, they would fill the Brooklyn Bridge with protesters and signs that read BLACK LIVES

MATTER. In Oakland, I joined a group of protesters at a friend's storefront and, as the protests raged outside, worked with children and their parents inside to create Black Lives Matter art.

> I hope somebody busts up this notion that if we only change ourselves, the world will change along with us—while saying close to nothing about upsetting these set ups that have our babies in cages and 6 feet under the ground. I been hearing this a lot today and it infuriates me that we are blaming ourselves for conditions we did not create. Stop that.
>
> Black people especially have NO BUSINESS using that tired line. COLLECTIVE ACTION will change the world we live in, not individual empowerment. And while spirit has our back, that doesn't happen without each of us having each other's backs. I believe in individual transformation; I struggle to transform every single day. But telling people to go volunteer is not going to change one thing about structural/institutional racism. And in telling Black people to change our individual behavior, we let a whole lotta folks off the hook for theirs. We know that for sure. Black people know that explicitly and distinctly. (Sunday, July 14, 2013, 2:50pm)

Black Lives Matter was quickly becoming a phenomenon. By Tuesday of the following week, Black Lives Matter had a social media presence, largely because of Opal Tometi, another activist, who reached out to me and said she had been following what was happening online and had seen my use of the hashtag and my description of it, and that it resonated with her. She asked if there was anything she could do to help, and we talked about creating opportunities where people could connect with one another online so that eventually they could take action together offline. Design Action Collective, a social justice graphic design shop, reached out to me to ask if there was anything they could do to help—they'd decided as a collective that they wanted to give design and labor to the growing phenomenon that was Black Lives Matter. Patrisse and I worked together with them on the logo, and Opal created the Facebook page, secured a website, and developed a Tumblr page, a Twitter page, and an Instagram account.

Patrisse and I had already started talking about the potential of Black Lives Matter as a political organization, how we could build an organizing project for Black people to come together and fight back, one that would welcome all Black people, without some of the phobias that can exist inside Black political spaces.

> #Blacklivesmatter is a collective affirmation and embracing of the resistance and resilience of Black people. It is a reminder and a demand that our lives be cherished, respected and able to access our full dignity and determination. It is a truth that we are called to embrace if our society is to become human again. It is a rallying cry. It is a prayer. The impact of embracing and defending the value of black life in particular has the potential to lift us all. #Blacklivesmatter asserts the truth of Black life that collective action builds collective power for collective transformation. (Tuesday, July 16, 2013, 3:58pm)

Within one week, I represented #BlackLivesMatter on *HuffPost Live,* a streaming news program, with the folks who created #WeAreNotTrayvonMartin, an anti-racist hashtag intended to educate white people about how racism played a role not just in Trayvon's murder but in racialized laws like Stand Your Ground. People were sharing their stories of anti-Black racism on our Tumblr page and looking for people to connect with through our Facebook page. I was mostly on Facebook (though I had a

Twitter account at the time, I rarely used it), while Patrisse and Opal vacillated between Facebook and Twitter. We were posting information about other cases across the country where vigilantes were active or where radicalized laws such as Stand Your Ground had created more violence or been applied unevenly— like the case of Marissa Alexander, who was jailed for three years for firing a warning shot in the air as she tried to fend off her abusive partner.

Black Lives Matter wouldn't actually become an organization until 2014—but Black Lives Matter (as a hashtag and a series of social media accounts by the same name) was already changing the lexicon in 2013. Patrisse, Opal, and I knew one another prior to creating Black Lives Matter. Patrisse and I met in 2005 when I'd first joined POWER—we became fast friends on a dance floor in Providence, Rhode Island. Opal and I met through a Black leadership network called Black Organizing for Leadership and Dignity (BOLD), when she had just become the director at the Black Alliance for Just Immigration. Patrisse, Opal, and I were a part of the BOLD network. One week after George Zimmerman was acquitted of Trayvon's murder, our BOLD network held a call with people across the country, and we discussed Black Lives Matter with about one hundred leaders nationwide. In October, the long-running and popular television show *Law & Order: Special Victims Unit* debuted an episode called "American Tragedy," a fictional remix of the Paula Deen controversy (Deen, a famous white southern chef, had been exposed for blatant acts of racism) and the killing of Trayvon Martin. During the episode's obligatory trial scene, the camera goes outside the courtroom to show a protest. The protesters are carrying signs that say BLACK LIVES MATTER.

The murders didn't begin or end with Trayvon Martin. A few short months later, nineteen-year-old Renisha McBride was killed in the middle of the night by fifty-five-year-old Ted

Wafer in Dearborn Heights, Michigan. McBride crashed into a parked car in the early-morning hours of November 2, 2013, and she went looking for help. At approximately 4:42 A.M., Renisha knocked on Wafer's door. Wafer opened the door and shot Renisha in the face. Wafer initially claimed self-defense, but the district attorney in the case finally agreed to press charges when Detroit resident dream hampton began to organize rallies, press conferences, and media coverage arguing that the case was being taken less seriously because McBride was a working-class Black girl from Detroit and the shooter was a white man in the suburbs.

Unlike in Trayvon's case, Wafer was convicted and sentenced to fifteen to thirty years in prison for second-degree murder, seven to fifteen years for manslaughter, and two years for a felony firearm charge—which means that Wafer will spend at least seventeen years in prison.

Many people, including members of Renisha's family, asserted that justice had been served, and yet we wondered about a system that swallowed people whole as a practice—Black people disproportionately, of course, but ultimately everyone who came into contact with it. It is likely that Ted Wafer will either die in prison or shortly after he is released. We used Black Lives Matter as a platform to have that conversation and hosted a dialogue with Darnell Moore, dream hampton, Thandisizwe Chimurenga, and Patrisse to talk about prison abolition, justice, and the contradictions in the movement. More than two hundred people from around the country joined that call, on less than two days' notice. For the rest of that year, we continued to use Black Lives Matter as a vehicle for activism, organizing, and analysis.

CHAPTER SEVEN

REBELLION AND RESISTANCE

EIGHTEEN-YEAR-OLD MICHAEL BROWN WAS KILLED ON AU-gust 9, 2014, in Canfield Green, a housing complex in Ferguson, Missouri. Ferguson police officer Darren Wilson shot Michael at least six times—twice in the head and four times in his right arm. After being murdered, Michael's body was left lying in the street for four and a half hours, just steps away from his mother's home. As people gathered, the community got angrier and angrier. Community members called for a protest at the Ferguson Police Department, and from there, an uprising ensued.

The National Guard was deployed to Ferguson to quell the uprising, but the images of tanks and soldiers in riot gear lobbing tear gas at largely peaceful protesters stained the hearts and minds of the world, which was watching on social media and television.

. . .

The uprising in Ferguson began around the same time Patrisse, Darnell Moore, and I put together the national conference call about Renisha McBride and the conviction of her killer, so together we processed what was happening in Ferguson after the call.

A few days later, I learned that a friend I'd met at a house party a year earlier was on the ground in Ferguson, providing support to organizations. I asked if I could be useful in any way, and he advised that I should come down to find out. I arrived in Missouri about a week later.

There were only two grassroots organizations present in St. Louis: Organization for Black Struggle (OBS), led by the indomitable Jamala Rogers, and Missourians Organizing for Reform and Empowerment (MORE), a former affiliate of the Association of Community Organizations for Reform Now (ACORN) focused on climate justice issues. Some of the activists had come through their work with the Fight for $15 campaign, which the Service Employees International Union launched in 2012. But the overwhelming majority of people who were engaged and involved in the protests were not affiliated with larger activist organizations. While they might have been paid on occasion to do short-term work like canvassing, mostly these individuals were not members of, and didn't trust, grassroots groups.

I spent my first week in Ferguson meeting the community. Already, local folks were wary of the people who had come in, wary of how the news media was portraying what was happening there, and wary of support—not the support itself but what that support might cost them and even the perception that they needed outside support at all.

In the meantime, Patrisse and Darnell had begun to plan a Black Lives Matter Freedom Ride to Ferguson. Modeled after the Freedom Rides that went through the south in the 1960s, bringing organizers and supporters to help register Black people to vote, the Black Lives Matter Freedom Ride was designed to gather Black people from other parts of the country to go to St. Louis and support the Black people there who were being attacked and maligned by the state for standing up for their right to live with dignity. We were told by people on the ground that the biggest needs were for media to come, to tell the story from the perspective of the community, so Patrisse and Darnell compiled an impressive list of Black media makers to go on the ride. All over the country, people organized rides in their local communities. In all, more than five hundred people from thirteen states joined the effort.

The Black Lives Matter Freedom Ride converged on Ferguson during Labor Day weekend. The local Black college that had agreed to host the group pulled out at the last minute, citing a "misunderstanding." But a local church, St. John's on the north side of St. Louis, agreed to host instead.

All weekend, the group convened: We built relationships, attended marches and protests, and joined community events designed to highlight local work. On our final day, we met at St. John's Church for a sermon delivered by the Reverend Starsky Wilson, "The Politics of Jesus"; its core message was that Jesus was a revolutionary too. The tension between the local community and outside activists and organizers didn't abate—and there were further tensions among different activists and organizations—but there was also a deep love and sense of community building from being in some shit together.

I came home from Ferguson and got a call from my friend there, asking me if I was willing to come back and help coordinate a national weekend of action as part of a coalition of local organizations. The activists in Ferguson had been impressed with the Freedom Ride; though it initially was viewed with some skepticism, in the aftermath folks felt that having a national presence and media attention there allowed people from St. Louis to tell their own stories.

I was reluctant to return. I'd just gotten home and already had a lot of travel ahead of me through my job with the National Domestic Workers Alliance—I'd just started working there full-time that July. Additionally, I was wary of getting caught up in the internal politics of Ferguson. I'd been a part of many national and international efforts by this time, including the last United States Social Forum, a major gathering of social justice activists that had taken place in Detroit a few years before. While those experiences had taught me a lot about how to build relationships with people with different backgrounds and agendas, that kind of work is also difficult. When you're an outsider, it's hard to build trust. And to pull off an event like the one they were proposing, people needed to work well together. Organizers wanted thousands of people to converge on Ferguson for the Weekend of Resistance, but I wanted to be sure they had the buy-in of all of their local partners before I agreed to help. I love organizing and believed in the mission, though, so I agreed, with the caveat that I wasn't going to get involved in local politics—I was there to help, not to get mired in factional power plays. There would need to be agreement from organizers that they were on board with my approach. They agreed, and I came.

My job was to run a canvass locally, to ensure that residents came out to the weekend events. This would also create a good opportunity for organizations to build their membership and increase long-term engagement even after the media left and the people from out of town went home.

All in all, I spent nearly five weeks in St. Louis. I worked with a team of seventeen people, all from the St. Louis area, including some from Ferguson. MORE hosted the canvass. For about two weeks, we worked as a team to engage local residents in the work that was being done in the aftermath of Michael Brown's death. Over time, we shifted the methodology of the canvass from handing out flyers and inviting people to specific events for the mass-action weekend to knocking on doors and having conversations with people in the community, asking them if they would be willing to join the movement—not just attend an event. We set up a series of house meetings leading up to the weekend, so that people could discover more about the organization, meet and build relationships with their neighbors, and learn about what it meant to join the movement.

We shifted the methodology because really engaging people in the movement wasn't going to be as easy as just handing them a flyer and talking about the victories we'd won on other campaigns. At that point, MORE's membership didn't include many people from Canfield Green, the apartment complex where Michael Brown was killed. I learned that they hadn't even been door knocking in Canfield; the rationale was that it was too difficult to organize there, because people tended not to attend meetings. To me, however, it made the most sense to start there, right in the heart of Ferguson, and work our way outward to the larger St. Louis area; the people who lived in that community would be more likely to get involved than people remote from the incident. Additionally, the Ferguson police shot Michael Brown. If this organization hoped to make any progress in holding them accountable, they needed to build a base of concerned community members who were willing to envision new solutions and fight for them.

In St. Louis, there are ninety different municipalities—and ten more unincorporated areas. They were all different: The Black people in some communities might not have suffered as much from predatory policing—and some municipalities didn't have Black people, period. We needed to focus on the municipalities closest to Ferguson, where Black people had experienced the police abuse we were protesting. Further, we needed to train community members *in those affected communities* to lead and sustain the movement when everyone else went home. We didn't need canvassers—we needed organizers.

As a team, we began to develop a different method of door knocking and base building. We did role-plays and troubleshot scenarios together: What if someone slams the door in your face? What if they don't want to give you their contact information? How do you turn a no into a yes? What are we asking people to do? What kinds of questions should we ask to get to know someone better? How do we find the people who may be looking for ways to get involved in the movement?

Each person was given turf to cover—meaning they had a map with a highlighted section and were to knock on every door within that highlighted area. Our instructions were to invite people to the house meeting, talk with them about their experiences around Michael Brown's death and any experiences they'd had with the Ferguson police, and ask them to join the movement.

Each day we would troubleshoot what had happened the day before and map out where we were headed or where we'd been. We also spent time together doing follow-up calls with interested neighbors, to answer questions and solidify their commitment to joining the movement.

In ten days we talked with more than fifteen hundred people and got nearly a thousand to commit not just to attending the weekend but also to joining the movement. We set up fifty house meetings and conducted the majority of them. I got to build with a crew of people who learned how to be organizers, together. Our team also learned that courageous action has consequences. We had doors slammed on us and other difficulties in the field; one member of the team was fired from his job for talking about the movement at work. But I saw them learn from and overcome these hurdles and transform in the process. These folks never made it on to the news. They never sat on a panel or spoke to a university. But those seventeen brave people took on the work of investing in themselves and their own community.

MORE, while white-led (the director and most of the staff were white), had become somewhat of the ground zero for folks coming in from out of town to lend support, as well as a hub for some protesters. But I'd felt a way about how much support I and others were providing the white-led organization when a Black-led organization just down the road wasn't getting the same attention, so I decided to also work on a training curriculum for that Black-led organization: OBS. The energy was different, to say the least. OBS was on a different side of town than MORE, one that was decidedly less gentrified. There weren't dozens of people in a bustling office like at MORE. It was largely quiet. Even here, in the middle of organizing for change, the discrepancies of the larger world crept in.

There's a story to tell about Ferguson, and it isn't mine to narrate. It's a story that needs to be told by multiple people because, depending on where you were, you may have a different perspective. There were many, many other people involved who led important efforts, who continue to lead organizing work there long after the cameras and the media attention to Ferguson have disappeared. MORE and OBS are important to the story of Ferguson, but so are Hands Up United and Action St. Louis. The story of what happened in Ferguson, and what is still happening in Ferguson specifically and St. Louis generally, must be told together by the people who led and continue to lead that fight. My story is not the story of the Ferguson uprising.

My story is only of my time there, what I saw, what I did, and what I experienced. It is the story of a group of imperfect people, drawn together by tragedy, trying to figure it out. I saw some people taking advantage of others, living out their revolutionary fantasies in a community that was in the spotlight for the first time, and I saw people earnestly trying to grapple with what it meant to fight for change. I saw egos and I saw competition, but I also saw cooperation and a beautiful spirit of trying to build a beloved community in the face of death and horror.

Most important for me, I got to work with a team of people who normally would have participated in the canvass just because they needed to make some extra money, and I watched as they transformed into people who genuinely cared about creating change in their community and wanted to play a leadership role in making that change happen. The Weekend of Resistance was a blur—I don't remember many of the details. I do, however, remember every detail of the team I worked with during those weeks. I remember shy people like Courtney coming out of their shells and really seeing themselves as agents of change. I remember queer people like Jan'ae and Nick not feeling like outsiders, for once. I remember Brian, who was doing this for his brand-new twin baby girls. Even Reginald, a master canvasser who'd probably collected more signatures than anyone I knew, transformed from a brilliant canvasser into an organizer—stopping to listen to what people had to say, encouraging them in each conversation to become braver, and becoming more brave himself.

The Black Lives Matter Freedom Ride and the Weekend of Resistance in Ferguson were moments of resistance that showed us how far we've come and how far we still have to travel, who we are and who we can be. St. Louis wasn't a story about middle-class Black people rising up—in fact, Ferguson helped a lot of people see that Black resistance rarely looks that way. St. Louis was working-class Black people, some with homes and some without, showing the world what it means to be Black in cities where the rules are designed by white people. And beyond that, Ferguson exposed what has happened to Black leadership; the rebellion was primarily against predatory policing but was also, implicitly, a rebuke of Black leadership that has forever changed how we look at resistance.

During the early period of what's commonly known as the civil rights movement, Black life was largely organized around the church, the core institution in Black communities across the country. This put church leaders in position to helm movements for social change, starting with the Reverend Dr. Martin Luther King, Jr., and the SCLC; religious leaders were, of course, demonized by white supremacists, but they were still seen as more palatable than organizers who didn't come from the church, like Ella Baker. And it started a tradition within the Black community that the face for popular movements would always be a religious leader. The two nationally recognized movement leaders who followed the civil rights movement were, for all their differences, cut from the same cloth: the Reverend Jesse Jackson and the Reverend Al Sharpton.

In the early days of the Ferguson rebellion, both Jackson and Sharpton arrived in the community to do what they'd become accustomed to doing—showing up at the site of a crisis or tragedy, articulating a set of demands while visibly supporting surviving family and community members, and, in cases where the situation was particularly dire, leading a march with other faith leaders and community members.

Ferguson deposed traditional Black leadership in an epic takedown. Jackson and Sharpton weren't deposed because they were leaders—they were deposed because of the kind of leadership they tried to exert.

While some of Michael Brown's family welcomed the support of the two clergymen, other friends of Brown and community members in Ferguson rejected it. Perhaps no one was more publicly criticized than Jackson, who arrived in Ferguson to a community angry and traumatized by the police's aggressive military-scale response to protests. Jackson gathered a crowd and asked for donations—for the church. Jackson was booed out of Ferguson, not to return. Similarly, though Sharpton befriended Brown's parents, he was widely criticized for his role in the Ferguson protests—namely, encouraging residents to calm down and vote.

That Ferguson protesters and activists refused to allow Jackson or Sharpton to speak on their behalf or advise them in their strategy to resist was significant because it denied them a place at the center of the controversy, where they had been in years past; it also did not allow their politics to define the politics of the uprising. While Sharpton denounced "bad apples" inside the Ferguson Police Department, local protesters went much further: They made the connection between the police tactics during the protests—attacking and penning in the community with military-grade weapons—and the predatory policing practices that created the need for the protests. In Ferguson, as in other police departments in that jurisdiction, the police preyed on poor Black residents through exorbitant fines and bail, which resulted in the further impoverishment and hyperincarceration of Black residents of St. Louis. In that context, it's obvious why Jackson's request for donations to sustain the church in a community where the per capita income was less than $21,000 a year and nearly a quarter of the residents lived below the poverty line was vehemently rejected.

Figures like Jackson and Sharpton are often criticized for embodying what is known as "respectability politics," a term coined by Evelyn Brooks Higginbotham. For Higginbotham, the politics of respectability consists of strategies that allow Black people to garner moral respect as a result of their tactics and actions. The politics of respectability is intended to demonstrate "good" moral character and allow Black people to be seen by whites as worthy of respect and thus worthy of the rights denied them.

Higginbotham would argue that the politics of respectability gives you the moral high ground, a notion that mistakenly assumes that the dehumanizing structures of racism have any moral nature to which to appeal.

In rejecting Jackson and Sharpton's approach and Higginbotham's respectability politics, the Ferguson rebellion marked a major shift, a moment when Black protesters stopped giving a fuck about what white people or "respectable" Black people thought about their uprising. This turning point did not hurt the growing movement, as figures like Higginbotham would claim—if anything, it helped open up new political space through which we could explore the pervasive nature of anti-Blackness and internalized white supremacy among Black communities. The Ferguson rebellion helped create room for a new common sense among Black people.

Had Black Lives Matter or the Ferguson rebellion or the subsequent Baltimore uprising heeded Higginbotham's advice about respectability, had folk listened to Al Sharpton asking them to go home and instead turn out to the polls or not to tear up their own community, there would have been no uprising, no reckoning, no calling to account—we would have simply continued in the same pattern as always. We would have traded tension for payoffs and public appearances—which, to be honest, did happen to some degree. But decentering Sharpton, Jackson, and their politics of respectability created the political and cultural space for a different approach. It was through this approach that people got to know and care about the lives and deaths of those whom the police and media would have painted as "unrespectable" and therefore unworthy of our attention. People like Freddie Gray, who'd been picked up on drug charges before, or Michael Brown, who was rumored to have stolen a pack of cigarillos prior to being shot six times by Darren Wilson. Or Jordan Davis, who refused to turn down his music, or Renisha McBride, who, it was suspected, was intoxicated when she had her car accident. By throwing respectability out the window, we recentered the conversation on the actions of corrupt or violent police and the larger corrupt and violent systems they protected—and on the inherent worth of Black lives.

Black Lives Matter, working alongside the activists and organizers who emerged from the Ferguson uprising, created political and cultural space for a more expansive version of Blackness to emerge. Black people did not have to wear their Sunday best to be considered worthy of respect, dignity, and humanity.

This isn't to say there are not significant conflicts. As the culture continues to change, this new common sense continues to be renegotiated and contested—even inside our own communities. Queer Black activists in Ferguson reported being on the front lines of protests with people who, away from the protests, would call them dykes, threaten to fuck them straight, and so on.

My first day in Ferguson, at a meeting with several men and one other woman, I was told that I wouldn't "fit in" with the community because I was a woman wearing a dress (a plain black cotton dress) and my hair was done (laid, I might add). It was implied by this man that I would be taken less seriously wearing a dress in a poor community.

To this day, some maintain that the visibility of the Ferguson uprising was "hijacked" by the so-called gay agenda. Indeed, change is slow—but it doesn't mean that it isn't happening. Change is always happening, whether or not we are ready for it or, for that matter, agree with it. It is significant that so many of the leaders of today's rebellions are women, that some are queer or lesbian or gay or bisexual or transgender or don't subscribe to gender at all.

There are quite a few barriers to becoming the movement we need to be. An uncomfortable truth is that those barriers are both external and internal. In the age of Trump and Trump-like politics around the country, increased repression, a retrenchment of systemic racism, and increasingly predatory forms of capitalism have and will continue to be significant barriers for our movement. But there's also something within our movement that keeps us from being all we could be.

Our movements must reflect the best of who we are and who we can be.

Most of my adult life, I have been actively engaged in building a movement in this country that transforms everything— a movement that transforms our economy from one that provides profit for some and pain for others; a movement that advances collaboration at home and cooperation around the world that is fair, just, and generative; a movement that upholds our right to participate in every decision that has an impact on our lives and the lives of the people we care for; a movement that brings out the best of who we can be, alone and together. Building that movement is the opposite of the conservative movement that threatens us right now. Their movement results in wealth being concentrated into the hands of a small few, rather than distributed in a way that gives us all a good life. It is based on the subjugation of nonwhite and working people. The conservative consensus is driven by the values of conservative Christianity and deadly economic policy, and it denies the majority access to basic human rights.

If we are to prevail, if we are to defeat the movement that has taken hold of our country and drives our relationships with the rest of the world, we must go from fragmented, divisive, and narrow to coordinated, collaborative, and broad. To quote Kanye West, I fear that we are "worried 'bout the wrong things" and content to be the God of small things.

Many of my teachers, trainers, and mentors have fallen into a pattern of making their political circles smaller and smaller rather than bigger and wider—whether that be in formal organizations or efforts that are organized but not housed in organizations. They look for people who think like them—who experience the same anxiety about having to engage in a world where not everyone thinks like you—and have adopted the idea that finding a group of people who think like you and being loud about your ideas is somehow building power. To be fair, we all to an extent look for our tribes, look for the places where we belong and where we can just be ourselves. But when it comes to politics, when it comes to governing, when it comes to building power, being small is something we cannot afford. And while I feel most comfortable around people who think like me and share my experiences, the longer I'm in the practice of building a movement, the more I realize that movement building isn't about finding your tribe—it's about growing your tribe across difference to focus on a common set of goals. It's about being able to solve real problems in people's lives, and it's about changing how we think about and express who we are together.

Think about it this way: The United States alone contains more than 329 million people. Let's assume that to take power in the United States, you need the engagement and allegiance of 10 percent of the total population. It's unlikely that all of these people will think the same about everything, so if our movements hope to have any influence whatsoever, they will need to compete for hearts and minds, which means abandoning the practice of building cliques and instead building groups of people who are committed to and motivated by moving people in their direction by the millions.

Hashtags don't build movements. People do. Now we have to learn how to build movements for the twenty-first century.

PART III

NOTES ON THE NEXT MOVEMENT

CHAPTER EIGHT

THE MEANING OF MOVEMENT

THESE DAYS, LOTS OF THINGS ARE CALLED MOVEMENTS THAT are not in fact movements. I am often asked how someone can start their own movement around something that they are passionate about—the humanity of women, the murders of trans people, animal rights, or senior care. My response is always the same: Find the people who care about the same things that you do, and join them.

Often, when people refer to movements they want to start, what they mean is that they want support in helping something go viral—getting more people to pay attention to something, giving something more visibility. But movements are not just visible or viral—they comprise people who are dedicated to achieving some kind of change. The change they (and we) seek cannot be accomplished by something going viral. The change we seek can only be accomplished through sustained organizing.

Movements are composed of individuals, organizations, and institutions. Movements bring people together to change laws and to change culture. Successful movements know how to use the tools of media and culture to communicate what they are for, and to help paint a picture of what an alternative world can look like, feel like, be like. They use media to communicate both to audiences that are already bought in and audiences that are on the fence.

Many believe that change happens because a few extraordinary people suddenly and miraculously mobilize millions—rather than through sustained participation and commitment with millions of people over a period of time, sometimes generations. If we reduce the last period of civil rights to the Reverend Dr. Martin Luther King, Jr., or Rosa Parks or even Malcolm X, we obscure the role that powerful organizations like the NAACP or the SCLC played as points of organization for the movement. Rosa Parks gets reduced to a lady who was tired after a long day of work. Similarly, the Montgomery Bus Boycott, one of the most powerful in history, gets reduced to a spontaneous action rather than an organized direct action with a strategy.

Organizations are a critical component of movements—they become the places where people can find community and learn about what's happening around them, why it's happening, who it benefits, and who it harms. Organizations are the places where we learn skills to take action, to organize to change the laws and change our culture. Organizations are where we come together to determine what we can do about the problems facing our communities. Some will argue that you don't need to be a part of an organization to be a part of a movement, and this is true. Yet if you want to be a part of a movement that is sustained and successful, you need organization.

Many confuse political organizations with nonprofit vehicles. I have been a part of a few nonprofit organizations that are more like "We Got Y'all" from Issa Rae's *Insecure*: led by white people with privilege, inauthentically connected to the communities they purport to serve, based solidly in a charity model that doesn't actually seek to solve problems as much as to maintain themselves and their funding. While many movement organizations don't fall into this category, there are far too many that do. A lack of strong, effective, strategic, and collaborative organizations and institutions that aim to shift policy and practice is what makes us weak in relation to the right—they have an intricate web of organizations and institutions that do everything from provide thought leadership to experimentation to policy development to engaging in the realm of culture.

Organizations also communicate to decision makers about your relative level of power. Imagine a labor union with two members negotiating with an employer of a thousand workers. Imagine teachers trying to negotiate a higher salary from the school district, and yet because the teachers are anti-organization, each teacher has their own demand for salary and benefits. Organizations encourage collaboration, but they also demonstrate a relative level of power and influence.

After protests die down, which they almost always do, where do people go to take sustained action? Where are people plugged in to develop their skills and learn more tools of organizing?

A commonly held assumption is that to build a movement, one must have a large following on social media. While having a lot of followers on Twitter can be influential, it is but one of many ingredients necessary for movements to be effective.

Case in point: In 2016, DeRay Mckesson, a social media personality, announced that he would be running in the Democratic primary for mayor of Baltimore. Having been born and raised there, and with more than 300,000 followers on Twitter, he assumed that he had enough name recognition and political credibility to win a mayoral primary. Jack'd, a popular app that facilitates intimate connections, sent a push notification encouraging all its users to vote for Mckesson. The results were telling—Mckesson won 2.6 percent of the vote, a total of 3,445 votes. The winner of the primary garnered 48,000 votes—fairly low in the context of an election, but high in relationship to their opponent's social media following.

Building a movement requires shifting people from spectators to strategists, from procrastinators to protagonists. What people are willing to do on social media doesn't always translate into what they're willing to do in their everyday lives. Movement building and participation require ongoing engagement, and the levels of engagement must continually shift and increase—from just showing up to signing a petition to getting nine friends involved to helping design strategy to pressuring a legislator to leading a group, and so on.

Successful movements also have broad appeal. They aren't just groups that everyone knows about; they are what everyone wants to join because they know that if that movement can win, it will change their quality of life. Movements embrace those who have been marginalized in one way or another, and movements move them from marginal to central. The shifts that movements advance are those that make visible those who have been invisible, those who our society and our economy and our government say are of no consequence to our future.

"Intersectionality" is a term that's been thrown around a lot—in good ways and bad—but more often than not is misunderstood. More than a theory, in practice, intersectionality results in unlearning and undoing segregation and thus interrupting the ways that power is consolidated in the hands of the few.

Coined by Dr. Kimberlé Crenshaw in the late 1980s, as I discussed earlier, intersectionality is a way to understand how power operates. It is also a way to ensure that no one, as Crenshaw states, gets left behind. It is a way of understanding both how and why people have been left behind, and it offers a road map for change by making visible those who are currently invisible. In doing so, we become better prepared to demand more, for the sake of winning more.

Some are surprised to learn that movements for justice can be guilty of the same dynamics they seek to challenge. I have been to thousands of meetings, conferences, convenings, gatherings, and campaigns that failed to live, in practice, the world they claimed to want to bring into existence. Even the most radical organizations often fall short of their stated ideals. I've lost count of how many times organizations would state a value like "sisters at the center" and then pretend not to notice that women did the bulk of the emotional and administrative work while men did the bulk of the intellectual work. More than that, I spent ten years of my life in an organization comprising a majority of women of color, from the membership to the staff, and yet the few men in the organization watched those women do the bulk of the work of building with members, recruiting new members, organizing community meetings, setting up for and cleaning up after those meetings, navigating the difficult dynamics of coalitions and alliances, raising money for the organization, and responding to crises in the membership, while they waxed poetic with other men about what the movement needed to be doing and where it needed to go.

I can't tell you how many times I've been referred to as sister, queen, and the like by my peers in movements and yet been offered no vision in those organizations for how the work we did would affect *my* quality of life. It seemed as though I was there not as a strategist, not as a tactician, not as a group builder but instead as a means to someone else's—usually a heterosexual man's—improved quality of life.

For me, intersectionality isn't an intellectual exercise. A movement is not intersectional if I am invited to join it but my concerns, my experiences, and my needs are not a part of what the organization or effort, as a whole, sees as its concerns and needs—or its path to power.

Intersectionality is at times used as a synonym for diversity or representation. I have heard people describe their car pools as intersectional, when they really mean that their car pool is diverse, and I have heard leaders claim that they are intersectional organizers, when they mean to say that they bring people together across race, class, and gender. Diversity is what happens when you have representation of various groups in a place. Representation is what happens when groups that haven't previously been included are included. Intersectionality is what happens when we do everything through the lens of making sure that no one is left behind. More than surface-level inclusion (or merely making sure everyone is represented), intersectionality is the practice of interrogating the power dynamics and rationales of how we can be, together.

The truth is, too many movements are not intersectional. It's a profound statement to make, and also a painful one. As Black people have fought and died for our right to dignity and opportunity, some of us try to get there by climbing on someone else's back without their consent rather than making sure that we form a chain, where all of us get there or none of us do. From voting rights to civil rights to abortion rights, we haven't quite grasped that if any of us are left behind, we have failed.

Intersectionality is not Oppression Olympics—that is, it avoids privileging one oppression over another. You can see this kind of competition when someone says, "I'm a Black woman, so you can't tell me anything," and so on. I hear some activists improperly using "intersectionality" as a way to designate who has the right to determine reality. Some use it to shut down valid criticisms of their own actions, behaviors, and impacts. I have even heard activists say things like "intersectionality is not for white women," which is a contradiction. For something to be intersectional, it must take into account the experiences of those who are marginalized in different ways. Crenshaw states:

> I am suggesting that Black women can experience discrimination in ways that are both similar to and different from those experienced by white women and Black men. Black women sometimes experience discrimination in ways similar to white women's experiences; sometimes they share very similar experiences with Black men. Yet often they experience double-discrimination—the combined effects of practices which discriminate on the basis of race, and on the basis of sex. And sometimes, they experience discrimination as Black women—not the sum of race and sex discrimination, but as Black women.

Crenshaw's point here is that intersectionality is a framework by which we examine how groups that experience double or triple discrimination get their needs met at the same time as, not in spite of, other groups in the same situation. This is important because it, again, exposes how and why we leave some people behind, and it forces us to acknowledge the ways in which we keep ourselves from reaping the opportunity to build movements that model the world we want to live in right now.

Intersectionality does not give us tickets to dismiss real concerns of other groups, and it does not determine whether or not you have the right to your experiences. Intersectionality does not say that the experiences of Black women are more important or more valid than those of white women, for example. Instead, intersectionality asks why white women's experiences are the standard that we use when addressing inequality based on gender. Intersectionality says two things: First, by looking at the world through a lens that is different from that of just white people, we can see how power is distributed unevenly and on what basis, and second, we need to ensure that the world that we fight for, the claim we lay to the future, is one that meets the needs of all those who have been marginalized.

What's at stake with intersectionality? Whether or not all of us are entitled to live a dignified life. Intersectionality asks us to consider why we do not give the same attention to the criminalization of Black women and girls as we do to the criminalization of Black men and boys. Intersectionality asks us to interrogate why Black people with disabilities—the group most likely to be killed by police—get little attention and physically able Black men who are killed by police get more attention. Intersectionality asks us to examine the places where we are marginalized, but it also demands that we examine how and why those of us who are marginalized can in turn exercise marginalization over others. It demands that we do better by one another so that we can be more powerful together.

CHAPTER NINE

UNITY AND SOLIDARITY

I S IT POSSIBLE TO BUILD MULTIRACIAL MOVEMENTS IF PEOPLE primarily organize their own demographic group? Is there a place for Black unity in a world of multiracial movements?

These are questions I've grappled with for a long time. On the one hand, I've engaged in this conversation with white people who are confused by why every organizing space can't be diverse, and by that they often mean: Why doesn't every organizing space include me? Isn't it racist to only organize within your own racial group? I've also encountered this question among multiracial efforts: If Black people organize among themselves, isn't that a threat to our ability to build a multiracial movement?

I was brought up in an organizing tradition that valued solidarity among oppressed people. Linda Burnham, leader of the Third World Women's Alliance, a dear friend and mentor, introduced the usage of the term "people of color" as a way to get people who were not white to see common cause with one another. To build a global movement for peace, a cooperative and nonexploitative economy, and a full democracy, it is critical that oppressed people see our common interests and experiences.

In my own work, I spent many years building solidarity, alliances, and movements in which Black people and Latino people specifically came together to fight for themselves and for one another. "Black and brown unity" was a common phrase used to describe this core alliance. Alliance building of this sort is a critical strategy for defeating white supremacy and creating real democracy—after all, people of color are the majority across the world and increasingly throughout the United States. Only through white supremacist policies and practices does the white minority rule over the majority—and a key to those practices is making sure that the nonwhite majority doesn't come together.

But for a long time, I've struggled with the nagging feeling that these alliances, as they are currently conceptualized and practiced, are often shallow and in some cases exploitative. Unity, of course, is important—but real unity cannot happen if we avoid addressing difficult contradictions, such as anti-Black sentiment and practice in Latino communities. Our alliances are often not rigorous enough in their attempt to define the basis upon which we come together—and what we need to learn and unlearn about one another in order for that unity to have depth and staying power. They assume that people of color have a connection on the basis of culture rather than on the basis of differently experienced yet connected exploitation and oppression. Too often, unity flattens the experiences of Black communities to that of Black American communities, which have unique and distinct experiences from, say, African immigrant communities or Afro-descended communities throughout Latin America and the Caribbean.

I was disappointed but not surprised when we first began to build out Black Lives Matter and learned that, for some, solidarity meant that Black people were intended to come together and organize under the watchful eye of what I call "Black and brown unity defenders"—people who felt that addressing specific instances of Black oppression somehow violated the alliance among people of color. For me, this calls into question what solidarity truly is: Is it a blurring of our experiences and our unique conditions for the sake of peace, or is it standing together in the muck of our differences and declaring that we refuse to be divided by the people who are responsible for our collective misery?

In 2014, I was part of an organization that came together to tackle the question of left strategy: What and who are needed to successfully interrupt the forces that cause so much misery in our communities? How can we build a force powerful enough to create the conditions for our communities to win? Gathered together were people who worked across various social issues—education equity and justice, economic justice and labor rights, climate justice and environmental racism—and who were hungry for a deeper structural understanding of relationships of power and a strategy, wielded collectively, to interrupt and transform those relationships.

There was a lot I loved about being a part of that group. I loved getting together with people who, like me, worked each day to create a better life for all of us, and I loved exploring complex theories of the economy, analyses of the strengths and weaknesses of current and prior social movements, and the work of defining what a freedom program could look like.

But I was far too often one of only a handful of Black people involved and contributing to shaping the strategy, approach, and practice of the group. There were rarely, if ever, working-class Black people present—much less in the leadership of the group.

On the rare occasion that a significant number of Black people were there, someone would inevitably say that we needed to pay more attention to making sure that Latinos were present too, under the premise that we must stay focused on building Black and brown unity.

Cue the sound of the needle being ripped off the record.

One afternoon, we met to discuss organizational business. On our agenda that day was developing topics for future political education; we were holding webinars to, in part, encourage people to join the organization. Also on the agenda, we were sharing ideas for organizations and individuals with whom to build relationships in order to grow beyond the Bay Area and California.

Around the table sat three African Americans (one man, two women), two Latinas, one white man, and one Asian man.

As we discussed political education, I suggested that we do a session on Black Lives Matter and Black resistance, which had begun to spread like wildfire across the country and the world. By then, Patrisse, Opal, and I had started the hashtag, built up social media platforms to connect people online so they could take action together offline, done a national conference call on Ted Wafer's trial for the murder of Renisha McBride, and organized the incredibly successful Black Lives Matter Freedom Ride to Ferguson. Black Lives Matter as an idea, as a demand, and newly as an organization had begun to flourish and capture the attention of the nation and the world.

One of the Latinas responded, "Actually, I think we've been doing a lot of content on Black people lately. I'm worried that the push for Black and brown unity will get lost if we aren't talking about it. Why don't we do something on immigration instead?"

I felt my face flush, and a wave of heat washed over my entire body. "I'm not sure I understand what you're saying. Black people across the country are engaged in active resistance to police and state violence, and you think that we're talking about it too much?"

"No, that's not what I'm saying," she stammered. "I just worry that we aren't talking enough about how Black and brown people need to stand together in this moment and really balance out an understanding of the fights that each community is facing."

This, of course, was an argument that had a zero-sum outcome. Talking about Black resistance did nothing to stand in the way of Black and brown unity. Nor should it have discouraged Latinos from joining this resistance movement. But the conversation was not focused on what we might do to strengthen the basis of alliance between our communities—it was instead focused on a narrow understanding of what issues impact whom, and how much airtime those issues are given. What does it mean to be a part of a project focused on building multiracial unity and be told that we're "talking too much about Black people" as Black people across the globe are rising up in resistance to challenge their murders by police and vigilantes?

To insinuate that talking about immigration is purely a Latino concern was equally infuriating. Were there not Black immigrants taking to the streets, bound in the double jeopardy of being criminalized because of their race and criminalized for lacking access to nationhood? What did it mean that in multiracial organizing, we could not sequence—that is, give proper attention and energy to an uprising among Black people across the world, the scale of which had not happened in at least four decades? What did it mean that instead of addressing the very blatant and basic form of anti-Blackness that had just occurred between us, we just moved on, as if the conflict was solely interpersonal and not also ideological and a manifestation of systemic dynamics?

It continued that way for several months—a tepid acknowledgment that Black people were resisting across the country, yet little focus on how to recruit more Black people specifically into the project that we were building together. Eventually, the few Black members formed a caucus to become more familiar with what was erupting across the country. To have to do that in a group formed for the purpose of building a freedom project felt devastating to me, in more ways than one, and yet I was grateful again for the ingenuity of Black people to carve out space for ourselves in a sea of flaccid multiracialism. Could there be socialism without the deep investment of Black people?

I have a deep suspicion of any effort that doesn't actively and loudly celebrate, study, and model Black resistance and our contributions to any movement for freedom worth a damn. It's not sufficient to herald Black leaders from the past. We must challenge our fear that Black people organizing means that the rest of us will be left behind. We must go further, to recognize that in this country, Black liberation is the key to everyone's liberation. More than that, we must be more diligent about building alliances that have depth and rigor. Shallow unity will always fall apart under pressure. We cannot be so concerned with coming together that we don't do the work to stay together. Like any good relationship, unity takes work—together, and apart.

Eventually, my discontent led me to leave the group, which I explained as a need to focus my limited personal time toward helping to build the next phase of the Black liberation movement. My split consciousness continues to this day—we have to build a viable left in this country, capable of ushering in a humane and dignified way of living for all of us. Yet there is no hope for a unified coalition or alliance that does not understand, viscerally and intellectually, that Black communities are critical, that Black communities are underorganized, and that Black communities are not just cultural cachet—the suppression of

Black communities is the fulcrum of how white supremacy is able to rule.

Multiracial organizing rooted in principles of representation, rather than strategy, is as dangerous as it is ineffective. Anyone who is serious about the project of building a multiracial movement must, as a matter of necessity and not just principle, work to uproot the anti-Blackness that exists in even the most radical of spaces. We have to acknowledge the ways in which all people of color are raised to understand themselves and their origin stories as in opposition to Blackness and Black people. Asians and Pacific Islanders are oppressed in this country, and yet many work hard to distance themselves from Black people and Blackness. All immigrants are taught to steer clear of Black people, lest they be considered one themselves. In a society where anti-Blackness is the fulcrum around which white supremacy functions, building multiracial organizations and movements without disrupting anti-Blackness in all of its forms is about as good for a movement as a bicycle is for a fish.

Black people coming together, protecting time with one another, and loving on one another outside the gaze of people who are not Black can be seen as threatening, to both white people and non-Black people of color. I have had too many conversations with people I love about why it's okay for Black people to seek each other out for healing, for bearing witness, for strategizing, for joy, without the watchful, and at times tokenizing, gaze of other communities. For some non-Black activists, that sort of congregating feels too exclusive, too divisive. They seem to feel as if Black people coming together to affirm one another's humanity, to fight for one another's dignity, to say to one another what we often find difficult or exhausting to say and explore with communities who are not Black, is somehow a threat to the possibility of building a movement that is multiracial.

The problem with this, of course, is that there can be no multiracial movement unless and until Black people specifically are a strong and vibrant component of that movement, and Black people cannot be strong and vibrant unless we too have the space we need to build with and challenge and comfort one another around what it means to live as a Black person in America.

It wasn't just white people offering "All Lives Matter" and "Blue Lives Matter"; non-Black people of color were deleting "Black" and inserting other identities. Brown Lives Matter. Asian Lives Matter. Native Lives Matter.

In some ways, I get it. The ways communities of color are marginalized are isolating and infuriating. We lack power in so many aspects of our lives that when any one group's unique dynamics of oppression or disenfranchisement break through the mainstream veil, we all try to attach to the moment to create more space for an expansive and nuanced conversation.

However, when Black Lives Matter broke through, the revisions of it were tinged with anti–Black racism, literally erasing the Black from Black Lives Matter. The irony of this, of course, is that it proved the point we set out to make.

It's important to understand that declaring that Black lives matter does not negate the significance of the lives of non-Black people, particularly non-Black people of color. But Black lives are uniquely and systematically attacked in our society. Black Lives Matter addresses its own necessity in the phrase itself: Black lives do not have value or merit in our society.

But the rhetoric of sameness in our movements leads to intentional and unintentional erasure of real experiences that deserve exploration. Why are Black people only 12 percent of the United States population but comprise 33 percent of people currently in prisons and jails? Why are Black women incarcerated at nearly twice the rate of white women? Why is maternal mortality for Black women so much higher than for other women?

Solidarity can never be expressed by hearing someone's pain and then turning the conversation back to yourself. Solidarity means trying to understand the ways our communities experience unique forms of oppression and marginalization. It means showing up for one another to bear witness and then expanding our fight to include the challenges faced by other communities besides our own. If my best friend tells me that she and her current partner are breaking up, solidarity is not interrupting her tearful testimony to say, "I too have had breakups! Let me tell you about my breakup!" Solidarity is listening, asking questions, and being there for her—for venting sessions, to help her figure out how to rebuild her life, and to offer support. And while going through a breakup is not the same as oppressed communities showing up for one another, the lessons of how to be a good friend are instructive on the broader social scale.

In some corners of our movements, solidarity is simply too shallow. It's the solidarity of proximity and empty slogans, without the work it takes for us to really have each other's backs in the face of oppression, dysfunction, and marginalization. We cannot effectively build global solidarity with oppressed people if we do not first practice authentic solidarity here.

If Black people are to become a powerful, organized political force, we have to come together, in all of our nuance and contradictions, to work out our differences. The work we have still to accomplish is significant. Black communities have divided ourselves in ways that are counterproductive—the shade of our skin, the size of our bodies, the things our bodies can and cannot do, whom we love and whom we are attracted to, the land that we originate from, our values and worldviews. If those relationships are not built and rebuilt, if the relationships among us are not transformed, we cannot effectively join others in a fight against our common oppression.

At the same time, there are important limitations to Black-only organizing efforts. Majoritarian movements are necessary to create change, but Black people are not the majority on our own. The worst versions of Black-only organizing operate not only as if Black communities can achieve change without solidarity but as if joining other oppressed and marginalized communities is a distraction from winning tangible, concrete changes for Black communities. This feeds the xenophobic idea that groups outside Black communities don't also exist within them. For example, I've had way too many arguments with Black people who claim that the "gay agenda" has hijacked the movement for Black liberation, as if this agenda (which does not exist, as far as I am aware) is the agenda of an "outside group" that is not also Black. Black people are not just Black—as a complex community, we are heterosexual and we are gay, lesbian, bisexual, we are cisgender and transgender. By "outside groups" who are getting their needs met before Black communities, these complainers often mean people who are lesbian, gay, bisexual, or transgender, or immigrant communities, or particular religious communities, like Muslims. This rhetoric is dangerous because it cloaks a reactionary politic inside a revolutionary one—in other words, it uses internal solidarity as a cover for exclusion and marginalization.

Another pitfall of Black-only organizing mirrors one all organizing can fall into: the creation of cliques and uniformity of thought. This happens when organizers adopt a shallow view of Blackness—Black people as a cool, inherently revolutionary monolith—while ignoring the people who fall outside this narrow definition. This point of view assumes that Black communities come into the world fully conscious of the systemic challenges we face and ready to dismantle them. They don't offer tools for those who are just awakening to these endeavors. These are the activists who wax poetic about Black power but don't acknowledge the impact of generations of exclusion, gaslighting, extraction, disenfranchisement, exploitation, domination, and oppression on Black communities.

Black-only organizing is not effective if it is isolationist or replicates the same barriers to entry that Black communities experience in other ways. These efforts, at their best, create space for us to examine our relationships to one another, with all of our contradictions. They can provide opportunities for healing old wounds, for affirming the connections among us, and for forging new connections. Doing this work together ensures that we can go out into the larger world, link arms with other communities who share a common cause, and advance our movements.

CHAPTER TEN

NEW MOVEMENTS, NEW LEADERSHIP

A MOVEMENT MUST GRAPPLE WITH DIFFERENT FORMS OF LEAD-ership that help it accomplish its objectives. When it comes to social change, leadership is often a contested territory. Who gets to be a leader? What does it mean to be a leader? Is leadership something people are born with, or is it a skill that is developed over time? Which forms of leadership best accomplish the goals, while also transforming the ways that power operates?

These questions do not have easy answers. As for me, I am drawn to forms of leadership that are grounded, effective, and take the best of many different approaches, leaving behind that which is problematic. No one form of leadership is superior—but the forms that we adopt must be honest and adaptable for the environment they are being deployed in. Whatever form of leadership is adopted, it should be deliberate—grounded in a strategy of how it gets your movement closest to the aims it hopes to achieve.

Black Lives Matter was often compared to Occupy Wall Street. However, there are some distinct differences between the two movements when it comes to the role and practice of leadership. Early on, Black Lives Matter was described as a "decentralized, leaderless movement." These are not words that we used to describe our own work—they are descriptors that were attached to us.

When we built the Black Lives Matter Global Network, we had ideas about how we thought leadership should function but weren't sure how it would work in practice.

Patrisse, Opal, and I never planned to be the "leaders" of Black Lives Matter. We'd planned to operate behind the scenes, connecting people who wanted to get involved in changing the world. After the Black Lives Matter Freedom Ride to Ferguson, we were faced with a dilemma: The people we'd organized to participate in the freedom ride began to agitate to start chapters. Further, Black organizations (and individuals) that did not share our vision began to claim the work that we had been doing, asserting that they'd "started Black Lives Matter" but then espousing values that were not in alignment with our vision. In order for our work not to be stolen out from underneath us, we had to make some quick decisions about how to proceed, to establish our work as distinct from traditional mainstream civil rights organizations but do so in a way that could help grow the work without us.

For us, then, decentralization was both practical and political. It was practical in the sense that we were each committed to our own work outside Black Lives Matter, as well as within it, and needed and wanted more hands to share the load of building a strong network. It was also political: Decentralization could level the playing field of power. It would allow people who are often marginalized or blocked from exercising leadership to lead in public and out loud. Decentralization would allow for a different practice of power, where many people rather than a small few determined the direction of the project.

Patrisse and I were trained in an organizing tradition in which activists are taught to develop other leaders; this philosophy asserts that many leaders are needed to create transformative change, and those leaders should come from communities that have traditionally been excluded from power. And yet we were a part of hierarchical organizations. Hierarchy can help with efficiency—making decisions and getting things done—but of course it is also racialized, gendered, and classed, and it often reflects existing power dynamics. Hierarchies also open themselves up to corruption and abuse when one person or a small group of people have too much power. There is good reason to be suspicious of hierarchies, particularly as they relate to Black people. Racism inherent in systems, structures, and practices in government, institutions, and the like has meant that Black people are often on the losing end of hierarchies.

Visible leadership within the Black liberation movement has historically skewed male, heterosexual, and charismatic, like the iconic trio of the Reverend Dr. Martin Luther King, Jr., Malcolm X, and Huey Newton. Each of these leaders oversaw decision-making and strategy for their respective organizations. For King, it was SCLC; for Malcolm X, it was the Nation of Islam; and for Huey Newton, it was the Black Panther Party for Self Defense. However, when each of these leaders was assassinated, so in large part were the movements they led. The struggle continued, but those specific movements, without their most recognizable leaders, were never the same. Since Black movements—particularly radical Black movements that challenge the state apparatus—are frequently targeted by the state for disruption, distortion, and destruction, considering different leadership models is as much strategic as it is political.

Decentralizing leadership, however, is not synonymous with having "no leaders." Decentralization means distributing leadership throughout the organization rather than concentrating it in one place or in one person or even a few people.

Occupy Wall Street designated itself as "leaderless." Everyone was a leader and no one was a leader. All that was required was that you showed up.

The problem, however, was that simply declaring that there were no leaders didn't mean there weren't any. And declaring that there were no leaders didn't address the fact that not only were there leaders but those leaders struggled to not replicate the leadership they were fighting against. Leadership was largely male, largely heterosexual, largely white, and largely educated at elite universities. If we perpetuate the same dynamics that we aim to disrupt in our movements for change, we are not interrupting power and we are not creating change—we are merely rebranding the same set of practices and the same dysfunctions.

Black Lives Matter designates itself a leader-full organization. That means that there isn't one leader but many. This isn't just rhetoric. Each chapter has chapter leads, and those leads develop leadership inside their chapters. They make decisions about the work of their own chapters, but they also help to make decisions about the activities and the positions of the larger network. And they reject the notion that one leader, or even three, can speak for all or make decisions for all. Trust me—I know this from firsthand experience. Leaders within Black Lives Matter will tell you that I am not the leader, and they will remind me of this fact as well if they believe I am unilaterally speaking for the network. I have become much more deliberate about being transparent about what opinions are mine and what statements are official— debated on and decided by the network itself.

Decentralization also has another purpose, however. It allows for an organization—or a group of people trying to accomplish something together, if you will—to get ideas, leadership, strategy, and input from more people. From that perspective, decentralization is simply smarter: It opens your organization to the contributions of everyone.

As an organizer, I see clear value and purpose in decentralized leadership. I value the input, opinions, and contributions of many, and decentralization can challenge the ways that we've been conditioned to value the input of some over others. It can also allow for a plurality of political worldviews, if constructed deliberately. But it's also a way to be strategic, to fight more effectively. Imagine if the Black Panther Party for Self Defense had functioned as a decentralized organization. Would it have been as easily decimated as it was under a centralized leadership framework?

At the same time, I do prefer working with some form of hierarchy, and I find some uses of hierarchy to be more efficient. Having many leaders, or rejecting the notion of leadership altogether, means that more process is necessary to get things done. Difficult decision-making practices are not inherent in decentralized models—but a lack of skill and practice in using decentralized methods can lead to a circular process that doesn't get anything done. One of the challenges that decentralized practices posed for Black Lives Matter was how to make quick decisions in an ever-changing environment. We did not have a model for how to make decisions, grounded in our values, in moments when we needed to respond quickly to changing conditions. In my experience, decentralization, or perhaps a misapplication of decentralized methods of leadership, has meant that we've had to let go of many opportunities to make important interventions because we relied so heavily on not making centralized decisions. Perhaps some of that could also be attributed to the wide range of political perspectives inside the organization, approaches that we simply did not have time to analyze and debate together—the newness of our relationships and connections being an important factor. I believe that in organizing, one has to be able to adapt or pivot with nimbleness. Upholding principle over purpose can be harmful under these circumstances.

I also know that not everyone is strong in everything. Imagine asking a person with no experience in the kitchen to become a chef at a Michelin-star restaurant, without the proper training, simply because our principles that everyone is a leader tell us that they can. A misapplication of decentralized practices can at times result in bringing a knife to a gunfight. Denying that not everyone is good at everything can be dangerous for what we are trying to accomplish. So, while everyone can, theoretically, lead, leadership is not only earned, it is a skill that is deliberately built over time. Movements need millions of leaders. Decentralization, along with other methods and models of leadership, can help us activate those leaders. Rather than claiming that leadership does not exist or is not valid, movements must determine which forms of leadership best help to accomplish the objectives they want to achieve.

CHAPTER ELEVEN

VOTING CAN BE A MOVEMENT

D O ELECTIONS MATTER? SOME HAVE ARGUED THAT THEY ARE futile, a charade that allows us to pretend that democracy actually exists, rigged in favor of the rich and powerful, white and male. The logic of those arguments points toward abstaining from the process altogether, either in protest or just to save ourselves from inevitable disappointment. As a result, some say it is better to build power outside the current system. Perhaps not engaging with the system at all will somehow cause it to just wither away.

I disagree with the idea of abstaining from voting or electoral politics, though I certainly understand why our communities are sick and tired of politics as it is. However, to me, building our movements only outside existing structures gets us no closer to where we need to go. Politics is a place where power operates, which means it's a place where there are opportunities to move our agenda. Politics is also a space for learning: It's a terrain where you can expose what priorities are dominant and who sets those priorities, and where you can battle for hearts and minds to reshape and reorganize those priorities.

Electoral power, and the way it's wielded, have major impacts on our lives. Our work to reimagine and build more radically democratic systems needs to happen in our most intimate spaces and our organizations first—but when applied at scale to electoral organizing, this same work can transform our society and our world. The world that we imagine will not come into existence if we are not courageous enough to challenge power where it operates at the largest scale, impacting the lives of millions, even billions of people. We need drastic change in the structures that are supposed to engage millions of people in making decisions that shape our lives, and we need shifts in the ways that we engage with those structures themselves—to change them, and to refuse to let them operate without our consent. An effective challenge requires pressure from the outside, pressure from the inside, and pressure against the structure of the system as a whole. Yet in 2020, another dimension is also required: a fight for the state—as we are no longer the only ones who want to change the role of government.

The 2016 presidential election marked more than a change in the White House. It also marked a change in governing philosophy, from neoliberalism to neofascism. In the 2016 election season, we were presented with a series of choices: most notably, on the Democratic Party side, the Clintons, whose relationship to Black communities was long, complicated, and dangerous, versus Bernie Sanders, a Democratic socialist from Vermont, where the Black population is 1.4 percent, for whom race seemed to be only a way to talk about class differences. On the Republican side, there were seventeen candidates in a primary that was likely the most diverse in history, including Texas senator Ted Cruz; Florida senator Marco Rubio; Carly Fiorina, a former CEO of Hewlett-Packard; Ben Carson, a retired pediatric neurosurgeon who gained popularity by comparing the Affordable Care Act to slavery during a National Prayer Breakfast in 2013 and only the third Black person in history to run for president on the Republican ticket; Bobby Jindal, then-governor of Louisiana and the first Indian American to run on the Republican ticket; and Donald Trump, a business mogul who was more than willing to mobilize white resentment and racism to build his political support.

In this new landscape, how would we influence decision makers and power brokers—policies and laws—to make Black lives matter?

Hillary Clinton was the front-runner to win the 2016 Democratic presidential nomination. The mainstream women's movement had already decided that she was their candidate and, more important, that it was her turn to be president. Many claimed that Clinton's career and political trajectory had been unfairly tarnished by the actions of her husband, unfairly diminished by and then judged through the lens of patriarchy. But while conceding that she was, at times, judged by the failures of her husband, we must still acknowledge that Hillary Clinton's worldview and politics were shaped and supported by dog-whistle racism and triangulation—an intentional political strategy of winning over swing voters by pushing off the left and positioning yourself as the one who can rise above ideology to pursue solutions.

Indeed, Clinton established her own pattern and practice of using tactics that relied on stereotypes relative to Black communities in order to influence white voters. During Clinton's first bid for president in 2008 against then–senator from Illinois Barack Obama, she dog-whistled to white voters that Obama was connected to Minister Louis Farrakhan via the Reverend Jeremiah Wright, who was criticized by some for a sermon he gave in which he declared "God damn America," among other seemingly controversial statements. Her campaign leaked a 2006 photo of Obama in Somali dress, a thinly veiled attempt to evoke fears about so-called Muslim terrorists in a post-9/11 context. During Clinton's second bid, she bristled at having to discuss policies she'd promoted that disproportionately impacted Black communities. To this day, the Clintons will assert that the core driver of their policies from the early 1990s until 2001 was Black communities themselves: The grandmother afraid to come out of her home because drug dealers had taken over her block. The church preacher who was tired of burying young community members. The family who had lost several members to gun violence. Michelle Alexander, the scholar and bestselling author of *The New Jim Crow,* wrote about these self-justifications in a scathing 2016 article, reminding voters that Clinton was active and not passive in promoting these types of stereotypes when her husband was president—actively countering the notion that she was being unfairly maligned:

> Some might argue that it's unfair to judge Hillary Clinton for the policies her husband championed years ago. But Hillary wasn't picking out china while she was first lady. She bravely broke the mold and redefined that job in ways no woman ever had before. She not only campaigned for Bill; she also wielded power and significant influence once he was elected, lobbying for legislation and other measures. . . . Of course, it can be said that it's unfair to criticize the Clin-

tons for punishing black people so harshly, given that many black people were on board with the "get tough" movement too. . . . What is often missed, however, is that most of those black activists and politicians weren't asking only for toughness. They were also demanding investment in their schools, better housing, jobs programs for young people, economic-stimulus packages, drug treatment on demand, and better access to healthcare. In the end, they wound up with police and prisons. To say that this was what black people wanted is misleading at best.

Unfortunately, the Clintons used real concerns, real fears, and real devastation as a way to advance their own political interests—and not to actually solve problems in Black communities. Cracking down on Black communities across America allowed the Clintons to become one of the most powerful and influential families in America, if not the world. From welfare reform to mass incarceration to Wall Street to war, the Clintons used Black America to advance their agenda and that of other powerful and aligned interests. The more they could be seen as a friend to Black communities, the better. But in truth, the Clintons did little good for Black communities.

Bernie Sanders became a formidable foe to Clinton in the Democratic primaries by galvanizing young voters, particularly young white ones. And yet nearly half of young Black voters cast their ballots for Clinton. Clinton pandered to Black voters, particularly older Black voters, while Sanders emphasized class over race. In the meantime, the right and the Republicans mobilized a different strategy—resentment and rage. The Republican field was diverse and represented different interests. The victor who emerged stood for a faction inside the Republican Party that had been gaining steam since Obama's reelection campaign, energized by their resentment of a Black president along with a clear playbook to take power and transform it to move their decades-long agenda to reduce the reach of the federal government.

Understandably, many within our network and inside the movement simply had no interest in getting involved in the election. Eight years of a Black president hadn't brought as much hope and change to Black America as had been promised. There were significant accomplishments during Obama's two terms in office: The release of more than 7,000 people from prison, the largest number in at least recent history by a sitting president. Increased oversight of jurisdictions with pattern and practice of racial discrimination in policing. Consent decrees with police departments across the country with the most egregious disparities and practices. Health insurance coverage that would have been impossible to achieve if left up to insurance companies and the market.

And yet there were also significant disappointments: The deportation of hundreds of thousands of immigrants—more than in any other administration, Republican or Democratic. Cabinet appointments like Rahm Emanuel as chief of staff and Arne Duncan as secretary of education, two officials who believed in the privatization of the most important resources in our communities. And while unemployment decreased overall, including among Black residents, there were no significant presidential economic initiatives to improve the quality of life of Black people in America—even though Black people, and Black women in particular, turned out at higher rates than any other racial or ethnic group or gender in both 2008 and 2012. Many in Black communities who had supported Obama quietly lamented that this wasn't quite the hope and change they'd voted for, even as they waited for a second term when he could really show Black communities what he would do when he wasn't under pressure to get reelected.

There was a stark contrast among the candidates of 2008,

2012, and 2016. For a generation emerging from eight years of the first Black presidency in the history of the United States, there was nothing inspiring about a sea of white candidates over the age of sixty talking about the middle class, a status that many Black voters had no hopes of reaching without a serious intervention. No candidate was able to meet the challenge of engaging and capturing the imagination of younger Black voters (and potential voters) who were in the midst of their own civil rights movement. Even though the movement was in full swing, no candidate could seem to talk about Black Lives Matter, or any policy solutions associated with it, without being forced to do so.

Black communities are woefully underorganized. There isn't (yet) an agreed-upon agenda or set of goals that the majority of us are moving toward together or collectively holding politicians accountable to. As a result, candidates who run for elected office don't feel accountable to Black people. Our demands are often diffuse and muted, and they are often rooted in what is already politically possible rather than setting the tone for what must be prioritized politically in order to gain the support of Black voters. In the 1990s, it was enough for Bill Clinton to go on Arsenio Hall's late-night talk show and play the saxophone to feel as though he'd done his outreach to Black voters. However, at no time did Clinton talk substantively about any policy agenda that would improve the lives of most Black people—despite the fact that they made up the core audience of Arsenio Hall's show.

Similarly, during the 2016 election, the bar was incredibly low. At least Barack Obama could excite Black people because he was Black himself and—maybe in an unconscious way—a lot of Black people felt he wouldn't abandon us, as George W. Bush had during Hurricane Katrina in 2005. And Obama, to his credit, knew he needed to engage Black communities—along with the rest of the country. But that wisdom went out the window with the 2016 election, when the Democratic nominee reverted to the strategies of the 1990s that had worked for Bill Clinton. Hillary Clinton went on talk shows and learned to do the "nae nae." She made a guest appearance at BET's *Black Girls Rock!* in the same year that Patrisse, Opal, and I received an award for being Community Change Agents. At her rallies, she told young Black activists who showed up to protest her that she believed in changing policies, not changing hearts or minds.

Bernie Sanders wasn't far behind. While he refrained from the most blatant forms of pandering, Sanders still made it a habit to talk about what he'd done to improve the lives of Black people during the civil rights movement, but as a senator from the nearly all-white state of Vermont, he didn't offer much for Black communities to consider with respect to how he would take on the deep-seated challenges Black communities were facing. Eventually, Sanders talked about criminal justice reform but didn't offer much substance beyond broad platitudes. Mainly, his political platform centered on improving the economy, and he seemed reluctant to acknowledge that improving the economy must also mean removing the systemic barriers that keep some people and their families from opportunity and mobility because of the color of their skin.

In June 2016, I realized the choices during this election would be impossible for Black people. We'd tried to organize a debate on the Democratic National Committee stage to address issues important to Black communities, but we were promptly shut down by then-chairwoman Debbie Wasserman Schultz, who stepped down from her position a few weeks later amid allegations that she had tried to influence the nomination process in favor of Clinton. We'd shared policy priorities with candidates and helped organize meetings as individuals, only to be met in some cases by staffers who did more to lecture us about the need to turn out to vote than they did to do that work with us, or without us. Though we'd built cultural cachet and Black Lives Matter was a household name, discussed over Sunday dinners and family phone calls, we were not yet solidified into a political force that candidates felt they dared not disappoint. The threat of a Trump presidency started to come into clearer focus, yet so did the ambivalence of many of our movement forces, inside and outside the Black Lives Matter Global Network. I felt a real sense of despair.

We also had to find a better balance between protesting the Democratic presidential candidates and pushing them to be accountable to us. Protest is an important pressure tactic, but there are many other pressure tactics that we could have employed. Organizers know that protest and direct action can be effective as a series of escalating tactics—but if you start with protest every time, without establishing a series of clear demands that you build wide support around, it's less likely that this tactic will be effective on its own. As a result, protest in some cases became predictable and something that candidates would prepare for and avoid rather than something that moved them to change their behavior. For example, on July 13, 2015, Sandra Bland was found hanging in a jail cell in Waller County, Texas—two years to the day after George Zimmerman was acquitted of the murder of Trayvon Martin. The day the news broke, protesters from the Black Lives Matter Global Network and other affiliated organizations confronted presidential candidates Bernie Sanders and Martin O'Malley at the progressive Democratic conference Netroots Nation in Phoenix, Arizona. When asked whether or not Black lives mattered, O'Malley responded, "Black lives matter. White lives matter. All lives matter." Sanders responded,

"Black lives, of course, matter. I've spent fifty years of my life fighting for civil rights and dignity, but if you don't want me to be here, that's okay. I don't want to outscream people." Clinton was not present at the conference.

A few weeks later, Sanders was confronted again at a campaign rally in Seattle, Washington, by three members of a Seattle chapter of Black Lives Matter. After Sanders dubbed Seattle "one of the most progressive cities in the United States," protesters took the stage to challenge that assertion. They asked the crowd to be silent for four and a half minutes to commemorate the life of Michael Brown, the eighteen-year-old Black man killed by police officer Darren Wilson in Ferguson, Missouri, the year before. They also criticized Sanders for his approach to the protest at Netroots Nation and urged the people at the rally, as well as Sanders, to take more action to counter police violence. Rather than responding to the issues that the protesters raised, Sanders left, declining to address the rally.

In early 2016, Clinton was confronted at a private event in Charleston, South Carolina, by a protester who held a sign that read WE HAVE TO BRING THEM TO HEEL; the protester told Clinton, "I am not a super-predator," and asked her to apologize for mass incarceration. Clinton responded, "Nobody's ever asked me before. You're the first person to ask me. And I'm happy to address it." Later that week, Clinton issued a statement about her "super-predator" speech:

> I shouldn't have used those words, and I wouldn't use them today. My life's work has been about lifting up children and young people who've been let down by the system or by society, kids who never got the chance they deserved. And unfortunately today, there are way too many of those kids, especially in African-American communities. We haven't done right by them. We need to.

A few days later, when Clinton was confronted by protesters from Black Lives Matter Boston about her role in the epidemic of mass incarceration, she took a different tone:

> Look, I don't believe you change hearts. I believe you change laws, you change allocation of resources, you change the way systems operate. You're not going to change every heart. You're not. But at the end of the day, we could do a whole lot to change some hearts and change some systems and create more opportunities for people who deserve to have them, to live up to their own God-given potential, to live safely without fear of violence in their own communities, to have a decent school, to have a decent house, to have a decent future.
>
> So we can do it one of many ways. You can keep the movement going, which you have started, and through it you may actually change some hearts. But if that's all that happens, we'll be back here in ten years having the same conversation. We will not have all the changes that you deserve to see happen in your lifetime because of your willingness to get out there and talk about this.

These protests were important and helped to move the candidates to address issues impacting Black people with more than campaign stump speeches. After being protested in Seattle, the Sanders campaign released a racial justice agenda, which they'd not had before. In it, Sanders agreed that five types of violence impacting Black, brown, and indigenous communities must be addressed—physical violence, political violence, legal violence, economic violence, and environmental violence—and spelled out a litany of ways to do that. Clinton, for the first time since

1996, addressed her super-predator comments and apologized for them. She then continued to address gun violence and policy violence through building a stronger relationship with the Mothers of the Movement—the mothers of Eric Garner (murdered by police in New York), Trayvon Martin (murdered by a racist vigilante in Florida), Jordan Davis (murdered by a racist vigilante in Florida), Michael Brown (murdered by police in Missouri), Sandra Bland (found hanged in a jail cell after a traffic stop in Texas), Hadiya Pendleton (shot in the back and killed in a park in Illinois), and Dontre Hamilton (a mentally ill man who was killed by police in Milwaukee)—and each of the mothers endorsed Hillary Clinton in the 2016 presidential election.

But what we learned was that protest is not enough to shift politics as much as we need them to shift. This is the work of governance: If we don't like the two-party system, if we know that democracy is not even close to what it needs to be for people to have a real say in what's happening in their lives, we have to protest, and we also have to step in to lead and govern.

Imagine if Black Lives Matter had a clear set of demands that we took on the campaign trail; in addition to holding Hillary Clinton accountable for her role in mass incarceration, what if we'd demanded she commit to an intervention, such as changing policies that led to more than seven million people being arrested for marijuana offenses in the last ten years? That would have been akin to Obama's release of more than 7,000 people incarcerated for nonviolent offenses. Imagine if the Movement for Black Lives had taken its Vision for Black Lives to every single candidate running for office and gotten them on the record discussing how they would address the issues outlined within it, from access to affordable housing to increasing workplace protections for the most vulnerable workers?

As Angela Davis notes, "radical" means "getting to the root."

Disengaging from politics as we know it is a failure to get to the root of how and on whose behalf decisions are made. Someone will be the president, whether we like it or not. And no matter who is president, chances are we will have to fight them, so we might as well weigh in on who we want to fight—choose our opponent and the terrain upon which we fight, rather than having them chosen for us.

It was important for Black Lives Matter, the organization and the movement, to challenge Democrats. Essential, really, because had there not been a pushing of Democrats to the left, we wouldn't have had much discussion of racial justice issues like criminal justice reform or police violence—even though the entire country had erupted with protests that outnumbered the number of protests during the last period of civil rights.

One critical part of the conversation that was missing, however, was the Republican strategy and agenda—and the movement engaging that agenda and strategy. During the course of the 2016 election, there were two major events that should have been a clear sign of what was to come.

On July 7, 2016, five Dallas police officers were killed. A little more than a week later, three police officers in Baton Rouge, Louisiana, were killed. Both shooters were Black and ex-military. A day before the Dallas shooting, video had emerged of Philando Castile being murdered by police in Falcon Heights, Minnesota. The day prior to Castile's murder, Alton Sterling was murdered by police in Baton Rouge. Ten people dead in two weeks.

Immediately, Donald Trump and the Republicans began to blame Black Lives Matter for the attacks on police, attempting to overshadow the murders of Alton Sterling and Philando Castile but also using these incidents as an opportunity to rev up their base around "law and order." Much was made of the Dallas shooter's affiliation with the New Black Panther Party. In the case of the Baton Rouge shooter, there were several attempts to affiliate him with an organization, even though he wrote that he wanted to take sole responsibility for the acts he'd committed. Trump responded:

> A brutal attack on our police force is an attack on our country and an attack on our families. We must stand in solidarity with law enforcement, which we must remember is the force between civilization and total chaos. Every American has the right to live in safety and peace.

These were coded messages designed as dog whistles to a white base already concerned with demographic changes in the country, social upheaval as a result of increased visibility of police and vigilante murders through the impact of the Black Lives Matter movement, and fear of economic decline. Here, Trump appealed directly to the Blue Lives Matter base, who largely believed that police, not Black communities, were under fire.

It was strategic and it went largely unchallenged. That, in part, was our failure. Not just of Black Lives Matter, but of all of us who want to see a better world.

Elections do matter—and they have consequences. It was to be expected that campaigns would have engaged this way. We're fighting for a different world, and we are building new muscles to do so. This level and manner of engagement are what has been acceptable to our communities and accepted by the major political parties—that their engagement with the Black community does not have to be substantive; that the parties do not need to come into our communities, build infrastructure, and sustain engagement during and between election cycles, and they do not have to answer for the failures of their leadership.

There was work that we did that was important, but there *was* also work we chose not to do—and the choice has had consequences. We could have developed a platform of values and core policy positions and then lobbied candidates and other elected officials to support those positions. We could have met with existing elected officials to see if they would use their influence to push candidates to talk about the things we cared about in an era that we were actively shaping. We could have and should have in that moment taken more seriously the need for an electoral strategy and the implications of not having one. We could have built a force that placed pressure on these candidates to be more responsive to the movement that was galvanizing the country. And we should have taken the threat from the candidate emerging from the other side more seriously—even if we had chosen, as we did, not to endorse a candidate as an organization.

Our movement was and is still in its infancy, with its members still getting to know one another and learning how to work together and reconcile the political position of the network relative to electoral politics. In short, the movement is still finding its way, and yet all eyes are on it to keep pushing the country toward justice, and those who do not want to see this movement succeed are attacking it and the structures that are supposed to protect us. It is hard to build a plane while you are flying it—while also under enemy fire. We hadn't yet learned how to struggle together politically in ways that could help us get sharper and have more of a unified position. And, as a result, we missed key opportunities to engage our communities and shift the balance of power.

With that being said, these challenges are not unique to this movement or to our organization. The left continues to be plagued by these questions and contradictions. We have a deep and reasonable distrust of government, and yet we want and need government to do more to play its designated role. We don't like politicians, and yet it is politicians who represent us and make decisions on our behalf. We don't like how power operates and so we shun power, but we need power in order to transform it. The contradictions themselves are not the problem. The problem lies in not being decisive about how we will impact politics so that we can change our own lives and the lives of millions who are suffering under our indecision.

At the time of this writing, the race for the White House is under way—well, sort of. The Democratic primary season started earlier than usual, and the field of candidates was the most diverse in history, with six women, two of whom were women of color, and twenty-two men, five of whom were men of color and one of whom was the first openly gay man to launch a major bid to become president of the United States. Having run a generally lackluster campaign, former vice president Joe Biden won handily in the South Carolina primary, with Congressman Jim Clyburn's endorsement. In a stunning upset, three of the seven other remaining candidates dropped out and threw their support behind Biden after it became clear that the progressive wing, led by Bernie Sanders and Elizabeth Warren, could potentially win the nomination. Warren, who started the primaries off strong but could not pull the votes she needed to have a path to the nomination, soon exited the race, leaving Sanders and Biden in a two-way race. A global coronavirus pandemic, known as COVID-19 but dubbed "the Rona" by Black people across America, effectively ended the Democratic primary, leaving Biden as the presumptive nominee.

While the coronavirus threw the primaries into chaos, the truth is, the state of the primaries was pretty rough before the introduction of COVID. The presence of two decidedly progressive candidates was an important opportunity to defeat the more moderate and conservative candidates in the primary, which ostensibly could have led to an epic battle in the general election between a white nationalist extremist and a progressive. Unfortunately, the result was much different. Sanders positioned himself as the furthest left on the spectrum, calling himself a "democratic socialist," while Warren positioned closer to the center, saying she was "a capitalist to [her] bones."

On the left, where many were relatively disengaged in the election of 2016 because Clinton was not progressive enough, it is notable that our movements were energized around Sanders and Warren, but in a way that was insufficient to build power, because that energy was largely focused on ideology rather than base building. Rather than focusing on defeating moderate and conservative candidates by building the largest coalition possible and energizing more voters to turn out—including those who did not consider themselves to be activists or a part of any movement—the left became focused on litmus tests around ideology and labels that were and are largely irrelevant for millions of people who are trying to decide where they are going to place their votes. To be clear, organizing around alternative forms of economy is an important task, and a long-term one. For example, many people in fact support socialist ideas, but they have been organized through a long and violent culture war to believe that socialism is a bad thing. Why die on the sword of socialism when you could put that energy into mobilizing more voters for your candidate—voters who might not show up on the basis of socialism but will show up on the basis of wanting and needing healthcare access, who will show up to put an end to the punishment economy that tears Black and white families apart with no recourse and no path to rehabilitation or restoration, who will show up for the promise of equal pay for equal work? This election, unfortunately, was not a referendum on whether or not capitalism would continue to exist—it was, as usual, an opportunity to demonstrate the power of your ideas by demonstrating how many people you can organize to your side. Both progressive candidates lost this battle.

With respect to organizing, there was one critical constituency that needed to be organized and motivated: Black voters—who soundly lined up behind former President Barack Obama's vice president.

CHAPTER TWELVE

THE POWER OF IDENTITY POLITICS

ONE EVENING, I ARRIVED AT MY LOCAL AIRPORT AFTER A VERY long flight from Washington, D.C. There were delays due to wildfires burning across California, making the air smoky and toxic and thick. I wanted and needed a nightcap after more than seven hours on an airplane, on a flight that should have taken no more than five. On my way home, I stopped at my favorite bar.

I usually go to this bar because it is a place where I can be anonymous—I don't have to engage with anyone really unless I want to, and luckily the regular patrons know that practice well. I thought that on this particular night it would be relatively empty, a solace I was seeking. It was, after all, a Monday after 9 P.M., and most people would be home, I assumed. Yet when I arrived, a crew of perhaps five or six people was there, somewhat intoxicated. All were white.

I bought my drink and went outside to the front patio of the bar for a smoke. As I looked for a seat to rest my weary body, I moved next to a woman I'd seen there before—young, white, hipsterish. I'd witnessed her, in all of her blond glory, getting too drunk and somewhat aggressively talking to people about her thoughts and opinions. I found her thoughts and opinions a bit obnoxious, and so I tended to leave her alone when I encountered her—as I did on this particular evening.

And yet even in a crowded bar, where it is difficult to hear yourself think, you can't help but sometimes hear the conversations of others. I listened to one that went something like this:

BLONDE: Oh, my favorite actor was in that movie. He's Egyptian.

WHITE GUY: He's Egyptian? I didn't know that. That's great—we need more people of color in movies.

BLONDE: He's a great actor, which is why he should be in more movies—not because he's a person of color. Also, I'm really sick of hearing all of that stuff. Black, white, blah blah blah. We need to stop doing that shit. It really gets on my nerves. When are we going to get around to being *human*!

Cue an eye roll from yours truly. She wasn't irate that people of color are underrepresented in film. She was irate at daring to name it, as if naming it somehow perpetuates the dynamic of underrepresentation.

It's not an uncommon occurrence, and in fact I've literally been accosted by white people in public places demanding to know why we identify ourselves in ways that divide us rather than just realizing we are all part of one human family. Once, a white woman berated me for about twenty minutes about how she was from France and there was no racism there and it was because

Black people identified with the nation and not their race. Mind you, this wasn't in relationship to any conversation I was having with her or anyone else for that matter—I was literally just sitting there by myself, waiting for a friend to come back from the bathroom, and she saw it as an opportunity to browbeat me about her ideas on race.

Aside from being annoying, these confrontations are examples of the persistence of an idea that remains common among white people, even white activists on the left, and is both naïve and dangerous. And so here is my earnest attempt to explain why identity politics has become so disparaged and why that matters for those of us working to build a better world.

Identity politics is both simple and hard to define, partially because it's been so demonized by American conservatives. Because identity politics is ultimately a political concept, to fully understand why identity politics is important, we should start by defining power. I define power as the ability to make decisions that affect your own life and the lives of others, the freedom to shape and determine the story of who we are. Power also means having the ability to reward and punish and decide how resources are distributed.

This is different, of course, from how most of us think about power, which is individualized. Most of us talk about power in relation to how we feel in any given moment. One can wake up in the morning feeling empowered—but empowerment is different from power. Power is about who makes the rules, and the reality is that most of us lack real power, even over the decisions that are closest to us. Sure, I am empowered to decide what I eat for breakfast today, but larger forces create the options I can choose from—or whether or not breakfast is even available to me. A lack of understanding of power is central to how power operates. Power prefers to operate in obscurity; if how power operates was fully transparent, I suspect many of us would rebel against it.

The blonde's insistence on ignoring power is a great example of how it operates. Those who have power rarely want to acknowledge that they have unearned benefits at the expense of others. Her plea just illustrates how power functions best—behind the curtain, unseen and unengaged. So-called identity politics tries to make that invisible power seen.

The term "identity politics" comes out of the last period of civil rights and is used as a way to describe the lived experiences of people who are not white, heterosexual, cisgender men. The "identity" in identity politics is a way of describing what it means to live outside what has been defined as the norm in the United States. When conducting a scientific experiment, in order to understand results, you need a control group and an experiment group. The control group is what happens when there is no change of what is constant. It is what has not been experimented on; it is what the experiment is compared to in order to see if there has been any change. In the United States, white people, white culture, and white experiences are the control against which everything else is compared. For people who are not white, this can be incredibly alienating—never seeing people who look like you in fashion magazines, not being able to get makeup that matches your skin tone. Whiteness as the control looks like clothes that fit only a certain type of body, as defined by whiteness. Whiteness as the control looks like nude tones on Band-Aids or pantyhose, or makeup being a certain shade of peach. Whiteness, white identity, is a core organizing principle for America.

Identity politics was developed by Black feminists who refused to be defined personally or politically by a set of standards that were not their own. The term first appears in the Combahee River Collective Statement, published in 1977 by a group of Black feminists attempting to locate themselves in social movements that purported to fight for their freedom but were constrained by their replication of the very dynamics they sought to destroy.

For the Combahee River Collective, their life experiences were shaped by what they called "interlocking oppressions"—racism, sexism, capitalism, heterosexism, and the like. They committed themselves to being anti-racist, unlike their white counterparts, and anti-sexist, unlike their white and Black male counterparts. The experiences they had in the women's movement led them to conclude that the movement was primarily designed for the freedom of white women and not for the freedom of all women. Similarly, the experience they had in the Black freedom movement was that it was primarily designed for the liberation of Black men and not for the freedom of all Black people. As such, they sought political spaces that would allow for the complexity of their experiences as Black, as Black women, as Black women who were lesbians. They realized that if they did not fight for themselves, no one was coming to fight for them. They coined the term "identity politics" to mean that they would form a politic based on their own experiences and the desire for their own liberation, as opposed to a politic that focused on the liberation of someone else.

> This focusing upon our own oppression is embodied in the concept of identity politics. We believe that the most profound and potentially most radical politics come directly out of our own identity, as opposed to working to end somebody else's oppression. . . . To be recognized as human, levelly human, is enough.
>
> . . . A political contribution which we feel we have already made is the expansion of the feminist principle that

the personal is political. . . . We have spent a great deal of energy delving into the cultural and experiential nature of our oppression out of necessity because none of these matters has ever been looked at before. No one before has ever examined the multilayered texture of Black women's lives.

"The personal is political" is an adage that comes out of the women's movement, and yet the members of the Combahee River Collective took that adage and made it specific to the lives of Black women. Identity politics in this case meant that Black women could not afford to cast aside Black men, because of their shared experiences of racism, and yet had to contend with the fact that Black men, white women, and white men all found benefit from the oppression of Black women. Identity politics, then, becomes a defiant rejection of the flattening of their lived experiences for the sake of uniformity or unity.

Black women could not and still cannot afford a women's movement that sees gender oppression only through the lens of white women. This has been an underlying principle of Black feminism—the notion that the experiences of Black women are unique and complex and must be seen as such in order to achieve the goal of eradicating those differences.

And yet many white feminists cannot understand why Black women don't just get in line. Why declare a separate racial identity? If whiteness is a kind of collective amnesia, then this kind of white feminism that asks Black women to forget is certainly one of its manifestations.

Should Black women forget that under slavery they were forced to nurse white children while neglecting their own? Should Black women forget the ire they faced from white women whose husbands lusted after Black women in subjugated positions? Should Black women forget Sojourner Truth's famous speech challenging contemporary white feminist heroes like Susan B. Anthony to see Black women as worthy of the right to participate? Historically speaking, there is little reason for Black women to have much faith that white women will fight for Black women to be free as they fight for themselves. Though there is much to gain from equity among all subjugated genders, it is also true that America has historically subordinated white women under white men but given them power and privilege over Black women.

Thus, identity politics is the radical notion that your worldview is shaped by your experiences and history and that those experiences will vary in relationship to the power a group or an individual has in the economy, society, or democracy. And given that America is powered by the politics of white identity, whiteness itself is the first and essential enactment of identity politics. America is built on white identity politics: the attempted genocide of indigenous people in the Americas in order to access the land and resources needed to build a white Christian nation; the enslavement of people from the African diaspora in order to secure free labor to build a white Christian nation; the exploitation, internment, and degradation of Chinese and other Asian and Pacific Islander and Latino/a immigrant labor in order to propel commerce forward, for the purposes of making the white Christian nation the most powerful in the world.

Why does this matter? Let's go back to the story of the blonde in the bar. It isn't fair to say that only white people express the notions declared by the blonde in the bar, but it is fair to say that white people who are irate about any group daring to declare that their experiences are different fail to understand the role that white people play in those experiences. I often laugh to myself when I hear sentiments like those expressed by the blonde in the bar, because the first thing that comes to mind is *You brought this on yourself.*

In other words, if white people had not created false classifications for people based on skin color or genitalia or class status in order to maintain power and privilege over others, would we even be having this conversation? If white people had not enacted a system of enslavement where Black people from the Caribbean, Africa, and Latin America were stolen and forced into subjugation for generations, would we be having this conversation? If the effects and impacts of maintaining that system of enslavement and subjugation—where Black people are seen as less than human and undeserving of compassion, resources, dignity, and in many cases life—were not ongoing, would there be any reason for Black people to seek safety in those who share their experiences?

Identity is the elephant in America's room.

Some might respond and say, "Yes, those are tragic events that are stains on America's past, but we must continue to move forward." But until we examine the ways the elephant in America's room continues to shape our lives, we have no real chance of moving past it. In fact, that's one of the effects of amnesia: The willful forgetting of traumatic experiences allows their harmful effects to continue. Forgetting that domestic workers don't currently have protections under many of America's labor laws obscures the reason they don't have those protections—racism—and thus, nearly one hundred years after domestic workers were denied access to most basic labor protections, they continue to exist precariously in the economy.

And here's why this amnesia really matters: The obscuring of identity politics when we map power deters us from changing how power operates in the first place. If we don't acknowledge that power works to the benefit of white, Christian, heterosexual, cisgender men, we will continue to blame those who are subjugated by that power for being subjugated, rather than working together to uproot the legacy of unevenly distributed power.

The same forces that deny health insurance to people with preexisting conditions, the same forces that want to deny women the right to decide when and if they reproduce, the same forces that want to deny protections to transgender people, the same forces that want to roll back voting rights for Black people, the same forces that want to deny each of us the right to live dignified lives are the ones that have invested a lot in making sure you don't understand that discrimination based on race and gender and sexuality and class are all strategies to keep the powerful in power and to deny those without power from accessing it. For more than forty years, the conservative movement has been fighting to capture hearts and minds and align those hearts and minds with an agenda that benefits a few at the expense of many. The conservative movement in this country has invested more in obscuring disparities by race and class and gender than the progressive movement has invested in highlighting them.

Many historians have described the last period of civil rights as a turbulent time when culture and politics were up for grabs. The growing power and unity of movements for civil rights, for human rights, for racial justice, for gender justice, for justice for queer and trans people threatened the established social and political fabric of this country. Women, gays, transgender people, Black people, Latino people, indigenous nations, Asian people, and some white people were all fighting for their social, political, and economic existence in a world where whiteness was the control. Just as those movements began to coalesce in such a way that they could have experienced more power together, they suffered some tremendous defeats and setbacks: Government-sponsored surveillance and disruption programs created deep rifts and tensions inside and between those social movements, going so far as to imprison leaders of these movements and, in some cases, murder their leaders. And conservatives began to take power in ways they hadn't before.

Part of taking power was about controlling the narrative and shaping cultural norms. The right has invested in new narratives about communities of color, specifically about Black people and immigrants of Latin descent. Black women became welfare queens taking advantage of the government; immigrants became dangerous predators; Black men became angry gun-toting radicals who wanted to disrupt our way of life. Women finally inching toward breaking that glass ceiling became the reason and the rationale for broken homes and families and a changing way of life.

Controlling the story of who we are and what makes us who we are is an exercise of power—the more people you can get to invest in that story, to make your story their own, the more powerful you become. This is the right's narrative: The story of America is about perseverance, rugged individualism, faith, and hard work. Inside that story are characters who threaten the success of the project, who were never meant to be included in it in the first place: Black people who were brought to this country enslaved and then fought for and won our freedom. Indigenous people who resist genocide and colonization, who refuse to cede their land and their way of life. Women who refuse to serve merely as breeding machines and keepers of the home. Lesbian, gay, bisexual, transgender, gender-variant, gender-nonconforming people who refuse the nuclear family, who refuse binaries like man and woman, gay and straight, who embrace the complexity of who we are and who we are becoming. Immigrants who refuse assimilation. The story is not meant to be challenged, yet it is being challenged each and every day, many times successfully.

Telling a new story requires that we accept the ways in which norms have changed, lifestyles have changed, and what is possible has changed. As Octavia Butler said, "The only lasting truth is Change." It is fascinating to be in a nation that claims to value innovation and yet is so resistant to change.

When Donald Trump became the president of the United States in 2017, a steady stream of articles, op-eds, and think pieces flooded both social media and other forms of media. A notable one—written, of course, by a white man—decried identity politics. His argument was that while it is a beautiful thing that America has become more diverse, there is an anxiety in those differences that can be resolved only by finding what unifies us. In short, the argument is the same as that of the blonde in the bar: The more we talk about our differences, the more we divide ourselves.

This too is white identity politics at work—dismissive of the experiences of the dispossessed and yet supportive of white communities that have not yet reaped all of the benefits of whiteness. Eager to take shortcuts to real power, progressive movements struggle to embrace the work necessary to make identity politics obsolete. It is often those who don't have to be faced with the politics of their identities—because power obscures their privileged identities—who decry identity politics in the first place, unable to acknowledge why there are those who cannot separate their lived experiences from the identities they have adopted and those that have been assigned, without choice or agency.

But America is a nation where those who are nonwhite, not Christian, not heterosexual, not cisgender, not male, are becoming the majority demographically, which signals the potential to become the majority politically, culturally, and socially. For white people, the anxiety of losing power is significant. But in that loss, in that anxiety, there is also possibility. It is not necessarily true that once those previously dispossessed come into power, those who previously held power will be dispossessed in the same way. Power doesn't have to be a seesaw, where one minute one group has power and elevates itself at the expense of other groups, and the next minute the group that didn't have power now has it and the other group is subjected to the same mistreatment.

What some white liberals and progressives get wrong about identity politics is that if power is only transactional, we will never unify those who lack power and those who fear losing power. A just reckoning isn't a simple shift in who gets to oppress whom—it will come when those who have been used to unparalleled power must reckon with what it means to distribute power more equally.

CHAPTER THIRTEEN

IMPOSTOR SYNDROME AND THE PATRIARCHY

WHEN I WRITE, I WANT TO ACCOMPLISH AN OUTCOME. I write when I feel that my throat is clogged and I cannot breathe. When I write, I offer what is weighing on my heart and on my spirit. I have learned that to block these impulses is detrimental to my physical, spiritual, and emotional health. When I write, words and sentences, phrases and metaphors, come together in my mind before they ever reach the terrifying blankness of a page. I can hear the cadence before the words arrange themselves, as if something outside me is pushing me to put it on the page. I tingle, my body electric with a spirit that moves from my chest, down my arms, and into my fingers. Sometimes I cry as my fingers fly across the keyboard, hot tears spilling on my lap. On any given day, I can be found writing notes to myself on my phone or on scraps of paper. For me, writing is a spiritual practice. It is a purging, a renewal, a call to action that I am unable to defy. It is the way I learned to communicate when there seemed to be no other options.

When I feel backed up and choked, it is often because I have been silenced. I have been told not to write, not to say what is missing, conveniently, from the popular lexicon. There is an indignation in being invisible, in being spoken for without being spoken to, that compels me to write and compels me to nourish my craft as a writer.

I struggle to call myself a writer, as opposed to someone who writes. I have been published many times in my life, in newspapers, magazines, and several books. And yet I have a hard time holding that both things can be true—that I can be someone who writes and someone who is in fact a writer. Someone for whom writing comes as naturally as my impulse to suck air into my lungs and then push it out again.

"Impostor syndrome" is a term derived from a 1978 study by Pauline Rose Clance and Suzanne Imes to describe a feeling of phoniness in people who believe that they are not intelligent, capable, or creative, despite evidence of high achievement. *The New York Times,* in describing their research, quoted them as saying that "while these people are highly motivated to achieve, they also live in fear of being 'found out' or exposed as frauds." To me, impostor syndrome can be simply described as a derivative of the patriarchy. As a Black queer woman, I can say confidently that I too am a survivor of impostor syndrome.

I'm a writer who doesn't know (or much care) about "literary society." I'm a radical who doesn't care much for the doctrinaire distinctions among leftists. I'm a Black girl who didn't grow up around a lot of other Black girls, except for my mama, who is the Blackest woman ever and who loves Black people fiercely. I'm a queer person who struggled more to out myself to the strangers and friends in my everyday life than I did with my family, who largely just kept it pushing when I came out to them. I'm a Black girl who came up mostly middle class, who had to work for everything I've ever had but was also given the world by my parents.

My mother always reinforced that I could do anything I set my mind to. I sometimes roll my eyes when she says that, institutional power being what it is, and yet I believe her both because she is my mama and because I have in fact done nearly everything I have set my mind to. I am an attractive, getting-close-to-forty-year-old Black woman who has a lot to offer the world, and I believe that I'm just getting started. Believe me, my self-esteem is intact. But self-esteem is not enough.

Impostor syndrome is a symptom of a larger phenomenon where Black women, especially queer Black women, seem to belong nowhere. We don't belong at the front of social movements, organizations, Congress, city councils, businesses, classrooms, or anywhere else you can name. Black women have always been the stepping-stone for someone else to take their so-called rightful place at the front of the line. We are taught that we belong nowhere.

Impostor syndrome for this Black girl is a literal feeling of inauthenticity, that I do not belong here. It would be easy and somewhat gratifying to call this self-doubt, curable by affirmations in the mirror and a few years on a therapist's couch. But no: My impostor syndrome is incurable by affirmations in the mirror, because as soon as I step away, this world reminds me that I have no business here.

I don't use self-help books or positive affirmations to fight my impostor-syndrome symptoms. I use good old-fashioned organizing and movement building, because Black women do in fact belong everywhere.

. . .

A very basic way to understand the patriarchy is that it is a system of power where men and male-bodied people gain power and privilege from the disadvantages that face women and woman-identified people. Fighting the patriarchy does not imply that all men are bad. Acknowledging the unearned power and privilege that men have garnered in this world, at the expense of the well-being and dignity of women and girls, doesn't make you a man-hater. In fact, the patriarchy has nothing to do with (and, frankly, doesn't give a shit about) whether or not you are a good or decent person or whether or not you hate men. Patriarchy is a system of power and privilege. It is not only about a deadly imbalance of power between cisgender men and cisgender women; it is also racialized. When I say patriarchy is racialized, what I mean, quite simply, is that not all patriarchy is created equal. To be racialized means that something is segregated or at least characterized by race. A racialized patriarchy allows white experiences to function as the control or the default for all experiences.

The racialized patriarchy is how Donald Trump could brag about grabbing women "by the pussy" and still—when it came to deciding between electing a sexual predator or Hillary Clinton, an adherent of neoliberal concepts and solutions with important ideas on how to advance the well-being of women—get the votes of 47 percent of white women who marked ballots. Because while patriarchy is terrible, white women were much angrier about the past eight years under Black leadership than they were about Trump grabbing vaginas for fun. It is why when we talk about the wage gap and equal pay and say that women make 81 cents to every dollar a man makes, we are actually talking about white men and white women. Black women make 66 cents to the 81 cents that white women make and to every dollar that a white man makes, and Latinas make 58 cents to the 81 cents that white women make and to every dollar that white men make. A racialized patriarchy means that white women are seen as deserving of protection, while Black women and women of color are seen as those from whom white women need to be protected.

I've spent much of my life fighting patriarchy, even when I didn't know it.

When I was a kid, I regularly defied patriarchy in my own home. My dad used to drink coffee like his life depended on it. He would wake up in the morning and drink a cup—lightened with half-and-half and sweetened with three Equal packets. I knew how to make it expertly, and so did my mother. "Lynette, make me some coffee!" was a common phrase in my home. Sometimes it would come for me. "Alicia!" my dad would bellow through the house. "Make me some coffee!"

I hated hearing it. Something about the demand to stop what I was doing, drop everything, and run to the kitchen to make an able-bodied man a cup of coffee made me angry, deep in my spirit. I was a child, so it wasn't like I was doing anything important. But in my eight-year-old mind, that wasn't the point. I hated hearing it said to my mother more than I hated having it said to me. My mother did everything in our home—she made sure the bills were paid, the house was clean, we were fed and taken care of. My dad ran the family business, which was also hard work, but in my mind he spent most of his time telling other people what to do, and we spent most of our time doing it. And it incensed me each and every time.

One day, I responded to my dad in a way that I hadn't before. "Make it yourself!" I yelled from my room. Needless to say, it didn't go over well—I'm pretty sure I was grounded and continued making cups of coffee for my dad on demand. But for me, it was a punishment well worth taking.

. . .

Every social movement that I've ever learned about or participated in has been infected by patriarchy. When people come together to solve problems, they do not automatically become immune to the distorted ways society and the economy are organized. We bring the things that shape us, consciously and unconsciously, everywhere we go. Unless we are intentional about interrupting what we've learned, we will perpetuate it, even as we are working hard for a better world.

As an organizer, I am used to environments where women, usually women of color, are carrying the lion's share of the work but are only a minuscule part of the visible leadership. Every membership organization that I have ever been a part of had women doing the administrative work, women doing the relationship-building work, women developing the strategies, and men acting as the visible and external leadership of the organization. The same patterns were reflected in our membership as well. The majority of our membership was always women— poor and working-class women of color, immigrant women, and queer women. But when men came to our community meetings, they would often take up the most space. They would talk the most, pontificate, and be quick to try to tell people what they "really needed to be doing."

The women we organized rarely approached work in that way. If they were taking time out of their lives to come and get involved with an organization, it was because they were ready to be a part of the solution—even if they weren't sure what the solution was. Now, that's not to say that these women didn't have ideas and strong opinions. These women ran households, took care of children and grandbabies, and treated every kid in the community like their own. They held down nephews who were in jail or otherwise street involved, yelled at the police to stop terrorizing the children and then yelled at the d-boys for selling drugs on the block. But they rarely came into community meetings with a fourteen-point theory about how to save Black America. Men did that.

As a young organizer, I was regularly hit on by men. Some would come to participate in community meetings because they thought that even though I was talking with them at their door about environmental racism and police violence, what I secretly wanted was for them to ask me out on a date or at least ask for my phone number. The first time I ever did outreach, I was locked in a house by a man who was high on what I assumed to be methamphetamines. The only way I got out of that house unscathed was by pretending that I was interested and then inviting the man to come outside with me and smoke a cigarette so "we can get to know each other better." Once we were outside, thankfully, the person I was doing outreach with, a man, was waiting for me.

In 2007, I attended the United States Social Forum, where more than 10,000 activists and organizers converged to share strategies to interrupt the systems of power that impacted our everyday lives. It was one of my first trips with POWER, and I was eager to prove myself by playing a role in helping to coordinate our delegation of about thirty members, along with the staff. One day, the director of the organization invited me to attend a meeting with him.

The meeting was of a new group of Black organizers from coalitions across the country, joining to work together in service of Black people in a new and more systematic way. I was excited about the potential of what could happen if this meeting was successful. I was becoming politicized in this organization, learning more about the history of Black people's efforts to live a dignified life, and I yearned to be part of a movement that had a specific focus on improving Black lives.

When we arrived, I looked around the room, and out of about a hundred people who were crowded together, there were only a handful of women. Literally: There were five Black women and approximately ninety-five Black men.

An older Black man called the meeting to order. I sat next to my co-worker, mesmerized and nervous. Why were there so few Black women here? I wondered. In our local organizing, most of the people who attended our meetings were Black women. The older Black man talked for about forty minutes. When he finally stopped talking, man after man spoke, long diatribes about what Black people needed to be doing, addressing our deficits as a result of a sleeping people who had lost our way from who we really were. That feeling I used to get as a kid when my dad would yell to my mother or me to make him coffee began to bubble up inside me. Nervous but resolute, I raised my hand.

"So," I began, "I appreciate what you all have had to say." I introduced myself and the organization I was a part of, and then I continued: "I believe in the liberation you believe in, and I work every day for that. I heard you say a lot, but I didn't hear you say anything about where women fit into this picture. Where do queer people fit in this vision you have for Black liberation?" I had just delivered my very own Sojourner Truth "Ain't I a Woman?" speech, and the room fell silent.

It was hot in there. The air hung heavy in the packed room. People shifted uncomfortably in their seats. Some of the men in the room refused to make eye contact with me. Had I said something wrong? In the forty minutes the older man had spent talking, and the additional forty minutes the other men took up agreeing profusely over the liberation of Black men, not one mention was made of how Black people as a whole find freedom. It was as if when they talked about Black men, one should automatically assume that meant all Black people. I looked at him, at first with shyness and then, increasingly, with defiance. He started to talk about how important "the sisters" were to the project of Black liberation, but by then, for me, it was too late. The point had already been made. And there my impostor syndrome kicked in again. Who did this Black girl think she was, questioning the vision and the leadership of this Black man?

Later, I asked my co-worker if I was off base or out of line. "No," he said. "It was a good and important question." Well, if it was a "good and important" question, why did I have to be the one to ask it? Why didn't it occur to men in the room, present company included, that women, queer people, and trans people were not only not present in the room but also not present in the vision of what freedom could look like for Black people?

Now, of course, these are sweeping generalizations. Not all men didn't help and not all women didn't pontificate. But the pattern was regular enough that organizers had to adjust our practice in order to address it explicitly and implicitly. We didn't always get it right, but we couldn't not address it just because we weren't confident it would be perfect. We had to be mindful about who was talking in the room, and we had to make sure that people took up work commensurate with what their neighbors were willing to do. We were deliberate about women taking leadership roles, and we were deliberate about building the capacity of women to hold those roles. We provided childcare at each of our meetings, so that women could participate, and we ensured that the children were being engaged and not just placed in front of a video. All of these efforts were made so that women could play meaningful roles in building a movement to potentially transform the conditions in their communities and to make sure that we could interrupt the systems of power that shaped us.

. . .

Studying the civil rights movement, the Black Power movement, and other milestones in the pursuit of Black liberation
shaped my understanding of movement building and why it was
important. It also strengthened my resolve not to repeat the er-
rors of the past. Through reading about and sitting at the feet of
those who are now elders but were my age when these movements were in full swing, I learned about how women were
written out of history and at times completely absent from the
strategies of these movements. How Rosa Parks was relegated to
being a woman whose feet were tired rather than a strategist and
an organizer who was a part of the NAACP. How fifteen-year-
old Claudette Colvin refused to give up her seat nine months
before Rosa Parks did. How Diane Nash and Ella Baker and
Fannie Lou Hamer were deprioritized in favor of Ralph Bunche,
the Reverend Dr. Martin Luther King, Jr., and Ralph Aberna-
thy. How Elaine Brown and Kathleen Cleaver, Ericka Huggins
and Janet Cyril, set strategy for the Black Panther Party, advanced their organization as the state continued to target co-
founder Huey Newton, and established programs that still exist
in some form more than fifty years later.

And while for some those are mistakes of the past, those mistakes seem to persist even to this day. It is still true that racialized
patriarchy is alive and well in our movements and that, unless we
are intentional about changing that, it will continue to persist
long after we are gone.

Just like in the 1960s and 1970s, in 2020 we are still looking
for male heroes and relegating women to support roles, refusing
to see the ways in which women anchor so much of what happens in our movements. It's how I can know that men in leadership roles of our movement abuse their wives physically and
emotionally behind doors that aren't so closed. It's how I can

show up to speak on behalf of my organization at a progressive conference for Congress members and be hit on by a popular progressive male congressperson just minutes before I take the stage. It's how I can be the director of an organization and still have funders looking for the man I must be sitting in for. It's how a young Black man in a blue Patagonia vest can be more palatable to older Black women than three fierce midthirties Black women with decades of experience in transforming conditions in our communities. It's how that same man can be recognized as "the" leader of Black Lives Matter even though he has absolutely no affiliation with the organization, and it is how Black Lives Matter today can still be described as "an effort to save Black men" as opposed to an organization working on behalf of all of us.

You see, impostor syndrome is something that women like me carry on our backs because the world tells us that our concerns, our experiences, our needs, and our dreams do not exist. I don't have impostor syndrome because I refuse to believe that I do good and important things in the world. I have impostor syndrome because the credit for what I do in the world will always be given to a man. If I am smart, it will be because a man made me that way. If I am strategic, it will be because a man repeated the same thing I already said and moved people to do what I said needed to be done. If I am innovative, the credit for my creativity will be given to a man.

So, this impostor syndrome survivor begs all of us not to repeat the mistakes of the past, in service to our vision for our future. We all have work to do to untangle ourselves from the racialized patriarchy. One way to do that is to remind ourselves that, as five-year-olds are known to say, white people are not the boss of us and they're not the center of the universe. Another way to think about that is to be intentional about decentering the experiences of white people as the experiences of everyone. Just like Band-Aids that say "flesh-colored" actually mean flesh-colored for white people, feminism that centers only on the experiences of white women is a feminism that will continue to leave out all other women. If you are incensed about the wage gap, make sure you work to address the wage gap from where it is the widest, so the greatest number of people can benefit. If you are outraged about sexual terror and violence, make sure you are just as outraged about poor Black women being raped and sexually assaulted by police officers and about Black trans women who are left for dead by the men who have sex with them in secret and then kill them.

The racialized patriarchy is not a one-directional phenomenon. It is not as simple as men being supported to curtail the dignity and well-being of women. I mean, yes, this is a big part of the problem, but there are other side effects, like the ways some women step on other women's necks for a few more crumbs. To me, though, one of the significant parts of why the racialized patriarchy completely sucks is the way in which it robs men and male-identified people of meaningful and intimate relationships with the people they care about. The racialized patriarchy prevents men and male-identified people from having relationships with other men and male-identified people that aren't rooted in violence of some kind. It robs men and male-identified people from meaningful relationships with their children. The racialized patriarchy tells men and male-identified people that they aren't real men if they cry or show any semblance of humanity, that they are gay if they hug or touch another man, or that they are weak if they attempt to shatter the prison of gender norms and roles.

. . .

Having a highly visible platform has taught me the most about how the racialized patriarchy works.

I expect Black men to use my presence or my leadership to try to reclaim their rightful place as kings of our communities (insert eye rolls here). There is something threatening about Black women in leadership, particularly for Black cisgender men. Perhaps it has something to do with the enduring legacy of slavery, a shame that rattles in our bones to this day. One culturally defining aspect of enslavement was denying Black cisgender men access to masculinity. Masculinity, in my estimation, is not an inherently patriarchal project. Masculinity has been appropriated by the racialized patriarchy. Deliberate moves like castration as a form of racialized sexual violence against Black men, a refusal to acknowledge Black families as legitimate, and a system that doesn't allow Black men to protect the people they love from extreme physical and sexual terror certainly and surely have long-lasting impacts. My grandmother's mother was enslaved—that's how close America's history of slavery remains.

I aim to be careful not to perpetuate dusty notions of Black manhood that harken back to the country of Africa, when men were kings and women were queens of our royal civilizations (tongue in cheek, of course, because Africa is not a country, and which civilizations exactly are we talking about?). I believe that all communities are inherently messy, that our perspective depends on whom we spend the most time talking to. And on a human level, there's been some serious damage done to Black masculinity in America. I believe Black men and Black masculine people deserve more than what they're getting too. If we are to build a healthy masculinity, we have to get rid of the racialized patriarchy.

Earlier, I made the assertion that being a feminist does not a man-hater make, and I mean that. I don't believe that taking men to task for their parasitic relationship to women is man-hating, but I also understand that for some, feminism is a hatred for men. My feminism is Black, it is queer, and it includes men, masculinity, and manhood that are sustainable and do not depend on the subjugation of women to exist.

Until we get there, I continue to expect men in general to sexualize me with or without my consent, will refuse to take me seriously, and take credit and be given credit for that to which they've made very little contribution. I expect them to have a propensity toward violence against me, even those men who claim to love me. And I work hard for the day when men who fight the racialized patriarchy are not the exception to the rule and, more than that, are not merely in solidarity with women. I work for the day when men understand that another masculinity is possible—but not under the racialized patriarchy.

The racialized patriarchy also comes in the form of Black women talking about #BlackGirlMagic in one breath and then in the next displaying an ambivalence, at best, to the idea of other Black women in leadership. Black women in leadership carry the unique dilemma of being seen as too tough and not tough enough. I once had someone I worked with tell me that I was "cold." When pressed further, they seemed comfortable with my being in a position of leadership only if it meant that we were friends and co-workers. I gently and firmly reminded them that we hadn't been friends previously, so the expectation that I would be calling them to hang out as opposed to calling them to check up on work we were doing together was an unrealistic one.

Far from being confined to this one person, this has been my frequent experience as a Black woman in leadership roles. I'm quite sure they would not have had this expectation had their boss been a white woman, or even another woman of color necessarily. As Black women, we are expected to take care of people, and the racialized patriarchy demands that we care for you before we care for ourselves. And, yes, quiet as it's kept, this is also true between and among Black women, even as we hashtag our selfies with #BlackGirlMagic. We're expected to be your homegirl who will understand why you just couldn't get it together today, and yet when we need to make sure that things are getting done, we are no longer your homegirl. We become those women whom you call cold, harsh, and the like.

My feminism calls bullshit when Black women are split into "nice" and "mean." Too often, "nice" means one person is getting what they need while the other is dimming their own light in order for the first's to be nourished, while "mean" is reserved for Black women with boundaries. But this dichotomy is especially problematic when it is propagated by Black women. Do we, as Black women, hold Black women to the same questionable expectations that we claim to abhor? Dismantling the racialized patriarchy and kicking it to the curb could mean that we would allow Black women to do their work without saddling them with the expectation to carry the weight for everyone else. Black women would not expect Black women to be superheroes and carry the world on our shoulders. Black women could take on what is right-sized for us as opposed to our assumed availability for everyone who desires to suck from our breasts, the way we were expected to nurse white women's babies as well as our own. High expectations are not the issue—instead, the issue lies in unrealistic expectations inside a racialized patriarchy, the expectation that Black women will be mules, not just for white people but for Black people too.

The Black radical tradition teaches us that an effective movement cannot be afraid of either leadership or Black women as leaders. Why repeat old mistakes when we could learn from them and make new ones that show we've learned a thing or two?

CHAPTER FOURTEEN

NO BASE, NO MOVEMENT

THE REAL STORY BEHIND ANY SUCCESSFUL MOVEMENT IS MANY people coming together to create the change they want to see in the world. This truth has been obscured by popular narratives of successful social change that tend to revolve around the courageous actions and moral clarity of one person, usually a cisgender heterosexual man. But lately, technology and social media have also obscured the fundamental means of organizing: building a base of affected people who learn together how to create real and lasting change.

As I discussed earlier, a base is a group of people united around an issue or a goal. A base should be distinguished from a constituency, which can include those groups but also include people who are impacted by an issue or a series of issues but aren't yet organized to fight them. For example, Black communities are a constituency: Black communities can include groups of people organized around an issue or a goal, like churches or unions or community organizations, but they will also include individuals and institutions who are not organized around an issue or a goal. A Black woman who has experienced domestic violence is a part of the constituency of Black communities, but if she has not become a part of an organizing effort to address domestic violence, she is not a part of a base.

Today, the internet connects us. The point of connection is usually personal: friends on Facebook or followers on Twitter. But people are also finding one another through groups in which members share an affinity, like Pantsuit Nation, an online discussion group that aimed to help get Hillary Clinton elected.

However, followers on Twitter and friends on Facebook are not the same as people who will actually come together to take action together on the ground.

Anything that reaches toward the sky must have a strong foundation to hold it up. That's how I think of movements—movements reach toward the sky to achieve what has been deemed impossible. And in order to stay sturdy, they need a base—people who keep the movements anchored in the needs, dreams, and lived experiences of those who are directly impacted by the problem at hand.

For example, POWER once ran a campaign to win free public transportation for young people in San Francisco. We heard from some of the parents in our organization that San Francisco Unified School District (SFUSD) had eliminated yellow school buses due to revenue shortfalls, and many were now scrambling to figure out how they would get their children to and from school. In a city where the cost of living was already astronomical, the only resort for many parents who used this service was to put their children on public transportation, increasing pressures on already stretched budgets.

So, what does one do in order to change this? An organizer

would say that we have to get people affected by the cuts together to state what we want done instead and then determine
who has the power to make the decision. If we want to influence the decision maker to either reverse the decision or do
something different, we have to demonstrate that this is something a lot of people care about and there will be consequences
if they don't do what we need them to do.

And that's what we did. We set out to find parents impacted
by the elimination of the yellow school buses by knocking on
doors in communities like Bayview Hunters Point and the Mission District, and we also found them through their children,
through the work we did with young people in high schools
throughout the city. We brought those parents together to understand the decision and discuss its implications. We brought
parents face-to-face with the SFUSD board, and we met with
the agency that oversees the public transportation system in San
Francisco. Together, we developed a plan to demand that the
Municipal Transportation Agency fully fund a pilot program
whereby young people under the age of eighteen get to ride the
city bus for free.

We met with decision makers, bringing along the affected
parents and young people. In our meetings, the youths and the
adults shared their stories of how they were being impacted by
these cuts, and then we offered a solution that would ease the
burden on them while promoting the use of public transportation throughout the city. Our youth members did presentations
to other students in their schools about the fight for free public
transportation. And we had people in our communities call
members of the Board of Supervisors, Transportation Commission, and school board to support our proposal.

We won the campaign because we had an organized base
who put pressure on decision makers. Yes, we used Facebook
and Twitter to get our message out. But we could not rely on

social media alone to win. We had to organize. We had to bring people together and advocate for ourselves.

There are many issues that people care about, and there is a lot at stake—but not enough of us are organized to make the impact we seek. Those of us who want to see healthcare for everyone, those of us who want to make sure that quality education stays accessible and affordable, those of us who want to ensure that we are protecting the environment, those of us who want to make sure that Black lives matter and that women are treated as people, are tasked with building a movement to win the world we dream of in our minds and in our hearts. To build that movement, we have to go about the task of building bases—ever-expanding groups of people organized around our vision for change.

How do we know when people are organized into a base? When there is intentional educational work being done to understand the problem and who is at fault. When they take action to bring more people into the fight. When they come together regularly to develop solutions and advocate for those solutions in homes, in workplaces, in places of worship, in schools, and to our government.

When Brett Kavanaugh was nominated to serve on the Supreme Court and Dr. Christine Blasey Ford came forward to recount her story of being sexually assaulted by him, women and men turned out en masse to protest his confirmation. These were people who had been galvanized by the Women's March in 2017 and by Harvey Weinstein's exposure as a serial predator through the #MeToo movement. They were inspired and even mobilized—but that isn't quite the same thing as being organized.

Mobilization is an opportunity to organize, to engage people in a consistent and deep way around issues. When Oscar Grant was murdered just a few blocks from my home in Oakland, I felt compelled to participate in a range of actions to hold the BART police officer who murdered him accountable for his crime. I marched through the streets. I chanted. I was teargassed and helped tend to others who were teargassed. And these efforts were successful in some respects. The coalition of people who came together accomplished a lot of short-term change: Johannes Mehserle was fired from the BART police force and charged with and convicted of involuntary manslaughter.

But was I organized into a lasting effort for systemic change? I was a supporter, but no organizers followed up with me and asked me why I had become involved. No organizers asked me how I wanted to be involved moving forward, and no organizers laid out a plan for me to get involved and stay involved. I was a part of a constituency of people who lived in Oakland and cared about what was happening in the place I lived, and I was mobilized and inspired, but I was not organized into a base that was ready to take action to achieve systemic change.

So, when building movements, we need to ask ourselves: How many new people brought into the fight consider themselves a part of an organized movement that we are building together? And how many of those people aren't people we are already connected to?

To build the kind of movement that we need to get the things we deserve, we can't be afraid to establish a base that is larger than the people we feel comfortable with. Movements and bases cannot be cliques of people who already know one another. We have to reach beyond the choir and take seriously the task of organizing the unorganized—the people who don't already speak the same language, the people who don't eat, sleep, and breathe social justice, the people who have everything at stake and are looking to be less isolated and more connected and who want to win changes in their lives and in the lives of the people they love.

There are some who argue that you don't need organizations to be a part of a movement. I find this idea misguided and ahistorical. Every successful social movement in history was undergirded by organizations: the suffrage movement, the anti-apartheid movement, the anti-war movement. Even in the age of technology, it is a fallacy to believe that organizations are un-important or unnecessary. Technology allows us to connect, but there is also some evidence that technology has in fact increased isolation—if we never have to be in the same physical space as the people we interact with, this can affect the value and depth of the relationships we build. I suspect as well that the relentless flow of information bombarding us all can make us dull to its effects and separate us from things happening in our own com-munities in real time—things that affect the lives of real people, not just for a minute or two in your timeline but for a lifetime or generations.

In social media environments, where everything moves fast, relationships are the first casualty. Many have observed the throwaway culture in our movements, the willingness to termi-nate or cancel people from movements for perceived deviations, but I think throwaway culture is really a manifestation of rela-tionships built through social media. On social media, if I don't like what someone has to say, I can block them, ignore them, or gather my friends to attack them online. I personally have spent hours on social media attacking and being attacked by people who didn't like what I had to say or who said things that I didn't like. Inevitably, the conversation ends by one of us blocking the other. These disagreements can bleed into our offline lives, when we take a disagreement about something online and use it to justify ending relationships with people who we previously believed shared our goals and objectives.

Today, there are some powerful organizations building a base of directly impacted people, who are coming together to change their conditions and transform how power operates—including organizations developed and grown by our opposition. These organizations are able to mobilize, activate, and engage millions of people on the issues that impact their lives. They are able to do this because they are intentional about building a political community for and with those who are disaffected by their political conditions and want to change those conditions. These organizations build community around and with their base, and these organizations invest in the lives of the members of their base. These organizations help the people who are a part of them combat feelings of isolation or loneliness by bringing them into community with those who have similar experiences.

Most important, these organizations offer a way forward. Organizations with a base don't allow for their members to stay disillusioned, to remain feeling powerless. These successful organizations give people a sense of their own power.

CHAPTER FIFTEEN

POLITICAL EDUCATION AND COMMON SENSE

I T WASN'T UNTIL I GOT TO COLLEGE THAT I REALLY BEGAN TO understand race. I had experienced racism, but—perhaps because my parents wanted to shield me from the complexity of race relations in America—I didn't develop a context for my experiences until I left home. Developing a context for my experiences meant that I felt less alone, less isolated, and less like there was something wrong with me. I learned that racism, like most systems of oppression, isn't about bad people doing terrible things to people who are different from them but instead is a way of maintaining power for certain groups at the expense of others. Knowing that oppression wasn't a function of people being mean to each other but instead was a means to an end helped me see that I'd better get to the business of fighting back and working to take and reshape power.

Now, of course, that leap didn't happen in an instant. And it definitely didn't all happen in college. It's still ongoing. But that experience was the beginning of my political education—and it prepared me to be a part of a movement and, eventually, someone who helps to shape movements.

Political education is a tool for understanding the political contexts we live in. It helps individuals and groups analyze the social and economic trends, the policies and the ideologies influencing our lives—and use this information to develop strategies to change the rules and transform power.

It comes in different forms. Popular education, developed by Brazilian educator Paulo Freire, is a form of political education where the "educator" and the "participants" engage in learning together to reflect on critical issues facing their communities and then take action to address those issues. I once participated in a workshop that used popular-education methods to explain exploitation in capitalism, and—despite two bachelor's degrees, in anthropology and sociology—my world completely opened up. I'd taken classes that explored Marxist theory but had never learned how it came to life through Third World liberation struggles, how poor people in Brazil and South Africa and Vietnam used those theories to change their governments, change the rules, and change their conditions. Had I learned about those theories in ways that actually applied to my life, my context, my experience, I probably would have analyzed and applied them differently. Because the information had little context that interested me, I could easily dismiss it (mostly because I didn't totally understand it) and miss an opportunity to see my world a little more clearly.

Peer-to-peer is another form of political education. Starting when I was just twelve years old, I became very involved in peer education—as a workshop facilitator, peer counselor, and sexual-health educator. Sexual-health education was a gateway for me to become involved in fighting for reproductive rights. My own sex education came when I was about eight or nine years old, when my mother, an avid coupon clipper, finally saved up enough UPC codes from tampon boxes to get a free copy of *The Miracle of Life,* a no-nonsense documentary about childbearing, from conception to birth. I was called inside the house from riding my bike up and down the street and placed in front of the television. It worked. From that point on, I was not afraid to discuss sex and wasn't embarrassed to say words like "vagina" or "penis."

When I was twelve, I learned that a lot of my peers were experimenting with sex for the first time. Many were uncomfortable talking about their bodies, embarrassed to ask questions about sex and intimacy and desire, much less discuss the potential of pregnancy or sexually transmitted diseases. It was a wealthy community, where some folks thought they were untouchable, especially by problems like teen pregnancy or STDs, which had long been coded as lower-class issues. Plus, many kids had not had open and honest conversations about sex with their parents. Instead, most got their sex information either from older siblings or from other kids—so it made sense that sexual-health education by someone in your peer group would be more effective than lectures from adults.

I did that work, through student clubs, health centers, and organizations, for about ten years, all the way through high school and college. Lots of the work we did was branded "teen pregnancy prevention." We saw ourselves as crusaders against an epidemic of teenagers getting pregnant and contracting sexually transmitted diseases due to a lack of accurate information. We had speakers come to class to bear witness to their confrontations with these scourges. Whether it was an abortion story or a story about contracting HIV, the message was always, at least in part: This could happen to you if you don't make better choices. It was done with good intentions, but delivering these messages sometimes felt coercive and stigmatizing—it was my least favorite part of our work.

My favorite part was that our approach was mostly rooted in principles of harm reduction and sex positivity. We did not engage in shaming, for the most part, of what got people off or what turned people on. We encouraged conversations about pleasure, as long as they were also about responsibility.

So, when I went away to college, I was excited to extend my education on a topic that I felt proficient in, even though I wasn't doing much of it myself: sex. In this way the political education that started with peer education was amplified and shaped by formal academic classwork. One of the texts in the course I took on the sociology of human sexuality was *Intimate Matters* by John D'Emilio and Estelle Freedman, which recounted key moments in the history of human sexuality. One such moment was the birth control movement led by Margaret Sanger.

The early birth control movement was firmly situated in the context of women's rights. During the Great Depression, activists were adamant that women should have control over their bodies and reproductive lives; controlling family planning had obvious economic implications during that time. So far, so good. But there was another side to the birth control movement, led by eugenicists who hijacked the movement to argue that birth control was necessary to keep undesirable races from reproducing. The logic of the eugenicists brought forced sterilizations to Black and Puerto Rican women during this period.

In class, we learned how Margaret Sanger became known as the mother of the birth control movement. Her work was supported by her wealthy husband, but that same rich husband was a proponent of eugenics—and Sanger joined him, later in life. The logic of eugenics that led to forced sterilizations also allowed the birth control pill to become widely available for most women, including women of color.

While taking this class, I was also working with a student organization run by Planned Parenthood. When they celebrated Margaret Sanger Day, I promptly stopped working with them and took a long break from reproductive justice work, especially work that didn't operate from a perspective of race, class, and gender. I looked more closely at other initiatives from Planned Parenthood and wondered whether or not these initiatives were supporting women of color or merely using women of color as window dressing. It became a lens I applied more frequently as the years went on.

Political education helps us see the world from different perspectives without elevating the viewpoint and perspective of white, Christian, heterosexual men over that of anyone else—including those groups whose presence, contributions, and history have suffered erasure. Political education is a part of the process of interrupting old power dynamics in our communities, the ones that privilege some experiences, perspectives, and tactics over others.

The conservative movement has also been looking at education for a few decades now, targeting curricula in high schools and universities to reach kids in their most formative years and shape how they understand the world. For example, a school district in Texas voted to change its curriculum to eliminate any material on the slave trade and instead teach young people that Black people freely chose to immigrate to the United States to find work, just as Europeans did. This is a vivid example of how the ability to control the stories that define us is a key form of power. Political education acknowledges that no education is neutral—that all information has a story behind it and an implicit agenda.

In this country, education has often been denied to parts of the population—for instance, Black students in the post–

Reconstruction and Jim Crow eras, or students today in under-financed and abandoned public schools. Given our complicated history with education, some people involved in movements for change don't like the idea of education or political education as a way to build a base. This form of anti-intellectualism—the tendency to avoid theory and study when building movements—is a response to the fact that not everyone has had an equal chance to learn. But education is still necessary.

For those of us who want to build a movement that can change our lives and the lives of the people we care about, we must ask ourselves: How can we use political education to help build the critical thinking skills and analysis of those with whom we are building a base? We cannot build a base or a movement without education.

Antonio Gramsci was an Italian Marxist philosopher and politician whose work offers some important ideas about the essential role of political education. Gramsci was born in 1891 in Sardinia, Italy. He co-founded the Italian Communist Party and was imprisoned by Benito Mussolini's fascist regime. While he was in prison, Gramsci wrote *Prison Notebooks,* a collection of more than thirty notebooks and 3,000 pages of theory, analysis, and history.

Gramsci is best known for his theories of cultural hegemony, a fancy term for how the state and ruling class instill values that are gradually accepted as "common sense"—in other words, what we consider to be normal or the status quo. Gramsci studied how people come to consent to the status quo. According to Gramsci, there are two ways that the state can persuade its subjects to do what it wants: through force and violence, or through consent. While the state does not hesitate to use force in pursuit of its agenda, it also knows that force is not a sustainable option for getting its subjects to do its will. Instead, the state relies on consent to move its agenda, and the state manufactures consent through hegemony, or through making its values, rules, and logic the "common sense" of the masses. In that way, individuals willingly go along with the state's program rather than having to be coerced through violence and force.

This doesn't mean that individuals are not also coerced through violence and force, particularly when daring to transgress the hegemony of the state. American hegemony is white, male, Christian, and heterosexual. That which does not support that common sense is aggressively surveilled and policed, sometimes through the direct violence of the state but most often through cultural hegemony.

For instance, people who identify as transgender are more prone to experience this violence, because they defy "common sense" about gender. At the time of this writing, at least twenty transgender people, predominantly Black transgender women, have been killed in hate crimes this year. In 2019, twenty-seven transgender or gender nonconforming people were murdered, and similarly, the murders were predominantly of Black transgender women. For people who identify as lesbian, gay, bisexual, and gender nonconforming, there are still more-startling statistics. The statistics are merely indicators of what happens when subjects defy the common sense of the state. In many cases, the state does not have to be the arbiter of force or violence when the hegemony is defied, because the subjects will enforce the status quo themselves, through vigilante violence.

Hegemony, in Gramsci's sense, is mostly developed and reinforced in the cultural realm, in ways that are largely invisible but carry great power and influence. For example, the notion that pink is for girls and blue is for boys is a pervasive idea reinforced throughout society. If you ever look for a toy or clothing for a newborn assigned either a male sex or male gender, you find a preponderance of blue items. If boys wear pink, they are sometimes ostracized. This binary of pink for girls and blue for boys helps maintain rigid gender roles, which in turn reinforce the power relationships between the sexes. Transgressions are not looked upon favorably, because to disrupt these rules would be to disrupt the distribution of power between the sexes. To dress a girl-identified child in blue or to dress a boy in pink causes consternation or even violence. These are powerful examples of hegemony at work—implicit rules that individuals in a society follow because they become common sense, "just the way things are" or "the way they're supposed to be."

Hegemony is important to understand because it informs how ideas are adopted, carried, and maintained. We can apply an understanding of hegemony to almost any social dynamic— racism, homophobia, heterosexism, sexism, ableism. We have to interrupt these toxic dynamics or they will eat away at our ability to build the kinds of movements that we need. But to interrupt these toxic dynamics requires that we figure out where the ideas come from in the first place.

For example, throughout the history of the women's movement, there have been numerous moments when white women failed to stand with their sisters of color and trans sisters. Behind this failure is a hegemonic idea: that their whiteness entitles them to privilege over their sisters of color and trans sisters. There are other ideas, often unsaid, within that hegemonic "common sense"—for instance, the idea that trans women are not women. Or that women of color are not fit to play leadership roles, or are too sensitive when it comes to race, or that privilege doesn't even exist between white women and women of color. We have to dig into the underlying ideas and make the hegemonic common sense visible to understand how we can create real unity and allyship in the women's movement.

There are examples unique to this political moment. Since the rise of the Black Lives Matter movement, hegemonic ideas have slowed our progress. One piece of hegemonic common sense is the idea that Black men are the central focus of Black Lives Matter and should be elevated at all times. The media rushed to anoint a young gay Black man as the founder of the movement, even though that was not the case. This same sort of prioritizing of Black men happened all over the country: young Black men elevated to the role of Black Lives Matter leaders, regardless of the work they'd actually put in. Why were they assigned these roles without justification? I believe it's because hegemony in the United States assigns leadership roles to men. In Black communities in particular, leadership is assigned to Black men even when Black women are carrying the work, designing the work, developing the strategy, and executing the strategy. Symbolism can often present as substance, yet they are not the same. This is a case where an unexamined hegemonic idea caused damage and distortion.

Yet another timely example is the rise of Donald Trump.

Trump's presidential campaign was a brilliant exercise in using hegemony to one's advantage. The Trump campaign successfully reached white people, particularly white men, who felt left out of the economy and the government. They felt left out not just because of the undue influence of the corporate class and the elite but also because they perceived that the wealth, access, and power promised to them were being distributed to women, people of color, and queer people. Trump's campaign relied on the hegemonic idea of who constituted the "real" America, who were the protagonists of this country's story and who were the villains. The protagonists were disaffected white people, both men and women, and the villains were people of color, with certain communities afforded their own unique piece of the story.

For example, the campaign's repetition of "law and order" was applied to a new generation of Black people demanding rights, respect, and self-determination, with Trump stoking age-old narratives of Black people as criminals and rule breakers who needed to be taught a lesson. "Illegals" and "aliens" were largely applied to Latino immigrants, though different groups of immigrants were caught up in it, especially those from the Islamic world. Illegals and border jumpers were coming to the United States and threatening our way of life, taking jobs meant for Americans and not following the rules. Meager but meaningful protections for trans people in the military would later be stripped under the guise of eliminating political correctness, subjecting a safeguarded class of people to regular and brutal discrimination and violence. Stripping away political correctness can also be seen in the campaign's promised return to the way things were—a time when things were more simple and certain groups of people knew their place.

These ideas are called hegemonic because they are embedded and reproduced in our culture. Wild West movies are an embodiment of the nation's origin story that paints white men as heroes and indigenous communities as savages in need of taming. The notion that white women are superior to Black women is codified in movies like *Driving Miss Daisy* and *The Help*, in which white women are portrayed as heroes and saviors while Black women play supporting roles or are the ones to be saved. It is codified in clothing ads, like the controversial Gap ad in which a white model is literally posing with her arm on top of a Black girl's head, as if she is a piece of furniture to prop her up.

This example points to the critical role of culture as an adjunct to political education.

Culture and policy affect and influence each other, so successful social movements must engage with both. This isn't a new idea—the right has been clear about the relationship between culture and policy for a very long time. It is one of the reasons they have invested so heavily in the realm of ideas and behavior. Right-wing campaigns have studied how to culturally frame their ideas and values as common sense.

Culture has long been lauded as an arena for social change—and yet organizers often dismiss culture as the soft work, while policy is the real work. But policy change can't happen without changing the complex web of ideas, values, and beliefs that undergird the status quo. When I was being trained as an organizer, culture work was believed to be for people who could not handle real organizing. Nobody would say it out loud, but there was a hierarchy—with community organizing on top and cultural organizing an afterthought.

To be fair, some cultural work did fall into this category. After all, posters and propaganda distributed among the coalition of the already willing weren't going to produce change as much as reinforce true believers.

When culture change happens, it is because movements have infiltrated the cultural arena and penetrated the veil beyond which every person encounters explicit and implicit messages about what is right and what is wrong, what is normal and what is abnormal, who belongs and who does not. When social movements engage in this arena, they subvert common ideas and compete with or replace them with new ideas that challenge so-called common sense.

Culture also offers an opportunity for the values and hegemony of the opposition to be exposed and interrogated. The veteran organizer and communications strategist Karlos Gauna Schmieder wrote that "we must lay claim to civil society, and fight for space in all the places where knowledge is produced and cultured." By laying claim to civil society, we assert that there is an alternative to the white, male, Christian, heterosexual "common sense" that is the status quo—and we work to produce new knowledge that not only reflects our vision for a new society but also includes a new vision for our relationships to one another and to the planet.

It is this challenge, to lay claim to civil society and to fight for space in all of the places where knowledge is produced and cultured, that movements must take on with vigor, just as right-wing movements have tried to lay claim to those places to build their movement. Culture, in this sense, is what makes right-wing movements strong and compelling. It is what lays the groundwork for effective, sustained policy change.

The marriage equality movement is a strong example of how progressive forces have laid claim to the places where knowledge is produced and cultured, in order to shift laws that impact the lives of millions of people.

For several decades, the right controlled public sentiment on sexuality and the family. The agenda of the right leans on compulsory heterosexuality, an agenda that asserts that all "normal" sexual relationships are between a man and a woman. Compulsory heterosexuality has been enforced rigorously by culture and policy. For decades, the widespread absence of LGBT characters on television, for example, was a way that compulsory heterosexuality was reinforced. When LGBT characters were portrayed on television, they were depicted with harmful stereotypes that further pushed the LGBT community to the margins.

The right launched a full-scale attack on queer sexualities in the 1980s and 1990s. The AIDS epidemic further stigmatized queer communities, as thousands of people died due to government inaction, prejudice, and discrimination. Being gay became synonymous with having a disease, and to make matters worse, any nonheterosexual relationship was also looked at as a sin against God, the two phenomena perpetuating the old idea that nonheterosexual sex deserved punishment, which in turn exacerbated inaction around the epidemic.

President George H. W. Bush was in leadership during the height of the AIDS crisis. Both he and Ronald Reagan, notoriously anti-LGBT, remained largely silent as more than 150,000 people died during their presidental terms. Funding for AIDS research, support for people living and dying of AIDS, and education on prevention and destigmatization lagged behind the unfolding of the crisis in communities across the nation. Along with gay men, Black people were disproportionately impacted by the AIDS epidemic.

It took years of advocacy and direct action to bring attention to the crisis into the mainstream. Groups like ACT UP were formed to place pressure on the administration to apply more resources to HIV/AIDS treatment and prevention. They also worked to ensure that the silence surrounding HIV and AIDS, rooted in homophobia, was broken.

But to make all of this change sustainable also took a cultural shift, a shift in the ideas that were considered status quo. Gay characters appeared on television, living the same kind of lives as heterosexual people. Gay characters began to be portrayed as having "normal" and meaningful relationships. Culture began to evolve from gay people being portrayed as pariahs and pedophiles to gay people being seen as a part of every community and every family.

This shift did not just happen on television, with shows like *Will & Grace, Ellen,* and *Grey's Anatomy.* It happened in comic books and in hip-hop and had ripple effects all the way up to the White House. The rapper and social entrepreneur Jay-Z came out in support of marriage equality in 2012, saying, "You can choose to love whoever you love." The musician Frank Ocean described his attraction to another young man when he was nineteen. Marvel and DC Comics reimagined the role of superhero to include characters who identified as LGBT, like Batwoman. In these ways, the common sense changes—not in a classroom or through peers but through the media.

Political education helps us make visible that which had been made invisible. We cannot expect to unravel common sense about how the world functions if we don't do that work. Political education helps us unearth our commonly held assumptions about the world that keep the same power dynamics functioning the way they always have. It supports our ability to dream of other worlds and to build them. And it gives us a clearer picture of all that we are up against.

CHAPTER SIXTEEN

UNITED FRONTS AND POPULAR FRONTS

M OVEMENTS REQUIRE PEOPLE TO COME TOGETHER, ACROSS difference, united in pursuit of a common goal. For some, movements comprise people who think alike and act alike—but in reality, movements come alive when those who are unlikely to come together do so for the sake of achieving something.

Sometimes, the ultimate goal is to create the conditions for coming together in ways that last, that can endure disagreements over direction, strategy, and more. Other times, this coming together is temporary.

I learned these lessons as the difference between united fronts and popular fronts, and the lessons have always proved useful to me when deciding with whom to ally and on what basis. They've allowed me to best understand how to build the team needed to accomplish a goal or a series of goals.

These days, I hear people clamoring to build a movement as if doing so is merely a case of adding water, oil, and milk to a premixed batter; after thirty minutes in the oven, a movement is baked. But building a movement isn't that simple. Building a movement means building alliances. Who we align with at any given time says a lot about what we are trying to build together and who we think is necessary to build it.

The question of alliances can be confusing. We might confuse short-term alliances with long-term ones. Or confuse whether the people we ally with on a single campaign need to be aligned with us on everything. But here's the truth of the matter: The people we need to build alliances with are not necessarily people we will agree with on everything or even most things. And yet having a strategy, a plan to win, asks us to do things differently than we've done them before.

In many movement-building efforts, there is a tendency to build alliances with only those we are the most comfortable with, those who already speak our language and share our views on the world. We can become so adamant about this that we chastise those who choose to cast a much wider net for the sake of building a broader movement. There's a righteousness that comes with that too. We can tell ourselves that everyone else isn't really about the business of building a movement, that we are the only ones who truly understand how to get to transformation.

I have fallen into this trap. I've spent a lot of my time as an organizer around people with radical politics, which sometimes makes me uncomfortable with people who might share my goal for a transformed world but don't share my politics.

I think we need to build a movement in the millions to create real change, and those millions must keep growing larger in order to maintain power and transform it. Too many of our social movements find comfort and solace in the small and homogenous. But when we look at some of the factors that have challenged the success of social movements, homogeneity is a problem.

This is why knowing the difference between popular fronts and united fronts is so important—it is a step toward understanding and practicing governance.

Popular fronts are alliances that come together across a range of political beliefs for the purpose of achieving a short-to-intermediate-term goal, while united fronts are long-term alliances based on the highest level of political alignment. The phrases are often used interchangeably but shouldn't be.

A lot of activist coalitions these days take the form of popular fronts and come together around achieving a short-to-intermediate-term objective. When I was organizing in Bayview Hunters Point, we built a popular front with the Nation of Islam, Greenaction for Health and Environmental Justice, and a few other smaller entities such as local churches and advocacy organizations like Environmental Justice Alliance and the Church of St. John Coltrane. We were united around advancing a ballot initiative to ensure that 50 percent of all new housing built in the community would be affordable to people making $40,000 a year or less. We had assets that we lent to one another. We were a small grassroots organization that would take thirty days to mobilize one hundred people, while the Nation of Islam could mobilize a thousand people with three days' notice.

There was a lot that we did not agree on politically.

At times, it was a source of tension between our organizations. For example, I was the lead organizer on the campaign, which meant that I made decisions on strategy and approach. In our meetings, I was often one of the only women, and certainly the only queer woman, in the group. But as the leadership in the campaign, I needed to sign off on decisions. This was different from how the Nation operated. Decisions were largely made by men, and as far as we knew there were no women, much less queer women, making decisions about the direction of their end of the campaign. When I would go to meetings at the mosque, women sat on one side of the room and men on the other. I, being me, would sit on the men's side of the room. We knew about and were aware of our differences politically—and we also knew that we needed one another to win. We would often remind one another that out of ten items on an agenda, we probably did not agree on nine of them—but if number ten was what we were united around, then we were committed to giving it everything we had.

Of course, it was not always possible to stay focused just on the task at hand. At times our membership was hostile to the idea of building a popular front with the Nation of Islam in particular. While our organization was nondenominational, our base was largely Christian. Similarly, our organization was pro-queer, anti-capitalist, intentionally multiracial, and feminist. We were advocates and practitioners of nonviolent direct action. The Nation of Islam differed from us on many of the political pillars that were the bedrock of our organization. The Nation was not anti-capitalist and in fact was pro-Black-capitalism. They were not pro-queer organizationally and they were not multiracial. Our stances on patriarchy differed substantially.

However, what allowed us to be dangerous together was that we were indivisible on the issue of the initiative. We demonstrated a respect for one another and our differences in ways that allowed us to appreciate the strengths that we brought to the table. And, more important, the community respected our unity: If two organizations that couldn't be more different politically could work together, surely this was a fight worth getting involved in. I will not forget a powerful sermon delivered by Minister Christopher Muhammad about queer liberation, in which he acknowledged the ways in which he had struggled with discriminating against queer people but had ultimately become convinced that we needed one another to get free. And as for us, we maintained our concerns and reservations around their politics that we did not and would not share. But our respect for their level of organization, the level of discipline within it, and the ways in which they prioritized organizing among the most downtrodden Black people deserved respect. As I got to know more of the members of the mosque and heard the stories of how they'd become members of the Nation, I came to realize that we could learn from elements of what they were doing in order to strengthen our organization.

We didn't look past our differences—we found the courage to look into them.

United fronts are alliances whose level of political alignment is much higher. United fronts bring together organizations that share a long-term vision for social change along with a shared theory for how social change happens.

When I first started at POWER, we helped to build a united front known as the May 1st Alliance for Land, Work, and Power. The united front comprised five grassroots organizations—the Chinese Progressive Association; POWER; St. Peter's Housing Committee; the San Francisco Day Labor Program and La Colectiva de Mujeres; and Coleman Advocates for Children and Youth—that came together because of our shared politics, our shared vision, and a shared organizing model. We spent time together doing organizing exchanges, studying political theory and social movements, learning from one another's organizing models, and taking action together. After about five years, this alliance grew into an even stronger one, known as San Francisco Rising—an electoral organizing vehicle designed to build and win real power for working-class San Francisco.

. . .

United fronts are helpful in a lot of ways, including being really clear about who is on the team. In some ways, united fronts are what we are working toward, why we organize: to build bigger and bigger teams of people aligned in strategy, vision, and values. But if I had to guess, I'd say that the next period will be characterized by a greater number of popular fronts, and I think this is a good thing.

Popular fronts help you engage with the world as it is, while united fronts offer the possibility of what could be. United fronts allow us to build new alternatives, to test new ideas together, because there is already a high level of trust, political clarity, and political unity. Popular fronts, however, teach us to be nimble, to build relationships across difference for the sake of our survival.

Popular fronts are important tools for organizers today. They match today's reality: that those of us who want to see a country and a world predicated on justice and equality and the ability to live well and with dignity are not well represented among those who are making decisions over our lives. We are a small proportion of people who currently serve in the U.S. Congress, a small percentage of people who are mayors and governors, and a small percentage of people moving resources on your city council or board of education.

We are not the majority of the decision makers, even though we likely represent the majority in terms of what we all want for our futures. It is tempting in these times to double down on those closest to you, who already share your vision, share your values, share your politics. But to get things done, we are tasked to find places of common ground, because that is how we can attain the political power we lack.

Many people are uncomfortable with popular fronts because they are afraid that working with their opponents will dilute their own politics. I agree that popular fronts without united fronts are dangerous for this exact reason—without an anchor,

without clarity about what you stand for and who you are accountable to, it can be difficult to maintain integrity and clarity
when working with people who do not share your values and
vision.

But I don't think the biggest challenge comes at us from the
opposite direction; I think we are so comfortable with those
who agree with us that we fear being challenged. It's natural to
seek safety and comfort, and yet, if we have a long-term vision
for our communities and the people we care about, we owe it to
ourselves to get a little uncomfortable.

We need movements that can hold complexity so that we can
learn how to reach for one another, even when reaching for one
another makes us uncomfortable. We need movements inside of
which millions of people can grow and learn, movements where
people can come as they are, as long as they are willing to be
transformed in the service of our full and complete liberation.
We need people who've never graduated from college. People
who come from fundamentalist religious backgrounds. We need
people who think that corporate approaches to solving problems
are the only way to change the world. We need people who
believe that charity will make the world a better place. We need
people who think all these ways, because without being part of
a movement that offers them the opportunity to see differently
and do differently, they will continue to see the world the way
that they do. Without being engaged somehow in a movement
for change, where would they get exposure to a different way of
seeing the world?

As an organizer, I was taught that we are looking for the
people who are looking for us. I think that's still true, and it's
something I carry with me each day. However, the success of the
conservative movement means that most of us are taught that the
problems that exist in the world are a function of individual failure rather than systemic success. The people who are looking

for us may or may not know that they are, but it is still our job to provide the light that helps them along their way. Popular fronts can be an important opportunity to bring us into proximity to those with whom we share aspirations but diverge on the best way to get there. It is through these relationships that we become open to new ways of seeing and interpreting our world.

CHAPTER SEVENTEEN

PLATFORMS, PEDESTALS, AND PROFILES

MOVEMENTS THAT ARE ABLE TO ENTER THE MAINSTREAM ARE likely to see their leaders thrust into the public eye—to be celebrated, to be admired, and to be scrutinized. Grappling with the issue of celebrity—of how to deal with the platforms, pedestals, and high profiles of leaders—is not a new question for social movements. The Reverend Dr. Martin Luther King, Jr., was not known by millions around the world when he began his career. He was a young minister working with a local community— but he gained prominence during the Montgomery bus boycott and was catapulted to national and international recognition. Malcolm X did not start off as an icon—in fact, before he was Malcolm X he was Malcolm Little, living a hard life before he found the Nation of Islam. Rosa Parks was a relatively unknown organizer for many years before anyone outside her immediate circle heard her name.

Aside from being leaders in the movement to gain civil and human rights, what they all had in common was their ability to communicate. Both their ideas and their images were essential in moving a strategy that advanced their cause. Rosa Parks was selected for the role she played because of the symbolism that she could project—a hardworking seamstress whose feet were tired after a long day was the perfect symbol for a lawsuit later filed by the NAACP on her behalf in an attempt to unravel segregation. King's appeal was that he was a man of faith, a moral compass for his parishioners and, later, for the soul of the nation. Malcolm X, finding Islam after having seen hard times, was able to provide answers for Black people on how to reclaim our own humanity. These three did not select themselves as figureheads—they were strategically selected by the movements that elevated them to communicate their vision and goals.

As a result of gaining prominence, these leaders—and many more not named here—had to make sense of the authenticity of their roles while at the same time trying to figure out how to use their new platforms for the collective good. And for some of these leaders, gaining a platform and increasing their public profile was accompanied by jealousy and ridicule from their peers, increased pressure, threats, and harassment from their opposition, and an onslaught of insecurity and self-doubt.

I've been organizing since I was twenty-two years old. When I was a local organizer, pounding the pavement, knocking on doors, and leading campaigns in Bayview Hunters Point, I was relatively unknown until I helped run a campaign that took on a major housing developer. In order to win our campaign, we had to operate on the same terrain that our opponent did— which meant we had to take our fight to the media. There were many leaders in that campaign, and why I was the one to gain visibility within it was likely the result of many factors, but a large part of it was an intentional strategy by our coalition. I had a formal education and two degrees from a highly ranked public university, which gave me particular skills, including the ability to write op-eds and articles about our work. I was not seen as a polarizing figure by the communities that we were organizing, or a figure who had an agenda—even though I did have one.

I was both a trained organizer and an organizer in training—which meant that I'd learned valuable tools for how to build relationships with people I'd never met before and how to agitate them to get involved in our campaign and eventually become leaders within it. As an organizer in training, I was taught how to effectively communicate through the media by three strategists from the Center for Media Justice; at that time, the center worked to help community-based organizations clearly communicate their vision, values, and alternatives through mainstream media platforms, which often did not share those views. When our opponent dropped nearly $3 million into a ballot measure campaign—on which we'd spent about $10,000—so they could run ads on BET and send weekly mailers to voters, we understood that we had to find our own ways to use mainstream platforms to win hearts and minds to our side.

Even though we knew that to win we needed to reach as many people as possible, we were still uncomfortable with what that meant.

I spent a lot of time during that campaign writing op-eds, talking on the radio, and debating our opponent in public forums. The local paper contacted me after the campaign to tell me that I'd been selected as a "Local Hero," which carried some prestige in the progressive organizing community. When I shared the news with a fellow organizer, they responded that it wasn't me who should be acknowledged, but everyone who worked on the campaign. Further, they argued, I should refuse the honor if the newspaper didn't agree to recognize the entire organization.

I was taken aback and a little hurt by this rebuff. It came from a person who would often shy away from playing any public role and would rationalize that it was inappropriate to do so because of their racial identity (they were white). I wasn't particularly keen on playing as public a role as I did, as I too felt some discomfort based on the advantages I felt I had. Yet after months of twelve-to-fourteen-hour days, numerous debates and public engagements, and the heartbreak of having ultimately lost the campaign, I accepted that there were those in my community who wanted to honor the work that I had done. As part of a coalition, I had been groomed to take on these roles. So, after putting in that work, why was I being punished for being effective and doing a good job in the role that I'd been given?

I won a number of awards in the progressive community for my work on that campaign. Some of those awards were presented to the organization, and some of them were presented to me specifically. But it has raised an important question for me ever since: How should movements approach platforms, pedestals, and profiles?

Technology and the rise of social media have made that question even more complex, shifting our understanding of leadership—and the responsibilities of a leader. Platforms, pedestals, and profiles are new versions of old models. A platform in King's day might have been a church congregation, whereas today a platform could be a social media page. Profiles in Parks's day revolved around who knew you and what they knew you for. Community members might have described Parks as a seamstress who became active in the NAACP in 1943, gaining the respect of her peers for her work registering Black people in Montgomery, Alabama, to vote. Today, a profile is still based on who knows you and what they know you for, but instead of your community knowing "who your people are," a profile might be a well-curated social media timeline of opinions and responses to the latest news, and the curation of relationships and visibility online. A pedestal is what we place people on because we hold them in high regard. Malcolm X was placed on a pedestal by Black communities in particular, mostly for his ability to speak unapologetically about the effects of white supremacy on Black society, and also for encouraging Black people to defend ourselves and seek liberation "by any means necessary." Placing people on pedestals can result in making people symbols without substance. Today, being placed on a pedestal can occur when you've built a strong enough brand—and yet the substance it's connected to may or may not be a part of, or accountable to, a movement.

When Patrisse, Opal, and I created Black Lives Matter, which would later become the Black Lives Matter Global Network, each of us also brought our own understanding of platforms, pedestals, and profiles. At that point, we'd all spent ten years as organizers and advocates for social justice. Our platforms and profiles, and perhaps even pedestals, come from the relationships we have in our communities, the networks we are a part of, and the work we've done for migrant rights, transit justice, racial justice, economic justice, and gender justice. For nearly a year, we operated silently, using our networks and our experiences as organizers to move people to action, to connect them to resources and analysis, and to engage those who were looking for a political home. Our work was to tell a new story of who Black people are and what we care about, in order to encourage and empower our communities to fight back against state-sanctioned violence—and that meant our primary role, initially, was to create the right spaces for that work and connect people who wanted to do the work of organizing for change.

But when a well-known mainstream civil rights organization began to claim our work as their own, while distorting the politics and the values behind it, we decided to take control of our own narrative and place ourselves more prominently in our own story.

Every day, I wonder whether we made the right decision. It was important for us to be protagonists in our own story, but there were and are consequences to that decision. We were concerned about making sure that the vision and values of the thing we created were not being watered down or misconstrued. I even wrote about it in 2014, in an article that was first published on the Feminist Wire with the encouragement of Darnell Moore. The article was initially titled "Erasing the Black from Black Lives Matter," but through the editing process, it came to be titled "A Herstory of the #BlackLivesMatter Movement." We did not want our work to be flattened, and while we wanted Black Lives Matter to have many different entry points, we did not want our work co-opted.

Having a platform, and a profile that results from it, places you on a pedestal that, while it may have been earned, is not always desired. Most of the organizers I know who have gained a level of visibility are actually very private people, uncomfortable in the spotlight and often shunning accolades. The reason we use a platform and a profile is to increase the visibility of the issues we care about, recruit new people into our fight, and continue to grow the movement that grew us.

I remember the first time Patrisse and I were on CNN. It was December 2014, and we were invited to respond to the refusal of a grand jury to press charges against Officer Darren Wilson for the murder of Michael Brown and, days later, the decision of a grand jury not to press charges against Officer Daniel Pantaleo in the murder of Eric Garner. We were already in New York to receive an award from Black Women's Blueprint, where Black women showed up to encourage us forward, to love on us, and to ensure that the work of Black women would not be erased. After a little bit of discussion, we agreed to appear on television.

At that time, there weren't many Black voices on major network news stations. Melissa Harris-Perry secured her own show on MSNBC in 2012. Harris-Perry used her show to discuss the movement that was launching across the country—and regularly invited activists and organizers to speak about the movement. Don Lemon has been a news anchor on CNN since 2006, but his position early on in the movement wasn't supportive—he seemed much more interested in sensationalizing it rather than helping his viewers make sense of it. Roland Martin was a regular contributor on CNN and had his own show on TV One, where he too regularly invited activists to appear. But aside from them, and a handful of others, Black anchors and commentators were few and far between.

The coverage of the movement was also a challenge. With few Black anchors willing to give the movement a positive platform, much of what was being portrayed at that time was unfavorable. There were shots of angry protesters and property destruction, but rarely in-depth interviews with protesters that could help people understand that there was more to the protests than angry people. Black media, while somewhat varied on the topic, at least did the work to get underneath the systemic issues facing Black people in America. It was Black media that elevated young Black people who were the architects of not just protests but organizations that were pushing demands to transform the systems that impacted our lives.

I remember arriving in Columbus Circle with Patrisse, unsure where we were going. At the time, CNN was located adjacent to a shopping mall with a subway station between them. I wore a red long-sleeved dress I'd bought the day before at a thrift store in Brooklyn. As we entered the building, after a few minutes of being completely disoriented, we arrived at the security desk, where we signed in and had our belongings scanned; then we proceeded through the security gates, into the elevators, and up to the designated floor. From there we were taken to get our hair and makeup done and then ushered onto the set for the taping.

Patrisse and I did a short segment with CNN host Brooke Baldwin. Everything looks much more impressive on television than it does in real life. Television studio sets are merely a table on an elevated platform in the middle of an office surrounded by desks and television cameras. On set, there are chairs behind the table and earpieces that allow guests and the host to hear producers and remote guests. Coffee cups are neatly placed at each seat, but often they do not contain coffee, or any beverage, for that matter. On television, it looks like everyone is in the same room, but in reality, there are three people in a newsroom looking into a teleprompter and another monitor with a feed.

I remember sitting next to Patrisse on that set, nervous but determined. The news cycle was intent on discouraging protests, encouraging people to accept the decision of the grand juries, but Baldwin was an amicable voice who genuinely weighed all options. There's never enough time in those segments to say everything that needs to be said. However, our media training was helpful in this regard—we were able to be clear on a few talking points that communicated that grand juries that refuse to bring charges against officers accused of murder are the norm and not the exception, that the families of the people who were killed deserve more than asking them to move on, and that Black Lives Matter would not stop fighting until we achieved justice for all of us.

When we unhooked our microphones and walked off the set, something had shifted in the trajectory of the movement. Black Lives Matter was no longer just a slogan that was being used across America. It was not just spontaneous rage that drove

Black Lives Matter, and it wasn't an aimless uprising without analysis, strategy, or agenda. As we were leaving, we were stopped in the newsroom by a producer for another show that wanted us on. Black Lives Matter had been talked *about* in the news media for months; suddenly the media had the people behind it to speak *for* it. Before we left that day, we'd taped three different segments on three different shows.

That was the beginning of a national and even international profile for the three of us as the co-founders of Black Lives Matter, individually and collectively. Profile was not something that any of us sought or seek for its own end. We didn't go on CNN to build our brands—we agreed to go on because there were things that needed to be said that weren't being said and troublesome assumptions that were not being challenged in the way they needed to be. We have sought to use media as a way to amplify not our own voices but the voices, hopes, and dreams of those who would not otherwise be heard. And with the development of those profiles and those platforms, we have been both placed on pedestals and besieged by those who hope to knock us off them.

When I was being trained as an organizer, social media forums were not yet as popular and as widely used as they are today. Debates over strategy, outcomes, or even grievances took place in the form of "open letters," often circulated through email. At the time, that world seemed vast and important, but in retrospect—compared to the global reach of social media—it was very, very small.

Yet even in my small corner of the world, there were those who went from being relatively unknown grassroots organizers to people with more power and influence. And I saw how the movement could be ambivalent toward its most visible members when those individuals were seen as having gone too far beyond the movement's own small imprint.

When Ai-jen Poo, currently the director of the National Domestic Workers Alliance and co-director of Caring Across Generations, built a profile and a platform based on her success leading domestic workers to win the first ever Domestic Workers Bill of Rights in New York State, it caused quiet rumblings within the movement that grew her. People were unsure if it was a good thing that her fame had outgrown our small corner of the world. When Van Jones remade himself from an ultra-left revolutionary into a bipartisan reformer who landed in the Obama administration as the "green jobs czar," the movement that grew him quickly disavowed him. Even when Patrisse Cullors began to grow a platform and a profile beyond the work I'd known her for at the Bus Riders Union, a project of the Labor/Community Strategy Center in Los Angeles, I received a call from one of her mentors questioning her ability to "lead the Black liberation movement." In one breath, movements in development and movements in full swing can become antagonistic to those who break through barriers to enter the mainstream, where they can expose the movement's ideas to new audiences.

There are valuable critiques of the rise of individuals within movements. Some would argue that profiles and platforms lead to a "cult of personality," whereby the larger movement can become overshadowed by a charismatic leader. And because individuals are fallible, there is a risk that too much attention on an individual can hurt the movement—particularly if that individual fails to represent the authentic aims and goals of the movement.

Another critique is that placing too much attention on individuals furthers the aims of the systems that we are trying to dismantle. Capitalism, a system that prioritizes profits over people, powered by the exploitation of labor and resources for the benefit of elites and corporations, follows the logic of individualism, which teaches that we must compete against one another to survive. Capitalism monetizes everything, creating a dynamic in which absolutely everything, including movements, can be bought or sold. When an individual becomes the face of a movement to the wider world, the movement can be perceived—sometimes by the individual—through a capitalist lens: The individual becomes a victor in a competition for leadership and visibility; the individual reaps the benefits of the labor of the movement. White supremacy, a system that prioritizes white people over communities of color, selects the leaders who are palatable to those uncomfortable with challenging the ways that racism continues to operate in our society. Those who are elevated are often those who can offer "cross appeal"—they can be seen as credible because of how they speak, how they present themselves, and what they present as solutions, which most of the time hinge on what makes white people comfortable or uncomfortable.

Another valuable critique is that some who gain platform and profile from movements do not have the best interests of those movements at heart, especially when they became famous before spending time building an organization and when their fame renders them unaccountable to any organization or constituency. They use their increased platform or profile within a movement as a springboard to become wealthy, to attain celebrity, or to gain proximity to celebrities rather than to directly and consistently challenge the structures that demean the lives of our communities.

These critiques pose valuable questions and contradictions for a movement to grapple with. Movements need to create change; that change is expressed sometimes through cultural shifts, sometimes through policy transformation. But either form of change requires power, and a movement's source of power is masses of people. This means movements must enter the arenas where millions of people engage—and those arenas are not always progressive.

But what would the last period of civil rights have accomplished if its tactics and leaders had not been broadcast into homes across the nation? Would there have been a Black Power movement if it had not been, in part, adopted by some members in Hollywood? Would the women's liberation movement of the 1970s have been as successful and widely known had there been no Gloria Steinem, no *Ms.* magazine? Can movements be content to be popular merely among those who are already familiar with them and those who directly benefit from them? Or do they need to create focal points—leaders, media, institutions—to become visible to the larger public?

We cannot know for sure, but those movements took advantage of the tools available to them to change the way of life for millions of people across the country.

So, the mistake is not in crossing over from relative obscurity to the mainstream—but is it a mistake to create pedestals for individual leaders and pin the fate of the movement to them? Is it a mistake for movement leaders to become celebrities, peddling the movement as a product that others can attain through proximity to that leader rather than to their work and contributions?

Every actor within a social movement has a role to play and contributions to offer that at some point should be recognized. But the pedestals we create for individuals have the opposite effect: They obscure people's contributions. They serve to situate the success of a movement inside one person, as opposed to that success being based on how much a movement grows beyond itself. At best, they turn people who are merely playing their roles into celebrities who are admired for their ability to "speak truth to power." At worst, they assign roles to people who don't deserve them—or to people who, in creating a cult of personality, themselves become a vestige of the social and economic systems we're trying to dismantle. Profiles and platforms are not inherently bad, and they can function as a helpful tool for movements to use. Pedestals, however, are rarely if ever of service in helping a movement achieve its goals and objectives.

I have traveled across the country talking with aspiring leaders who hope to make change in their communities. I'll admit I die a little inside when people ask me, "How can I build my platform?"

Or when they introduce themselves to me as an "influencer." No joke: A brilliant young Black sister recently handed me a business card that identified her as a "student influencer."

My response, sometimes through gritted teeth, is this: "For what and for whom are you building a platform and profile?"

I still do not believe that Twitter followers and Facebook friends represent the amount of influence you have. My friends who are digital organizers will kill me for saying this, and believe me, I mean no disrespect. If you have a million followers on Twitter, you are influencing something and someone. And yet the question remains: for whom, and for what?

Black Lives Matter started as a hashtag and then grew into a series of social media pages that connected people online. But it was when masses of people began to move in service of Black Lives Matter that it became effective. Imagine if we merely continued to tweet about our dissatisfaction without taking that displeasure directly to decision makers? Imagine if we had continued to just write about what's wrong online without showing up at campaign fundraisers and news conferences, without establishing encampments in front of city halls and police stations. What impact would we have had? Would this even be considered a movement?

Black Lives Matter brought people together online to take action together offline. Solely organizing, educating, or pontificating online was never something that we considered to be effective organizing. But more than that, bringing people together offline requires building the relationships and infrastructure that can help grow the movement. Protests are never enough to build a movement. Protests need planning and preparation. Outreach and attendance. Follow-up. Security and safety plans. Messaging and targets. Demands. Cultural components. All of that requires vehicles that can give people things to be involved in between protests and off-camera.

For me, the only use for a platform or a profile is in the service of the strategy of a movement. It doesn't matter how many people follow me on social media if I am not moving them to do something amazing together offline—which is the only hope to achieve the changes we so desperately need and deserve. It doesn't matter if someone wants to "be like me" but doesn't want to do the work that I do that makes me *me*—and that work is situated inside the context of a movement. It is not work that I do in isolation or on my own. Can I move the people who follow me on Twitter into votes that oust problematic decision makers and instill people with vision and a plan? Can I transform my Facebook friends into leagues of democracy defenders in fifty states—people who ensure that every voice is counted? If not, frankly, fuck a platform and fuck a profile. Platforms and profiles are only as useful as what they are in service of.

I worry that we are encouraging people to build profiles and platforms without a strategy to win the changes we want to see in the world—to think they can change the world according to how many people follow them on social media. I've learned we need bases, not brands.

DeRay Mckesson is often credited with launching the Black Lives Matter movement along with the work that Patrisse, Opal, and I initiated. However, Mckesson offers a sharp lesson on pedestals, platforms, and profiles—and why we need to be careful about assigning roles that are inaccurate and untrue.

Mckesson is someone I first met in Ferguson, Missouri, a full year after Patrisse, Opal, and I launched Black Lives Matter. How we met matters. Patrisse and Darnell Moore had organized a freedom ride whereby Black organizers, healers, lawyers, teachers, medics, and journalists gathered from all over the country to make their way to Ferguson. I flew to St. Louis to help support another organization on the ground there. The freedom ride coincided with the time I spent in St. Louis, and as I was being given the rundown on the landscape during my first few days there, I was told about a young man named DeRay Mckesson.

Mckesson played the role of a community journalist on the ground in Ferguson. He and Johnetta Elzie had started a newsletter called *This Is the Movement,* and I remember Mckesson approaching me at a meeting convened by what has since become the Movement for Black Lives and asking if they could interview the three of us about Black Lives Matter. They even featured us and a link to buy our T-shirts in their newsletter. In Issue No. 29, they highlighted a talk given by Patrisse "from #BlackLivesMatter" at St. John's Church during the freedom ride. (The church was the freedom riders' home base in St. Louis.)

The next time I saw Mckesson, he showed up at a mediation

that Patrisse organized among some young women who had formed an activist group in the wake of the protests. This mediation took place in St. Louis when we were all there together for the Weekend of Resistance, a month or so after the freedom ride that took place on Labor Day weekend of 2014. The young women were friends, but the pressure of the ongoing protests, along with other factors, had caused a rift among them. Patrisse, being the healer she is, tried to bring the young women together so the group could talk out their differences in person rather than attacking one another on social media, which they had already begun doing. Elzie was a part of the activist group for a time, and she'd brought Mckesson for support. Patrisse had enlisted me to help her hold the conversation.

When Mckesson arrived, I asked if he and another woman who'd come with them would mind waiting outside so that the young women could have an honest conversation and not feel they had to perform for an audience. He was annoyed, to be sure, but at the time, I wasn't that concerned. I didn't know him, so I was fine with being the bad guy if it meant that these women could have the space they needed to iron out their differences.

When I left Ferguson, I'd all but forgotten about Mckesson. So I was surprised the next time I saw him, in his blue Patagonia vest, bragging on Twitter that he was the only activist who was followed on social media by Beyoncé.

Then I started to catch wind of barbs he had been throwing at our work. I have a social media following, but I don't obsess over social media. Perhaps it's my age, or perhaps it's because the time I spend in meetings with other organizers and on phone calls with other organizers, funders, policymakers, and elected officials doesn't leave me much time to monitor what's happening on social media. I would learn about something he'd said on social media only because someone would text me asking for my opinion.

One post I remember in particular was an assertion that you don't have to be part of an organization to be part of a movement. He was criticizing Black Lives Matter, which was, at that time, fending off attacks from right-wing operatives who were trying to pin on us the actions of activists who had begun to call themselves Black Lives Matter but had not been a part of the organizing efforts we were building through a network structure that had chapters. These activists had led a march where people in the crowd were chanting "Pigs in a blanket, fry 'em like bacon." The news media had been stirred up like a beehive over the comments, and our team was working furiously to clarify that not everyone who identifies as Black Lives Matter is a part of the formal organization. It wasn't the first time reporters would do that—when two police officers in Brooklyn were ambushed and killed, conservative media attempted to connect their murders to Black Lives Matter and then quickly had to walk it back when it was discovered that the shooter, who was also killed, had written on social media that Black Lives Matter was "too soft" for him. We had no relationship to these protesters, and we were growing increasingly concerned that a lack of strong, formalized structure would put the organization at risk for infiltration, and worse yet, make us responsible for risks we hadn't collectively agreed to take.

Instead of attacking Mckesson on social media, I went through my network to find a way to get in touch with him. I called him on the phone and we had what I thought was a good conversation. I asked him what the intent of his comments was and explained what we were trying to do as Black Lives Matter. I also explained to him the role that organizations play in movements, how I'd come to understand the importance of organizations, and that our organization was not intended to be exclusive—it was intended rather to clarify values and objectives, vision and strategy. We ended the call agreeing to keep the lines of communication open, and I explicitly remember saying that if he ever had a question about something we were doing or saying, that I was always open to talking with him. I said I felt that social media was often an ineffective way of communicating disagreements, and he agreed.

A few weeks later, in an act of good faith, I invited Mckesson and Elzie to a gathering that I organized in Upstate New York, bringing together an intergenerational group of organizers, activists, theorists, and practitioners to build stronger relationships with one another. Mckesson was clearly uncomfortable in the space, and he stuck to Elzie for the two days we were gathered. They mostly kept to themselves, unwilling to build relationships. I was admittedly turned off by his behavior there and felt that perhaps it had been a mistake to invite him. I admonished myself that I wouldn't do that again.

The next time I saw Mckesson, he was meeting with Hillary Clinton and her team at a 2016 conference that the Movement for Black Lives organized—despite an explicit request that candidates not attend the conference. The Movement for Black Lives is a coalition of Black-led organizations across the country that coordinate to advance the goals and objectives of the Black freedom movement. Black Lives Matter Global Network was a member of the Movement for Black Lives. The conference organizers were upset, and so was I. After all the shit-talking he had done about Black Lives Matter, why would he show up at a movement conference and arrange a meeting that the conference organizers had explicitly asked not take place there, out of a desire to keep a level of independence from presidential candidates seeking a stage to generate votes? Why wouldn't he reach out to the conference organizers to consult them before doing it, given that they'd spent months fundraising for the conference, planning the workshops and activities? Furthermore, why would he have that meeting at the conference, yet not invite the organizations that had put the conference on?

I'd just landed in New York after having left the Movement for Black Lives conference in Cleveland, Ohio. The experience was beautiful, but it had ended in a tough way, as a group of us sat for a restorative circle with a group of Ferguson activists who were upset at the profile that Black Lives Matter was getting, at the confusion between Ferguson and Black Lives Matter, and at the lack of attention paid to local activists and organizers. A friend sent me a news article headlined CLINTON TO MEET WITH BLACK LIVES MATTER ACTIVISTS IN CLEVELAND and I nearly hit the roof. Reading the article, it was clear that the Black Lives Matter activists who were being described included Mckesson. They did not, however, include the dozens of leaders who had led the protests in Ferguson or in cities across the country. I learned later that they were never even invited or made aware that the meeting was taking place.

Black Lives Matter has indeed become a generic label for organizing and activism related to police violence. That is caused, in part, by laziness among journalists and other actors in the news media—describing everything related to Black people and protest as Black Lives Matter rather than being precise about Black Lives Matter being an organization, and a movement bigger than our organization, that has swept the country and the world.

One could argue that it's difficult to distinguish, particularly when there are so many people who identify with the principles and values of Black Lives Matter. But those of us who are involved in the movement know the difference—we know the difference because we work with one another. We share the same ecosystem. We know the difference between the Movement for Black Lives, and the wide range of organizations that comprise that alliance, and the larger movement for Black liberation.

There is a difference between feeling alignment with the values of something and claiming that you play (or allowing others to refer to you as playing) a role that you do not play. If I allowed someone to tell you that I am the head of the NAACP and didn't correct them, I am complicit. People often confuse Patrisse and me, even though we don't look alike, and she lives in Los Angeles and I in the Bay Area. If someone calls me Patrisse, I correct them. If I know they're looking for Patrisse and they reach out to me mistakenly, I connect them directly and get out of the way. Not telling the truth and lying are different ways of talking about the same thing.

I cannot tell you how many times I have been at events where someone will approach me to say that they know the other cofounder of Black Lives Matter, DeRay Mckesson. Recently, I was a speaker at a gala for the NAACP. I took a quick restroom break and was washing my hands when a young white woman, leaving her stall, approached me at the sink and gushed about how important Black Lives Matter was to our country. She told me that she worked at Salesforce and that "the other co-founder of Black Lives Matter, DeRay Mckesson," had come to the company to speak. I left her agape in the restroom when I explained to her that while Mckesson was an activist, he was not a co-founder of Black Lives Matter.

I wish that these were innocent mistakes, but they're not. Characterizing these misstatements as misunderstandings is gaslighting of the highest degree. Mckesson was a speaker at a *Forbes* magazine event, "Forbes 30 under 30," and was listed in the program as the co-founder of Black Lives Matter, yet he wasn't in a rush to correct the mistake—and certainly didn't address the mistake in any comments he made that day. There was an outcry on social media, which forced Mckesson to contact the planners and have them change the description. But had there not been an outcry by people sick of watching the misleading dynamic, there wouldn't have been any change.

Tarana Burke wrote an article about this misrepresentation in 2016 in *The Root,* a year before the #MeToo movement swept the country, criticizing Mckesson for allowing his role to be overstated. She cites a *Vanity Fair* "new establishment" leaders list on which Mckesson is No. 86 and accompanied by the following text:

Crowning achievement: Transforming a Twitter hashtag, #BlackLivesMatter, into a sustained, multi-year, national movement calling for the end of police killings of African-Americans. He may have lost a bid to become Baltimore's next mayor, but he is the leader of a movement.

Burke goes on to write, "I have seen Mckesson and some of his people go on social media tirades about how they are not a part of Black Lives Matter. That is, until someone from the press says it—then there is no correction. If he won't do it, those who know better need to do so, or else, when this comes up in civics classes 20 years from now, there will be more lies and erasure happening."

Burke knows what she's talking about. A year later, Alyssa Milano tweeted #MeToo in an attempt to show solidarity with those who are survivors of sexual violence. The actress then went on to be designated as the founder of #MeToo—though Burke had created #MeToo a decade earlier. Burke is now widely understood to be the creator of the #MeToo movement; however, it took a lot of work to get that to happen—including Milano herself using her platform to acknowledge that she was neither the creator of the hashtag nor the instigator of the movement.

Some will be tempted to dismiss this recounting as petty, or selfish, or perhaps more a function of ego than the unity that is needed to accomplish the goals of a movement. The problem with that view is that conflicts and contradictions are also a part of movements, and ignoring them or just pleading for everyone to get along doesn't deal with the issues—it buries them for the sake of comfort, at the expense of the clarity that is needed to really understand our ecosystem and the wide range of practices, politics, values, and degrees of accountability inside it.

Movements must grapple with the narration of our stories—particularly when we are not the ones telling them. Movements must grapple with their own boundaries, clarifying who falls within them and who falls outside them. Movements must be able to hold conflict with clarity. When in his book Mckesson credits a relatively unknown UCLA professor with the creation of the #BlackLivesMatter hashtag, he doesn't do so for the purpose of clarity—he does it to unseat and deliberately discredit the roles that Patrisse, Opal, and I, along with many, many others, have played in bringing people together to take action and engaging our communities around a new theory of who Black life encompasses and why that matters for our liberation. And in many ways he does it for the purpose of attempting to justify the ways in which he inflates his own role in Black Lives Matter.

In 2017, Patrisse, Opal, Mckesson, Elzie, and I were the subjects of a lawsuit by a Louisiana police officer who was injured in a protest in Baton Rouge. The charge: inciting violence. The officer sued the hashtag, and each of us individually became a defendant in the case.

I'm not aware of many protests that Mckesson has organized,

but the Baton Rouge one was certainly organized by him—or at least he'd claimed it was on social media. Neither Patrisse nor Opal nor I was present, participated in any planning of it, nor recruited anyone to be a part of it. Nothing was organized in Louisiana by or on behalf of the Network, and I have the same understanding with respect to the Movement for Black Lives. Yet here we were facing a lawsuit because of actions that were not ours. Mckesson quickly distanced himself from the protests that he took part in organizing and promoting, and from responsibility for organizing them.

The lawsuit was eventually thrown out, with the judge citing that it was not possible to sue a hashtag, among other reasons for dismissing the suit. But the point remains: After years of death threats and targeting, we became even more wary. It is one thing to use Black Lives Matter and a perception that you are the leader of it for your benefit and gain; it is quite another to then abandon it when the heat is turned up. Patrisse, Opal, and I had excellent legal support that worked quickly to protect us from the suit. But what if we hadn't? Might I, we, or the Network have ended up the subject of a lawsuit for an action that we did not participate in? What if Black Lives Matter, the organization, had become liable for that action despite not having had anything to do with it?

There will likely always be contestations over where the Black Lives Matter movement began. Beginnings and endings are a function of position and experience, and this movement is no different. Many of us were doing work at the same time for the same reason and didn't know about one another until nearly a year later. I met Charlene Carruthers, the first national director of the Black Youth Project 100, when I was still the executive director at POWER in San Francisco. I had no idea that the Black Youth Project would establish itself as a leading organization in the Movement for Black Lives until nearly two years after they were founded. As we were launching Black Lives Matter as a series of online platforms, the Dream Defenders, with which I was unfamiliar, and Power U, with which I was very familiar, were taking over the Florida State Capitol, demanding an end to the Stand Your Ground law. I met the director of the Dream Defenders, at that time Phillip Agnew, at a Black Alliance for Just Immigration gathering in Miami in 2014, just a few months before Ferguson erupted. I remember being in Ferguson when a young activist asked me with distrust if I'd ever heard of the Organization for Black Struggle. I had, of course, not only heard of them but sat at the feet of a well-known leader of that organization, "Mama" Jamala Rogers. Our reality is shaped by where and when we enter at any given moment. For some, the movement begins in 2014 in Ferguson, Missouri. For others, the movement begins in 2013 with the acquittal of George Zimmerman for the murder of Trayvon Martin. For even others, the movement begins when Oscar Grant was murdered in 2009. And still for others, the movement begins when Black people were left to die on roofs in Orleans Parish during Hurricane Katrina, or when Rodney King was brutally beaten by Los Angeles police officers and it was caught on video, or when Sean Bell was murdered on his wedding day, or when Amadou Diallo was shot forty-one times. But there is no sidestepping that there is something unsavory about these kinds of omissions—and something strategic as well.

What have we learned from the movements that have preceded us? Why do we continue to search for the second coming of the Reverend Dr. Martin Luther King, Jr.? My take on this is that our search has less to do with wanting to lift up the leaders than it does with our laziness and gullibility, and with our unwillingness to grapple with the ways in which hegemonic ideas, even and especially in Black communities, assign leadership to men, regardless of their actual contribution.

We have allowed Mckesson to overstate his role, influence, and impact on the Black Lives Matter movement because he is, in many ways, more palatable than the many people who helped to kick-start this iteration of the movement. He is well branded, with his trademark blue Patagonia vest that helps you identify him in a sea of people all claiming to represent Black Lives Matter. He is not controversial in the least, rarely pushing the public to move beyond deeply and widely held beliefs about power, leadership, and impact. He is edgy enough in his willingness to document protests and through that documentation claim that he played a larger role in them than he did, and yet complaisant enough to go along to get along. He does not make power uncomfortable. Mckesson is exactly the kind of Black Lives Matter representative that makes White House officials feel comfortable. He gladly met with the Obamas and senior officials in the Obama administration like Valerie Jarrett and David Axelrod—after Black Lives Matter declined to attend a meeting pitched to us as "off the record" yet had a press release sent out about it the day after we agreed initially to attend. We were not willing to be used as symbols—we wanted to engage in real, unscripted, unstaged discussion about the changes that were necessary. He is also willing to translate the movement to those in the entertainment industry, many of whom are themselves shielded from politics by an industry that is okay with you being political as long as it's on brand.

Some are too lazy to question platforms, pedestals, and profiles when they fit our notions of who we think should be leading movements—and when the people who purport to lead them make us more comfortable than the people who actually are leading those movements. Even though Mckesson is gay and faces discrimination within and outside his activist work, there must at some point be an acknowledgment of the historical power dynamic that puts men on pedestals for work women do.

This is more than a question of who is willing to play different roles. There would be nothing at all wrong with a coordinated strategy inside Black Lives Matter that dispatched some activists to meet with the president and his senior advisers and others to protest outside the meeting. The challenge here is that because Mckesson is an at-large activist, and not in coordination with the many activists who did the work of building enough pressure to force those meetings to happen in the first place, he is often at protests in the role of a documentarian—not in the role of a protester. He is using the Black Lives Matter platform and profile for access—but we don't know who that access is for because we are unclear who he organizes, who he is accountable to, and who elevated him as a leader of this movement in the first place.

In many ways, Mckesson continues to play an important role, documenting and translating for people who are new to our movements what is happening and how they can be involved. He is filling a space that our movements have left open, and I often say to his critics that if you don't like what he is doing and how he is doing it, it is imperative that you outorganize him, not merely talk about him behind his back. But Mckesson and his antics offer an important opportunity to look at platforms, profiles, and pedestals in a different way than we have before. It is up to us to stop looking for the next coming of the Reverend Dr. Martin Luther King, Jr., and instead take on the important questions outlined here.

For the most part, it no longer bothers me to be questioned about why I, for example, have a profile and a platform. It is troubling, however, that it seems we have not learned much from the lessons offered us through past mistakes other movements have made. These lessons were hard fought and hard won, intended to sharpen the movements of the future, which are the movements of right now.

One of those lessons is worth being explicit about here: We have to start crediting the work of Black women and stop handing that credit to Black men. We can wax poetic about how the movement belongs to no one and still interrogate why we credit Black men like DeRay Mckesson as its founder, or the founder of the organization that Patrisse, Opal, and I created. Crediting Mckesson with the growth or development of this movement is like crediting the Reverend Dr. Martin Luther King, Jr., with refusing to sit in the back of the bus. It's ahistorical and it serves to only perpetuate the erasure of Black women's labor, strategy, and existence.

Movements that have their eyes set on victory know that in our society, people tend to place more importance on the daily lives of celebrities than we do on the decisions being made every day by the people who run the country. Movements that are afraid to enter the mainstream will have an increasingly hard time being relevant or accessible to the millions of people who are looking for them, and some movements are in denial about that. In many ways, we are more comfortable talking to one another and to people who already agree with us than we are with taking on every corner of society, the economy, and the government. We need to push past our comfort zones and get creative about how to use our platforms and profiles for politics and power rather than as pedestals.

CHAPTER EIGHTEEN

IN THE END: POWER

TODAY, I'M OBSESSED WITH POWER—BLACK POWER, TO BE specific.

I believe that Black communities have the potential to unlock a new democracy, a new civil society, and a new economy in the United States. I believe that Black communities have the power not just to save the country but to lead the country.

I used to be a cynic. As I was developing my worldview, developing my ideas, working in communities, I used to believe that there was no saving America, and I had no desire to lead America.

Over the last decade, that cynicism has transformed into a profound hope. It's not the kind of hope that merely believes that there is something better out there somewhere, like the great land of Oz. It is a hope that is clear-eyed, a hope that propels me. It is the hope that organizers carry, a hope that understands that what we are up against is mighty and what we are up against will not go away quietly into the night just because we will it so.

No, it is a hope that knows that we have no other choice but to fight, to try to unlock the potential of real change.

I know there is hope because I have helped to unlock a potential that I did not really think was possible, even as I pushed for it— the potential for other Black people to see that we are worthy beyond measure and to allow that hope, that merciless hope, to push us forward. I have seen what can happen when we crack the code that allows others to believe that they are exactly who we need in order to bring about change in this country. We can transform power so that it is no longer producing misery around the world.

These days, I spend my time building new political projects, like the Black Futures Lab, an innovation and experimentation lab that tests new ways to build, drive, and transform Black power in the United States. At the BFL, we believe that Black people can be powerful in every aspect of our lives, and politics is no exception.

I was called to launch this organization after the 2016 presidential election. After three years of building the Black Lives Matter Global Network and fifteen years of grassroots organizing in Black communities, I felt strongly that our movement to ensure popular participation, justice, and equity needed relevant institutions that could respond to a legacy of racism and disenfranchisement while also proactively engaging politics as it is in order to create the conditions to win politics as we want it to be. And there simply are not enough Black-centered and Black-focused organizations that work at the scale we need them to and that are not just interested in sitting at the table but are ready to set the table and determine the rules of what happens at the table. For nearly twenty years now I have been sitting at tables and muttering under my breath about what wasn't working, what could be happening, and what needed to be done. Finally I decided to stop complaining about what didn't exist, what wasn't working, what needed investment, and instead create what didn't exist, try the strategies I thought could work, invest in what I thought needed investment, and dare to do what I thought wasn't being done well enough, by enough people, or loud enough.

The Black Futures Lab works to make Black people powerful in politics. We collect recent and relevant data on the complex lives of Black people in order to win policy and shape policy in cities and states. We organize influencers and celebrities to use their platforms for politics and not just for products. We equip Black communities with the tools we need in order to be powerful in politics, developing leaders and training them not only to alter the balance of power but also to govern and to lead. We work to close the gap between Black elected officials and the Black communities they serve. We invest in Black-led organizations to build their capacity to lead and to serve. And we invest in Black people who are running for office who share our vision for how to make Black communities powerful in politics.

When the 2016 elections were over, I vowed that I would step away from the limelight and go back to working quietly behind the scenes at the National Domestic Workers Alliance, with women who clean homes, care for other people's children, care for our aging loved ones, and support independence for our loved ones with disabilities. Yet there was something that continued to nag at me—in particular, the ambivalence of activists and organizers about the importance of elections. Each day, as the president announced yet another damaging initiative geared toward vulnerable members of society, I would stew about the fact that those best positioned to make change are largely absent from the mechanisms that bring about change. No amount of Twitter followers or protests would shift the balance of power in the United States. Further, building smaller and smaller fiefdoms of people who were already of like mind would not create the kind of movement that would have any chance of winning the changes we need for Black lives to matter in our society, our economy, and our democracy.

The only way for me to break through the fear, uncertainty, and frustration that resulted from the 2016 election was to work to build the kind of vehicle I think we need to make real change in America, for and by Black people. Part of that work involves changing how we understand who Black people are, telling more stories and more nuanced stories about Black people as a way to create sea change for Black life. Part of that work involves building the capacity of Black communities to change policy, driven by the people who disproportionately experience the impacts of existing policies that serve to criminalize, contort, and contain the lives of Black communities.

For the majority of 2018, the Black Futures Lab worked to mobilize the largest data project to date focused on the lives of Black people. We called it the Black Census Project and set out to talk to as many Black people as possible about what we experience in the economy, in society, and in democracy. We also asked a fundamental question that is rarely asked of Black communities: What do you want in your future?

We talked to more than 30,000 Black people across the

United States: Black people from different geographies, political ideologies, sexualities, and countries of origin, and Black people who were currently incarcerated and who were once incarcerated. A comprehensive survey such as this had not been conducted in more than 154 years. We partnered with more than forty Black-led organizations across the nation and trained more than one hundred Black organizers in the art and science of community organizing. We collected responses online and offline.

What I've learned through this endeavor is that the conditions for building effective and responsive social movements not only exist but are in their prime at this very moment. In just a year, we engaged with more than 100,000 Black people through our various initiatives. That number felt small in proportion to how many we could be touching, and yet it felt large in relationship to how many Black people our partners were engaging with in any given moment.

The most common response we hear from Black people who have been touched by our project is that they have never been asked what they want their future to look like, what they want the future to hold for them. Indeed, for many Black communities, the future seems predetermined, and we are left to make the best of an untenable series of factors that limit our life chances and shorten our life outcomes. In 2018 alone, without even trying, we built an engagement list of more than 11,000 people.

We have launched a policy institute focused on building the capacity of Black communities to design, develop, negotiate, win, and implement policy in cities and states. We are building vehicles to impact the outcomes of elections across the nation. We have our eyes set on Hollywood, working to organize influencers and celebrities to use their platforms to call attention to some of the biggest issues impacting Black communities and to get people who follow them to take action on the issues they care about.

We've also created political vehicles that can contend for power inside the electoral arena. I created the Black to the Future Action Fund and the Our Future Is Black PAC to invest in Black leaders who have a strong vision for what transforming our communities can look like, leaders who are willing to govern with Black communities to address some of the biggest challenges facing our society today. We don't believe in supporting leaders who are Black simply because they are Black. To do so would be supporting the state of politics that we have today. We support Black leaders who have a transformative vision, who believe that politics should be about engaging as many people as possible in the project of governance.

Effective and transformational governance in this period requires the participation and engagement of more and more people, as opposed to fewer and fewer. For politics to change, for the conditions in Black communities to change, Black communities must not only be engaged but must also shape the decisions that impact our lives. We must be involved in our own governance.

At the Black Futures Lab, governance is what we are fighting for. We are fighting for the right to make decisions for our own lives and to ensure that right for others. Right now our communities are governed by corporations and financial capital. Our leaders know that they have to address the needs and concerns of these influences if they want to keep their jobs. Today, elected officials are careful not to disappoint these forces, knowing that to do so would mean they would reap intolerable consequences. But what if our leaders knew that to leave Black communities behind would reap intolerable consequences? What if our leaders were as afraid to disappoint Black people as they were afraid to disappoint lobbyists, banks, and other corporate actors?

Governance is power. It is the place where we get to decide who makes what decision, it is the place where we get to decide the values upon which we make decisions, and it is the place where we get to choose if it is to be governance by the many or governance by the few.

We do this work in service of building a movement that is bigger than hashtags, bigger than social media followings. We do this work because we believe that Black communities deserve to be powerful in every aspect of our lives, and politics should be no exception.

When we declare that our future is Black, what we mean is that addressing the needs, concerns, hopes, and aspirations of Black people will bring about a better future for all of us. Addressing the needs, concerns, hopes, and aspirations of Black people will change how and who can access healthcare, education, jobs, and housing. Paying attention to what Black people need will keep people out of prisons and jails and will require investments in supporting people to put their lives back together—accessing mental and emotional health services, finding new solutions to address what happens when human beings harm one another, and addressing racist sentencing practices that criminalize Black life. Actualizing the dreams of Black communities means addressing inequities in immigration laws, expanding the opportunities for Black families of all kinds to be assured that their children could grow up to be adults, and allowing America to be reconstructed to get closer to what it promises—freedom, justice, and liberty for all.

We are but a small part of the infrastructure that must be built in America to change the conditions that Black communities experience. In our freedom dreams, there is a whole web of institutions that work to change the story of what Black communities are, design policies to protect Black families from being preyed upon, and support Black communities to thrive. There are institutions that work to make Black communities whole again, and they are nurtured as much as is humanly possible by the full engagement and participation of Black communities. In our freedom dreams, Black communities are powerful beyond measure, and we are free to exercise that power in service of our goals, in service of meeting our needs, and in collaboration with other communities that, like us, are working to heal from the harm that the American project has inflicted upon generations.

It will not be easy, and we will encounter resistance. To get even close, we have a much bigger project on our hands, which is protecting the country from sliding backward into the Dark Ages. The rise of fascist politics in America is dangerous and will have impacts far into the next decade, and more is at stake now than ever before. But now is not the time to be cynical—now is the time to reimagine what else can connect us beyond fear, and violence, and poverty, and environmental degradation.

It is always easiest to point out what is wrong. Where we fall short is always easily accessible. If today's hashtag is Make America Great Again, then the movement we need to build is one that will force America to be great for the first time. A movement where we recognize that we need one another to survive and that our survival can be interdependent rather than parasitic. A movement where we remind ourselves of what really connects all of us—a desire to be seen and valued, to make each day count, to be loved and to love in return. A movement where we resist replicating the same dynamics that we fight against.

I don't believe in utopias. There is not a scenario where suddenly everybody gets it and starts organizing with an intersectional lens, politics sheds its corruption, and corporations reverse their death grip on the economy and civil society. What is more likely is that there will be one step forward and a few more steps back, and, like an onion, each layer we peel back exposes more questions, more contradictions, more challenges that we did not anticipate. That is the hard and beautiful work of movement building—figuring out how to solve the problem of how to be who we need to be in this moment so that we can be powerful together. It's figuring out who the "we" must be for us to unlock the next level. And in a nation that is built from colonialism, genocide, enslavement, and theft, it will be easier for us to pick one another apart than it will be to roll up our sleeves and look honestly at the task in front of us.

Every morning when I wake up, I pray. I place my head against the floor and I thank my God for allowing me to see another day. I give thanks for the blessings that I have received in life, I ask for forgiveness for all of the ways in which I am not yet the person I want to be, and I ask for the continued blessings of life so that I can work to get closer to where I want to be. And in my prayers, I ask my God to remind me that the goal is not to get ahead of anyone else but instead to live my life in such a way that I remember we must make it to the other side together.

Not everyone will make it. Not everyone will want to. But for those of us who do want to make it to the other side, together, we will have to remember that we are in it for the long haul, that we need one another, and that we can be more than the worst thing we've ever done, we can be better than the worst we've ever been. I pray that I remember to believe in myself, to believe in us, and that the future is not only Black, it is ours to shape.

When you finish this book, if you've made it this far, I hope that you too will summon your faith to build an America like we've never seen before. Making America great is forcing America to live up to its promise for the first time. Making America great is ensuring that America remembers that each of us is but a tiny speck on this planet who must learn how to coexist in ways that allow others to live well too. Making America great is making right all that has been done wrong in the name of progress and profit. And at its core, making America great is a commitment to ensuring that everyone can have a good life.

EPILOGUE: TAKE CARE OF YOURSELF

D URING THE COURSE OF MY WRITING THIS BOOK, MY MOTHER died suddenly.

I can't be sure what milestone I will have hit by the time this book is in your hands, but what I can tell you is that it's likely that whatever the timeline (at the time of this writing it's been two years), the grief won't be the same, but it will still be there. It may not be as sharp, as poignant and pointed, as it is in this moment, but it will be there, accompanying me like an overzealous security detail.

Every day without my mother has literally ached. Her illness felt sudden and short, though it's likely that she was sick for a while and her disease just went undetected. From diagnosis to death was a harrowing seven weeks.

I'll never forget the day my dad called. I'd just landed in San Francisco and was headed to a new bookstore on Haight Street to interview Brittney Cooper about her new book, *Eloquent Rage,* in front of a live audience. I was concerned that I might be late to the event, as I'd landed at the worst possible time in the Bay Area—rush hour. I ended up there early, thanks to a savvy rideshare driver.

Soon people began to arrive. I stood outside, as usual, getting my last few minutes alone before the event (it's the introvert in me). Just as I was preparing to go inside, my phone rang, with "Dad" emblazoned on the screen. I sent the call to voicemail, and then I received a text:

Call me when you can.

Kk I'm heading into an event right now. Should be done at 8:30— will call then.

Thanks!

The event went well, and Brittney and I had a great time, clowning around about the absurdity of whiteness. Afterward, after the last person had left, I called a rideshare to take me home, and then thought I'd better take myself out for a nightcap after such a great event.

Just as I was about to walk into the bar, I called my dad.

He picked up on the first ring. He explained to me that my mother wasn't herself, that she was forgetful, was getting lost in the house they'd lived in together for the past two years, and that the other night he'd seen her putting towels in the refrigerator.

My heart started to pound. What could be wrong with Moms? Perhaps she'd had a stroke of some type. I advised my dad to take her to the doctor the next day and demand an MRI. Let them know her symptoms, I said, and tell them you're increasingly concerned about her confusion and memory loss. He mentioned being worried that their insurance needed to approve the procedure; I reassured him that if the doctor was concerned enough about the state of her health, they would have the upper hand in convincing the insurance company that the procedure was needed. I told him to call me first thing in the morning and let me know what the doctor said.

The next morning, I woke up and went about my regular routine. A package had come to the house from my mother earlier in the week while I was traveling. I sat on the couch and opened it, unsure what to expect, laughing when I found a box full of individually wrapped lemons from her lemon tree, along with a note in her beautiful handwriting. In the note, she explained that she didn't want the lemons to go to waste and freeze, so she was sending them to me and I must be sure to share them with my partner. She also thanked me for letting her know about a Black History Month special I'd been a part of on the local news station, because I rarely would talk about interviews I'd done or events I'd appeared at. I put the lemons aside, smiled at the note, and went on with my day.

Later that afternoon, I was rushing through my apartment. I was supposed to be making an appearance at a local event, and as usual, I was running late. As I tore through the house, holding my too-high heels in my hand, the phone rang.

"Hey, Dad," I said breathlessly. "What's up?" The sounds on the other end were unlike any I'd heard him make before. He was crying hard.

"Y-y-y-your mo-mo-mom," he stammered.

"Take a deep breath. What's happening?"

It was a few minutes before I could get him to say the sentence.

They'd found a tumor in my mom's brain. I crumpled to the floor and joined my dad in producing sounds I'd never heard myself make before.

.   .   .

The next seven weeks were surreal. In just a few days, my mom went from being able to walk and talk to being in the ICU for more than a week with fluid on her brain that needed to be drained immediately if she were to live, so that they could determine whether treatment was even possible. There were surgeries, doctors, nurses, other patients, family members I hadn't seen in years, and then, there was me. I mostly canceled everything I was responsible for, except caring for myself, and even that was a challenge. We waded through paperwork, trying to figure out what my mom wanted because she often could not talk, and when she did, it didn't always make sense. Some days I would arrive at the hospital and she would seem close to her old self—awake, laughing and flashing her million-dollar smile, clowning around with the nurses, and eating lemon pound cake. But most days, she was not conscious, or she was quiet. She had a hard time sleeping and would stay up for days on end, forcing the doctors to drug her so she wouldn't continue in a state of delirium. In seven weeks, we moved from the doctor's office to the ICU to the acute floor to hospice. Seven weeks and we were forced to make decisions no family wants to make. On one of her lucid days, I asked her about her final wishes, and she looked at me with bewilderment and exclaimed tenderly, "Baby girl— I'm not ready to die!" Moments like those are heartbreaks that I will always carry with me. They are moments that I replay at night when I close my eyes, or at times when I least expect those memories to emerge. I can be in the middle of a conversation and hear her voice telling me that she didn't want to die, that she wasn't ready.

She shouldn't have been ready. She was sixty-three years old, and I thought she would live forever.

. . .

Losing my mother, my best friend, to cancer so suddenly has been the greatest personal trauma of my life. I am thirty-nine years old at the time of this writing. I have access to resources for healing, for staring my grief and my trauma in the face and letting them know that they too are welcome here. And yet, because I have those resources, because I have been fortunate enough to see the many sides of grief and trauma and not merely be a recipient of them, I am fully aware that to leave grief and trauma unaddressed, unwelcomed, and unhealed can quite literally kill you.

Most of us have experienced trauma of some type. And right now, as of this writing, we are in the middle of an acute national trauma: a global pandemic exposing a desperate public health crisis, a worsening economic crisis careening toward an economic depression, and a crisis in our democracy, where elections have been interrupted and voting in person is increasingly unsafe, while voting at all is becoming increasingly inaccessible. There is pain all around us, a widening gyre of trauma.

Everyone, every single one of us, moves through life in need of connection and intimacy. Trauma and grief will undoubtedly threaten your ability to connect with others. Trauma and grief are like dragons that lie in wait beneath the bridges of our lives—just when you find yourself halfway across the bridge, they emerge and breathe fire, burning the foundation beneath your feet. And they are never alone—trauma and grief are a posse, accompanied by self-doubt, rage, and addiction, to name just a few of their fearsome minions.

Through many years of work, I've come to understand that I have lived a good life and I am eager to live more of it, in spite of the hurt and pain I've encountered along the way. I have been sexually assaulted, as a teenager, by someone I knew and trusted. I've been in multiple abusive relationships, from family members to lovers. Each day, I experience the trauma of systems like racism, patriarchy, capitalism, homophobia, and more that invite me to close down the possibility of connection. And every single day, every moment of it, I am given the choice, the opportunity, to stay open to connection, because I know that I need it, and that I deserve it. We all do.

I imagine—no, I know—that there are those among us who never get a break from trauma or grief. Knowing now the pain of losing my mother, I think often of those in my life for whom both parents are dead or in jail, or who never knew their parents at all. I think often of those in my life and those whom I don't even know who every day experience a variety of traumas, from death to despair and desperation to addiction. No one can avoid trauma, but some of us experience more of it than others, as a result of inequities in our society. For some of us, grief and trauma are the air we breathe, not a single incident that shapes our lives.

I can see the impact of trauma and grief in our work. The heartbreak of working with a family who you know will be evicted and you can't stop it. The wail of a mother who has just lost her only child to violence at the hands of her community or violence at the hands of the police or even violence by suicide. Often, we can link our trauma and our grief to the trauma and grief of others, finding common cause in our misery, working together to make sure we can build a world as free as possible of the pain that we all endure. Many of those who are drawn to social change work are attracted to it because at times they find human connection in and through trauma. Trauma and grief, and the endurance of them, can be what connect us. Yet it is never enough to organize because you are angry, because you are grieving. Trauma bonding is corrosive to the practice of building power. The question facing us is this:

What can we do to remain resilient in the face of crisis and chaos? How do we keep coming back to that which moves us, that which grounds us, when seemingly everything is falling apart around us, among us, and inside us?

Audre Lorde is often quoted for saying, "Caring for myself is not self-indulgence, it is self-preservation, and that is an act of political warfare." Indeed, "self-care" has become a popular refrain for organizers and activists alike, and yet sometimes I wonder whether the concept itself might be self-defeating, at least in the ways that we have interpreted Lorde's words and put them into practice.

When I was being trained as an organizer, self-care was seen as indulgent, something that was reserved only for those who had the financial or social means to take care of themselves while the world was going to hell around them. When someone I worked with would say that they needed to take care of themselves, I would imagine Marie Antoinette proclaiming from her decadent palace, "Let them eat cake!" In other words, how selfish is it that you want to take a break while the rest of us are burning the candle at both ends? Burnout was not uncommon among the people I built political community with, and in fact, if you hadn't burned out, perhaps you just weren't working hard enough or doing enough for "the people."

In 2003, I was doing an organizing internship at a local community-based organization. It was summertime in Oakland, and temperatures would rise above 80 degrees. I would arrive at the office around 11 A.M., participate in trainings and role-plays for a few hours, and then grab my clipboard, pen, and materials and go door knocking in one of the surrounding communities. On my way out the door, it was common to step over my then-boss, who would be lying on the ground, unable to move because their back went out. I remember being puzzled by this: Why not just stop working? But as time went on, it wasn't so baffling to me anymore. Endless commitments, meetings, events, hearings, and rallies left no time for catching a cold or tending to a sore back. Working through illness and other catastrophe became the norm. If I was forced to stay at home because of the severity of an illness, or to avoid infecting others, I would feel anxious. What haven't I completed for today? Who else was I forcing to do my work for me?

It took me a while to realize that my colds were becoming more common because I never let myself take the time I needed to fully recover. My body was shutting down on me and my heart was being broken each and every day, yet with all the work I was doing, I was neglecting the work I needed to do on myself. Luckily there were people in my community who worried about me. I participated in programs designed to help organizers and activists learn to better balance all of the demands of our work. Time management training was part of it, but the other part of it was looking at how trauma and grief shape how we show up in our interactions with others. These programs were important and made an impact on me. But when I took a sabbatical—dedicated time away from work, social media, family demands, and life demands—I truly began to understand the benefits of self-care.

I spent six weeks away from work. The first few days were grueling, to say the least. I was tired. My first day away I felt like a fish out of water, tucked away in the mountains of Washington State, in a beautiful house with two other people I'd never met before and wasn't sure I would like. I brought a suitcase full of books, convinced that I would read the time away. But what I learned during that time was that self-care wasn't about filling my time with recreation. Nor was it about completing tasks. It was having time to dream. Being (relatively) sober. Completing ten-mile hikes when I'd never hiked before in my entire life. Taking long drives with no purpose and no destination. It was during that time that I was inspired to leave my job and move toward my vision. That was in April 2013. A few months later, Black Lives Matter was born.

When I returned from sabbatical, I'd never been more clear about my purpose. Even though I'd spent ten years in an organization that I loved and that was my political home, I was clear that I was ready for a new phase in my life. I didn't keep all of the practices I developed—but I did hold on to a sense of how to get to my purpose, over and over again.

Across the country, new activists ask me how I balance everything, and my answer is: I don't. I have plenty of days where everything doesn't get done, and if it does get done it's not the way I would have wanted it to. The secret is that getting things done isn't about your ability to do it, it's about the fact that the society we live in inherently creates problems that replicate themselves endlessly, because problems are built into systems in which everything can be bought or sold but some people will never have the money, access, or social capital to afford what they need to take care of themselves.

When my mother was sick, we received access to exquisite hospice care—because a kind social worker in the hospital where my mom had spent weeks knew who I was and admired the work of Black Lives Matter. That hospice care would have cost more than $11,000 per week, a cost that is completely inaccessible for most people in this country. My mother and my family needed that care, care that was essential to our social fabric during a time of incredible crisis and pain. And yet I often thought about the fact that there were many people who needed exactly that kind of care who would never be able to access it, because the cost was prohibitive and they didn't happen to know someone willing to help. What is self-care without the care of the community?

This is why it breaks my heart to see activists and organizers lashing out at one another, angry about money and power and credit, acting out our traumas over and over again with those and against those who were not involved in their creation. Self-awareness and tools for dealing with trauma and grief and loss are one part of the battle; the other part is healing the systems that create inequity and feed on trauma like a parasite.

My hope for us is that we begin to intimately understand that living in a society where everything can be bought or sold but not everyone can buy or sell is harmful to our health, physically, emotionally, and spiritually. That the best way to care for ourselves is in the manner that Audre Lorde described: to connect with each other in ways that propel all of us toward care—for ourselves and one another.

But with that hope, I also see reality. I believe with all my heart that change is possible and inevitable, but my honest estimation is that we are far from that change.

And that means, for me, that we need to treat our work as if it is in fact hospice care for that which is dying and prenatal care for that which is being born.

In hospice, care is the most important thing, the principle around which everything is organized. When my mother was in hospice, everything was geared toward meeting her needs for an improved quality of life, which was important for a woman who was dying of cancer that had localized itself in the form of a tumor in her temporal lobe and had spread across her entire brain. Our society is no different—the cancer has localized itself in particular communities but also spreads across all of our communities in unique ways, and we need to think seriously about how we care for those communities, how we address the ongoing assaults of racism and sexism and homophobia and poverty. That is our hospice work.

But the prenatal work is what a lot of this book and a lot of my life are about—the work of dreaming and acting to create the world we deserve. It's about opening our imagination and putting ourselves on the line to create and enact solutions to our problems and the deepest needs of connection and community at the base of all human existence.

Hope is not the absence of despair—it is the ability to come back to our purpose, again and again. My purpose is to build political power for my community so that we can be powerful in every aspect of our lives. My work is to transform grief and despair and rage into the love that we need to push us forward. I am not, and we are not, defined by what we lack—we are defined by how we come together when we fall apart.

AFTERWORD FOR THE PAPERBACK EDITION

I was putting the finishing touches on this manuscript when COVID-19 reached the United States. I did not know then what we all know now—that crises would collide and combine to create a chaos unseen and unheard of in my lifetime. More than half a million people have had their lives stolen from them and from us. Mismanagement and neglect at the highest levels of government, made more acute by decades of racist disinvestment in communities across America, placed a bull's-eye on Black, Latino, and Asian communities in particular. From the start, then-president Donald Trump dubbed COVID-19 the "China virus," making Asian communities targets of racist violence and misplaced blame. Black and Latino communities were, and are still, overrepresented in case numbers of COVID-19 and deaths resulting from the virus. More than 40 percent of Black-owned businesses have permanently closed, as opposed to 17 percent of white-owned businesses. It is a catastrophe we will not soon forget.

I also didn't know that the Black Lives Matter movement would explode again, years after it first emerged in 2013 and just a few short months after the pandemic tightened its grip on the country.

Ahmaud Arbery was jogging in Georgia when he was gunned down in broad daylight by a white father-son vigilante duo. Breonna Taylor was shot in the middle of the night during a police raid of her Louisville, Kentucky, home. George Floyd was murdered in Minneapolis, Minnesota, by Officer Derek Chauvin. Floyd's death was captured on video—a Black man more than six feet tall under the knee of a white officer who kept one hand in his pocket as Floyd called out for his mother, just breaths before his last one. Protests exploded here—and across the world—in such massive numbers that Black Lives Matter became the largest social movement in the history of the United States.

Movements, as I say earlier in this book, are not reserved for those of us who want to see peace and justice. In response to the uprisings, white nationalists also mobilized for the future of America. They set fires at police stations, posing as protesters. They drove cars through protests, running over people who had taken to the streets to demand an end to the senseless murders of our people. They shot and killed protesters: Seventeen-year-old Kyle Rittenhouse, armed with a Smith & Wesson AR-15-style rifle, shot three people at a protest in Kenosha, Wisconsin, killing two. Their president joined in, having protesters in Washington, D.C., tear-gassed to clear a path for him to pose for a staged photo, Bible in hand, at St. John's Episcopal Church, which had been damaged by fire during a protest the night before.

Meanwhile, the most important election in a generation loomed and Black voters were the pivotal bloc in deciding who would contend for power, with former vice president Joe Biden emerging as the victor.

In so many ways, Black communities have been the protagonists in the definitive events of this new decade. Black people, activated and enraged by police and vigilante violence, economic instability, and attacks on our democracy, are setting the terms of the debate. Black people took our protest to the streets and took our protest to the polls for the sake of ourselves, daring America to embody for the first time its promise of freedom, liberty, and justice for all. Millions of people took action to change the course of this country, and this time, those protests were decisively multiracial.

Never in my lifetime have I seen this country have the kind of epiphany around race that it is having now. These days, it is difficult to ignore. One evening, after a long day of work, I ended the last of what felt like a hundred phone calls and collapsed, exhausted, onto the couch. I turned on the television to watch some of my favorite reality shows—to escape my own reality of running two organizations and being thrust into the center of a new conversation about Black Lives Matter. My dreams were dashed. Every single channel I turned to featured a conversation about race, white privilege, Black lives, and what can be done to address generations of rigged rules that leave Black communities behind.

We are in a moment of great transformation. Many of the political, economic, and social dynamics today are reminiscent of the post–Civil War Reconstruction era. Reconstruction is generally understood to be the period between 1865 and 1877, the turning point when a country divided by race and anxious about the future embarked on an experiment to answer two questions: How do you put a broken nation together again? And who gets to be a part of it?

There is much we can learn from this period that must inform our next steps as we struggle to come back together.

. . .

More than 620,000 people were killed and thousands more injured in the Civil War, and by the end, the South was in shambles. Many farms were decimated, and transportation infrastructure was in ruins. The enormous cost of the war to the Confederacy seriously damaged the economic infrastructure of the South.

All of Southern society shifted. Many newly emancipated Black people left rural areas and migrated to cities. Almost a quarter of Southern white men of military age were killed during the war, leaving many families destitute and eliminating a large chunk of the Southern white workforce. Slavery had come to an end; racial terror, however, had not.

The end of the Civil War brought intensified racial violence. On December 24, 1865, the Ku Klux Klan was founded. The next year, in Memphis, Tennessee, a shoot-out occurred between white policemen and Black veterans of the Union Army. In response, mobs of white vigilantes and police sacked Black neighborhoods, attacking and killing Black soldiers, robbing Black families, and torching their homes. Federal troops were sent in to quell the violence, and in the end, most of those injured or killed were Black. The racial terror was so effective that Black families left Memphis in droves; five years later, the city's Black population had plummeted. That same year in New Orleans, a peaceful protest by freedmen was attacked by a white mob, many of whom had been soldiers for the Confederacy. The backdrop of the protest was tensions between Republicans and conservative Democrats over political power and the conditions of freedmen. When all was said and done, 38 people were killed and 146 people were injured—most of whom were Black.

In early 1865, Congress established the Freedmen's Bureau—a federal agency to protect the rights of newly emancipated Black people by negotiating labor contracts, providing shelter and medical care, and establishing schools and churches. After

President Abraham Lincoln's assassination, his successor, Andrew Johnson, vetoed legislation to renew the Freedmen's Bureau. But after the elections of 1866 gave Republicans the majority to override vetoes, the Freedmen's Bureau was successfully renewed.

The Ku Klux Klan was increasingly active during this period, using racial violence to terrorize newly emancipated Black citizens as well as white abolitionists and elected officials who passed laws that granted suffrage to Black men and allowed Black people to serve on juries and hold elected office. Black codes and other racialized restrictions were enacted, designed to keep newly freed Blacks from exercising these new rights.

In response, Congress passed a series of Enforcement Acts— three pieces of legislation that established rights for emancipated Black people. Legislators also made three amendments to the U.S. Constitution: The Thirteenth Amendment abolished slavery and involuntary servitude, except as punishment for a crime; the Fourteenth Amendment established citizenship for all people born or naturalized in the United States (with the exception of Indigenous people); and the Fifteenth Amendment prohibited the federal government and states from denying citizens their right to vote based on race or previous servitude.

Increased protection resulted in increased political participation. In 1868, more than 700,000 newly freed Blacks voted, delivering the 300,000 votes necessary to push President Ulysses S. Grant, who ran on a platform of civil rights, to victory. Grant strengthened the ability of the government to intervene to protect citizenship rights for Black people. In 1870, he established the Justice Department, creating attorney general and solicitor general positions to prosecute the Klan. In 1871, the Ku Klux Klan Act authorized the president to impose martial law and suspend habeas corpus. The federal government went after the KKK with rigor, essentially ending the Klan for a period of time.

But support for Reconstruction began to wither as political power shifted in the Southern states. Though Grant was successful in targeting the Klan, other paramilitary racist vigilante groups picked up where the Klan left off. And while there were Republicans who supported Black civil rights, there were also those who adamantly opposed them. White politicians in the North and South united in their quest to rebuild white supremacy when even Republicans abandoned the project of enfranchising Black citizens, who were once again terrorized by paramilitary organizations, now in league with the Democratic Party that dominated the South. With the Compromise Act of 1877, Reconstruction was effectively over, and the re-entrenchment of second-class citizenship for Black people was under way.

In this country today, it feels as if we have just ended a war. This time, anxiety about changing demographics has resulted in a struggle over the existence of and role for government. Multiple crises are colliding—a global public health crisis, a crisis of democracy, a growing economic crisis, and a crisis of national identity. In the first Reconstruction era, colliding crises brought a restructuring of the economy, the enfranchisement of hundreds of thousands of people, and new rules and resources dedicated to the protection of those newly established rights.

What will this era of Reconstruction bring?

For the past decade, we have, knowingly or unknowingly, battled over what the future will hold for ourselves, for our families, and for our communities. The contest, in so many ways, is between the same forces that battled in the post–Civil War Reconstruction: those who would fight for the enfranchisement of all people—making innovations to government and democracy to allow for full and free participation—and those who would rather dismantle the project altogether before allowing, much less helping to create, liberty and justice for all.

We saw this struggle dramatized when throngs of Trump supporters stormed the U.S. Capitol on January 6, 2021, to protest the certification of the presidential election results that declared Joe Biden, elected with Black political power, the winner. Those supporters were so angry at Black political power that they smeared feces on the inside of the Capitol while fighting police officers and killing one.

As at the end of the Civil War, we are in the midst of a great transformation as a nation, one that will lead to an expansion of rights, dignity, and respect—or one that will see them wither away. The struggle between these two forces is not always as visible as the Capitol riots, though.

The battle over the unwritten rules that guide a society is an important one. The culture wars of my childhood shaped the policy and practice of government. And now we see yesterday's "moral majority" and "focus on the family" morph into a new movement that no longer even pretends to claim any moral high ground, given whom it has lined up behind. Today's movement—a collusion among conspiracy theorists, right-wing nationalists, and the Republican Party—works hard to push back against the positive changes that have occurred in our society, like expanding rights for queer and trans people, like uprooting systemic racism, like fighting back against police violence, like expanding voting rights. To them, holding people and systems accountable for racism or sexism is "cancel culture"; expanding or extending rights for the first time is a Marxist/socialist/Communist plot or agenda; adhering to public health requirements, like wearing a mask in public, is government tyranny; and Black Lives Matter is either a vehicle for patronage politics within the Democratic Party or in an alliance with antifa—or sometimes, improbably, both.

These same people are strangely silent when it comes to white nationalist violence.

It would be easy to dismiss the sudden fixation on "cancel culture" as the temper tantrums of a vocal minority, but what history tells us is that these seeds, when nurtured, grow into vines that strangle American possibility. There are already efforts under way to prevent the power delivered by Black voters from being used to benefit Black voters. At the time of this writing, no fewer than 250 voter suppression bills are moving through legislatures in 43 states, aimed at preventing Black communities from having their say in our collective future. In Florida, the state where Trayvon Martin was killed, the governor is pushing to pass an anti-protest bill that would be the harshest in the nation, making it a felony offense to participate in protests that result in property damage or blocked roads. Anyone who even donates to a protest where this happens could be charged under the state's racketeering laws. At the same time, the law grants amnesty to people who drive their cars through such protests and cuts state funding to localities that reduce budgets for police departments.

Incensed by the election of the one and only Black president, followed by the stinging defeat of their white nationalist champion's reelection bid, this coalition has gone into overdrive, committed to reestablishing white supremacy as the organizing principle of America. They fight to maintain and advance a way of life that benefits only a few, even if they have to deconstruct democracy, the basic constitutional mechanism for distributing and protecting access to resources.

In the period after emancipation, Black communities unlocked previously unseen potential in America. The enfranchisement of hundreds of thousands of Black men helped usher in new laws and practices that pushed America closer to what it had always promised. Expanding and protecting rights for Black people eventually meant expanded rights for others—women, immigrants, queer and trans people, people with disabilities, and even white people.

Today, Black communities have again unlocked the potential for a new society, a new democracy, and a new economy. As with the election of Ulysses S. Grant, where Black communities changed the political terrain, Black voters in the 2020 presidential election provided the margin of victory for Joe Biden, as they did for the Democratic candidates in runoff elections for Georgia's two Senate seats. Black communities today are still waiting to see if there will be massive policy shifts to re-enfranchise Black communities and make America work for us—in part by having the United States government intervene in the racial terror that continues today.

If we are in another period of Reconstruction—where we can use the mandate delivered by Black voters, joined by a multiracial coalition—what will we build, and what kind of architects will we be? What are the values that will accompany this rebuilding, and what will be the new story of who we are and who we can be together?

What the Freedmen's Bureau accomplished—establishing schools and churches for Black communities, providing legal support to negotiate labor contracts, providing food and clothing and fuel, and helping Black communities participate in the decisions that impacted their lives—was a critical component of rebuilding America after it had been torn apart. The Bureau was an acknowledgment that the government needed to play a stronger role in addressing the impacts of white supremacy on the equitable distribution of resources. It intervened militarily in the affairs of the Confederacy, as the South—which was in shambles as a result of the war and in need of rebuilding—held tight to white supremacy at the expense of the economy it claimed to care so much about. It was an acknowledgment that governance, even more than government, meant ensuring that we all had a right to shape the conditions of our lives.

Governance under Reconstruction understood that racist violence was a hindrance to the effort to enfranchise Black people. The vigorous prosecution of the Ku Klux Klan served to drive it underground. It was, for a short time, an institutional acknowledgment that the rules had been rigged in favor of white, propertied people and that new rules must be made to provide a counterbalance. It was not enough to turn away from the violence and hope it would disappear on its own. These governments understood that to prevent violence against Black people who dared to be free, they would need to protect and defend those rights on behalf of the government itself.

Today, as it was then and as it was during my own childhood, white nationalist violence is on the rise. As reported in *The Washington Post,* FBI director Christopher Wray recently reconfirmed to the Senate Judiciary Committee that white nationalist militia organizations were the greatest domestic terror threat in the United States: "I would certainly say, as I think I've said consistently in the past, that racially motivated violent extremism, specifically of the sort that advocates for the superiority of the white race, is a persistent, evolving threat. It's the biggest chunk of our racially motivated violent extremism cases for sure. And racially motivated violent extremism is the biggest chunk of our domestic terrorism portfolio, if you will, overall."

In this new period of Reconstruction, will we establish governance that is truly for and by all people? Or, under the guise of compromise, will we instead allow the heirs of the Confederacy to continue to wither away the expansion and protection of rights we fought so hard for?

The opportunity of today's America is much greater than my

mother thought was possible, than my grandmother thought was possible, and than my great-grandmother, born into enslavement, could even imagine. Perhaps, then, the purpose of power is realizing and making power more than a promise, but a reality, in such a way that my family and yours might one day soon experience what it is like to be powerful in every part of our lives.

ACKNOWLEDGMENTS

Writing a book is probably the most adult thing I've done. When my mother died, I thought this project was over—far from it! My mom was with me every step of the way when I was writing this book. Every time I wanted to quit, every time I was unsure, she was right there. I'm sorry for all the times I got exasperated when you asked me how the book was coming along and when it would be published. I completed this for you— thank you for pushing me, even from wherever you are now.

My editor, Chris Jackson, believed in this project from the very first minute we talked. You impressed me, you took the time to listen to me, and you were a steady hand at all stages— thank you. Thank you to the team at One World / Random House for working so hard to move this book in the midst of a global pandemic: not a small feat. Thank you to the Skai Blue Media team—Rakia, aren't we so glad we met on the baseball field? Thank you to Hedgebrook for giving me respite to write the very first words, and to Hollis Wong Wear for introducing me to radical hospitality. To Rashad Robinson and Heather McGhee, who helped me get it done, my way. To Bayview Hunters Point, which grew me all the way up. To Willie and Mary Ratcliff, who encouraged me to write, all the time, about everything. To all of my teachers—thank you for being patient with me. To my community—thank you for lifting me up, for having my back, and for riding with me.

To my love, Malachi. Words can't express anything that must be said, so suffice it to say thank you. For believing in me when I didn't believe in myself. For encouraging me. For holding up the mirror to me. For providing fertile ground for me to grow into myself, without apology. Life is better with you in it.

This book would not have been possible without a whole team of people—but everything and anything that you find abhorrent about it is my responsibility and mine alone.

INDEX

ALICIA GARZA founded the Black Futures Lab to make Black communities powerful in politics. In 2018, the Black Futures Lab conducted the largest survey of Black communities in over 150 years.

Alicia believes that Black communities deserve what all communities deserve—to be powerful in every aspect of their lives. An innovator, strategist, organizer, and cheeseburger enthusiast, she is the co-creator of #BlackLivesMatter and the Black Lives Matter Global Network, an international organizing project to end state violence and oppression against Black people. The Black Lives Matter Global Network now has forty chapters in four countries.

Alicia serves as the strategy and partnerships director for the National Domestic Workers Alliance, the nation's premier voice for millions of domestic workers in the United States. She is also the co-founder of Supermajority, a new home for women's activism. She shares her thoughts on the women transforming power in *Marie Claire* magazine every month.

She lives with her partner in Oakland, California.

Facebook.com/ChasingGarza
Twitter: @aliciagarza